This book offers a fresh examination of key seventeenth-century writers in the context of their common interest in the republican, libertarian, and oppositional potential of the philosophical tradition of Stoicism. The Stoic ethos embraced several paradoxical moral and political concepts, notably "constancy" accompanied by a fascination with violence, "indifference" that mirrors extremities of anger, and "retirement" that involves quests for honor and authority. Indeed, Stoicism in England involved not actual withdrawal from society but an intense kind of literacy – reading and writing focused on Seneca, Tacitus, Lucan, and Lipsius as they could be seen to comment on contemporary political situations and ideological problems. Through subtly nuanced close readings of Marvell, Katherine Philips, and Milton, Andrew Shifflett shows that these writers had more in common than previous philosophical, political, and aesthetic categories have allowed, both in their keen Stoic interests and in the struggle to wrest this tradition from absolutist interpretations.

STOICISM, POLITICS, AND LITERATURE
IN THE AGE OF MILTON

STOICISM, POLITICS, AND LITERATURE IN THE AGE OF MILTON

War and peace reconciled

ANDREW SHIFFLETT

CAMBRIDGE
UNIVERSITY PRESS

PUBLISHED BY THE PRESS SYNDICATE OF THE UNIVERSITY OF CAMBRIDGE
The Pitt Building, Trumpington Street, Cambridge CB2 1RP, United Kingdom

CAMBRIDGE UNIVERSITY PRESS
The Edinburgh Building, Cambridge CB2 2RU, United Kingdom
40 West 20th Street, New York, NY 10011–4211, USA
10 Stamford Road, Oakleigh, Melbourne 3166, Australia

First published 1998

Printed in the United Kingdom at the University Press, Cambridge

Typeset in Baskerville 11/12½ pt.   [VN]

A catalogue record for this book is available from the British Library

Library of Congress cataloguing in publication data

Shifflett, Andrew Eric, 1964–
Stoicism, politics, and literature in the age of Milton:
war and peace reconciled / Andrew Shifflett.
p.   cm.
Includes bibliographical references and index.
ISBN 0 521 59203 8 (hardback)
1. English literature – Early modern, 1500–1700 – History and criticism.
2. Politics and literature – Great Britain – History – 17th century.
3. Great Britain – History – Civil War, 1642–1649 – Literature and the war.
4. Great Britain – Politics and government – 1603–1714.
5. Milton, John, 1608–1674 – Contemporaries.   6. English literature –
Classical influences. 7. Philosophy, Ancient, in literature.
8. Stoics in literature. 9. Peace in literature. 10. War in literature.
11. Stoics – Influence.
I. Title.
PR438.P65S53   1998
820.9'358–dc21   97-28830   CIP

ISBN 0521 59203 8 hardback

To the Memory of My Father
John Sterling Shifflett

Contents

Figures

Acknowledgments

I have received many gifts in the course of writing this book. I am indebted to Princeton University for a University Fellowship from 1988 through 1992 and an additional Charlotte Elizabeth Procter Dissertation Fellowship in 1991–92; to the University of Cincinnati for a Charles Phelps Taft Postdoctoral Fellowship in 1994–95; and to the University of South Carolina for its continuing support of this and other projects. In the early stages of the writing I was guided by two justly admired scholars, Victoria Kahn and Earl Miner, whose keen criticism and common sense helped me both to finish a dissertation and to get a job. More recently I have benefited from the insights and encouragement of my friends Robert Epstein, Paula Loscocco, William Ostrem, and John Stevens, as well my new colleagues Lawrence Rhu and Philip Rollinson. Several seminar groups and conference audiences at Princeton University, the Modern Language Association Convention, the University of Cincinnati, and the University of Michigan-Dearborn have helped me to clarify my views. I also wish to thank the readers for Cambridge University Press for their detailed reports and, of course, Josie Dixon, who provided thoughtful assistance throughout the entire review and production processes. But my greatest debts in this and all other things are to my wife Audrey, to my mother Elizabeth, and to my late father John. "A benefit endures," says Seneca, "even after that through which it was manifested has been lost; for it is a virtuous act, and no power can undo it."

An earlier version of chapter 3 was published as " 'How Many Virtues Must I Hate': Katherine Philips and the Politics of Clemency," in *Studies in Philology* 94 (1997): 103–35. An earlier version of chapter 4 was published as " 'By *Lucan* Driv'n About': A Jonsonian Marvell's Lucanic Milton," in *Renaissance Quarterly* 49 (1996): 803–23. I am grateful to the editors for permission to use work which originally appeared in their journals.

Introduction

In his magisterial *Foundations of Modern Political Thought* Quentin Skinner argues that the Stoicism of Montaigne, Guillaume Du Vair, and Justus Lipsius "carried with it a distinctive set of political implications, the most important being the idea that everyone has a duty to submit himself to the existing order of things, never resisting the prevailing government but accepting and where necessary enduring it with fortitude."[1] He finds it "hardly surprising" that these "stoic moralists were vehemently opposed to any attempt to vindicate the lawfulness of political resistance."[2] This interpretation is exemplary in both negative and positive senses, and Skinner may serve to represent what I take to be the ideal, if initially unwilling, readers of this book: those interested in seventeenth-century English literature and politics, and particularly in the interdisciplinary work now being done by such scholars as Victoria Kahn, David Norbrook, Annabel Patterson, Stephen Zwicker, and, of course, by Skinner himself; and those also who share his widely accepted but to my mind quite inadequate understanding of early modern Stoicism.

In England, at least, Stoicism was seldom about "never resisting the prevailing government" and blindly accepting things as they were. Even in its least resolute forms, it could be a subtle casuistry of political activism. A convenient if none too distinguished example of English Neostoic prose is a text that Skinner cites, *A Buckler against Adversity* (1622). This translation by Andrew Court of a dialogue by Du Vair is not "vehemently opposed to any attempt to vindicate the lawfulness of political resistance." It does not argue in any absolute sense for inaction but instructs readers to consider action as seriously as they possibly can given their actual psychological, political, and military situations. In book 3, for instance, the moderator asks the wise Linus a rather difficult question:

I would desire to know of you, which of the two we ought rather to imitate: and if we see the striving of Vertue against Violence, to prove unprofitable to the publike, and hurtful to our selves; whether we ought to forsake all publike actions, and withdraw us wholly from businesse; or whether Vertue ought even amidst the greatest stormes keep on her course, and rather suffer herself to bee overwhelmed then goe back; or whether there bee ever a middle path between an obstinate austeritie, and a shamefull servitude, by the which an innocent prudence may bee saved harmelesse from these civill broyles, and cragged cliffes, wherewith we are on all sides environed.[3]

Linus proceeds to map out the "middle path" as the one most useful to know in the worst situations. This is not a path to be taken in every situation: there are more active and less active responses that might be chosen, but of course the decision is always up to the actor and should always be made by taking actual situations into account. Perhaps it is the shared ease of the modern liberal democracies that has led scholars to read only pessimism in such texts as *A Buckler against Adversity*, to see so insistently in them a separation between "fortitude" and "resistance" when those terms are so often united in an "innocent" but also politically meaningful "prudence." Their only defender of late, to my knowledge, has been Markku Peltonen, who in *Classical Humanism and Republicanism in English Political Thought* is willing to see humane, "Ciceronian" ideals even in Lipsius's *Politicorum sive Civilis Doctrinae Libri Sex* (1589), a work usually dismissed as a handbook for early modern despots: "It was 'civil life' attained by virtues which formed Lipsius's chief aim" in that work; and the "same values of the virtuous active life" are said by Peltonen to permeate *A Buckler against Adversity*.[4] More often, however, "Stoic" designates defeat, hopelessness, inertia, old-age, or something worse – as when a Miltonist refers to "the isolated, discrete rational individual . . . pushed towards . . . a purely private and personal stoicism in the face of an irrational world."[5] It may be too late to renew interest in the Stoics' conception of the world, its inhabitants, and its history as a vibrant organism amid so much misinformation, but something can be done to recover the relevance of Stoicism to seventeenth-century men and women. Indeed, a central argument of this book is that the Stoic "middle path" was conceived more and more during the seventeenth century as a matter of writing and publication within the "republic of letters" – an "ideal" but also quite real "community," writes David Norbrook in an essay on John Donne, "to which entry was freely offered to those with ability and whose values were critical of tradition, struggling to replace the arbitrary exercise of power by rational political debate."[6] In a sense, this "middle path" led back to the philosophical projects that Cicero speaks of in *De Oratore* 1.1 and elsewhere, and which Seneca speaks of with such ardor in letters and treatises written during the reign of Nero; but it was also to literalize and substantiate such projects in the age of the printing press and occasional poem. Moreover, if the rigorous Stoic *otium* does sometimes seem too convenient, one should take care to consider just what sort of *negotium* it was that seventeenth-century Stoics were turning away from. As Maurizio Viroli reminds us in *From Politics to Reason of State*, the classical "language of politics" in which political activity was held to foster the collective virtue of citizens had been giving way, "between the end of the sixteenth century and the beginning of the seventeenth century," to the theories and practices of "reason of state."[7] Stoic retirement often meant retreat from the state, not from political action. Moreover, retirement could itself be a decisive act of political rhetoric and a tacit but hard to ignore plea for a return to virtue-centered politics.

My goal is thus at once to understand the rhetorical and philosophical bases of a literary movement and to sketch some suggestions for a new map of political discourse during the middle decades of the seventeenth century. By focusing on Andrew Marvell, Katherine Philips, and John Milton I hope to show that these poets and friends within the republic of letters have more in common than the usual philosophical, political, and aesthetic categories have allowed. Although they were by no means ideologically identical – I understand that associating Smectymnuous and Orinda may seem perverse to some readers – each was keenly interested in the republican, libertarian, and oppositional possibilities of the Stoic tradition and each struggled to wrest that tradition from pessimistic and absolutist interpretations. Because these struggles in the name of constancy do not always reveal constant personalities and alliances, I wish to make it clear at the outset that this book is not intended to be a survey of philosophical and political doctrines. Nor am I interested in determining which texts are truly Stoic and which are not. Even if such a survey were within my abilities it would, I believe, be antipathetic to these writers who so rightly exploited the casuistical tendencies of Stoicism to the fullest. The ethical biases of Stoicism ensured that doctrines were always held responsible to the lives of individual readers and writers, and its paradoxical rhetoric ensured that they were always open to internal critique and the complexities of literary figuration.[8] One sees in the texts of Marvell, Philips, and Milton just how contested and nuanced Stoic rhetoric could be during this period. One also begins to understand that Stoicism in its most powerful forms is not about actual withdrawal from the world but about the meaning of action and the manipulation of anger for political ends.

Although or perhaps because Stoicism advised such emotional control, it was often thought to have radical political implications.

The Stoic ethos involved several paradoxical literary and political concepts, most notably constancy accompanied by a fascination with violence, indifference mirroring extremities of anger, and retirement involving quests for honor and authority. I argue in chapter 1 that this politically charged and insistently paradoxical rhetoric was a means to assert the honor of the willful, aristocratic self amid the factional and ideological struggles that characterized Elizabeth's last years and the reigns of James I and Charles I. This did not involve withdrawal but a certain kind of literacy: reading and writing focused especially on Seneca, Tacitus, Lucan, and Lipsius as they could be made to comment on contemporary political situations and ideological issues. From the first English translation of Lipsius's *De Constantia* in 1594, striking homologies were perceived between the content of Stoic privacy and civil war itself. Stoic literacy and imitation theory thus mirrored the competitive tensions that Gordon Braden has discerned at the core of the Stoic soul in his study of *Renaissance Tragedy and the Senecan Tradition*.[9] But while the ancient Stoic often turned away from war and politics toward inwardly directed battles of honor, the seventeenth-century Stoic directed those battles outwardly and symbolically in the literary "arena."

Braden's approach has thus been both very influential to me and something of a problem as I have come to terms with the productivity and vitality of early modern Stoicism in England. Inwardly directed battles of honor are likely to lead, as Braden argues they do, to the abyss. "Between the Stoic and the Skeptic there is not always that much distance," he writes; "the self aspires to be an imitation of the cosmos, but it might as well be an arbitrary stand taken against a meaningless reality that has value only as an opportunity for proving ourselves and enjoying our self-esteem." Indeed, "the pattern of Stoic retreat" drives "relentlessly toward the ultimate Stoic act: suicide."[10] If we take this prognosis too far, we might conclude that it was only their common Christian faith that saved such political opposites as Bishop Joseph Hall, "Our English Seneca," and the Restoration Milton from early, self-inflicted deaths. But Stoicism usually led in the seventeenth century, not to suicide or paralysis, but to *literature* and *publication*. This involved in part the publication of privacy, the commercialization of the withdrawn personality in such texts as Sir William Cornwallis's *Essayes* (1600–01), Donne's *Letters to Severall Persons of Honour* (1651), and Abraham Cowley's remarkable *Essays, in Verse and Prose* (1668). In Cornwallis, at the dawn of the century, we see that the fashion for privacy is coeval with the conception that the things and inhabitants of this world are, as the Stoic says, "things indifferent." Judgment of these things counts for every-thing – as Milton was to argue in *Areopagitica* – and judgment is typically a matter of *reading* and *writing*. Thus, in "Of Resolution" Cornwallis writes: "The world is a booke; the wordes and actions of men Commen-taries upon that volume; the former like manuscriptes private; the latter common, like things printed."[11] Cornwallis turns the world, its persons, resolutions, and actions into texts; he only makes surfaces to be scratched, but this is not for him an *aporia*. "Si philospharis, bene est," writes Seneca in *Epistulae Morales* 15, and when you are philosophizing with Seneca and Senecans you are exchanging words, letters, and books on matters of mutual importance.

But the literature of Stoic retirement was much more than a literature of privacy. We cannot begin to understand the fascination that Stoicism held for seventeenth-century writers until we take seriously the cosmo-politan ideals of the Stoics. One of the fullest statements of these ideals is found in Seneca's *De Tranquillitate Animi* 4.1–4, where he writes:

I confesse well that we ought sometimes to retire ourselves, but leasurely, and with a secure retreat, our ensignes displaied, and without empeachment of our worldly dignitie. They are more valiant and more assured than their Con-querours that make a faire and honest retreat. So in my opinion ought vertue to behave her self, and if the inconstancy of worldly affaires disturbe all, and taketh away from a vertuous man the meanes to doe good; yet for all this ought he not to turne his back, nor to cast away his weapons to save himselfe by flight, and to thrust him selfe in a secret place, as if there could be any corner where fortune could not find him out: but he ought to be less busie in affaires, and find out some expedient with judgement to make himself profitable to his Countrie. Is it not lawfull for him to beare armes? Let him aspire to some publique charge . . . Is he put to silence? Let him helpe his Citizens by his private counsell. Is it dangerous for him to enter the judgement place? Let him shew himself a faithfull friend, a gracious companion, a temperate guest in houses, in The-aters, at feasts. If hee have lost the office of Citizen? Let him use that of a man. And therefore with a great mind have we not shut ourselves within the walls of one Citty, but have thrust ourselves into the conversation of the whole world, and have professed that the world is our Countrey, that wee might give vertue a more spacious field to shew her self in.[12]

The literature of Stoic retirement was a literature not only of private selves but also of community. It was a record of what Seneca called *res publica magna et vere publica* and what his dedicated translator, Thomas

Lodge, called "the conversation of the whole world." Having temporarily retired to the study or garden, the Stoic does not cease acting in the world; the world of retirement is really a much larger world than the one that has been left. For all their talk about the masculinity of virtue, ancient and early modern Stoics tended to emphasize the intellectual equivalency of the sexes and sought to bridge moral if not economic gaps between rich and poor. Whatever the "office . . . of a man" really is – answers to this question in the sixteenth and seventeenth centuries are always fascinating – it is not something likely to be contained by arbitrary boundaries. The world is a living organism for the Stoic, and each person can serve it wisely and well when they recognize that, as *humans*, they share the same fate as all other persons.[13] The Stoics, writes Ludwig Edelstein, "asked the individual to learn that it is necessary for him to live for others and that he is born for human society at large, of which he must always feel himself to be a member rather than a fragment separated off. Here in humanity and not in the state, in the moral community of man, he is truly at home."[14] The history of the literary culture of seventeenth-century England is, among all the other things that it is, a history of Stoic cosmopolitanism – an ideal that because of social and technological realities had never before been achieved in practice although it had been professed since the time of Zeno.

Thus, while I am indebted to Braden's recovery of the *anger* within the Stoic tradition, and while chapter 1 deals with the rhetorical combination of Stoicism and war in seventeenth-century English culture, the following chapters are guided by journeys from violence and rage to the paradoxical engagements of retirement. By retiring strategically in a Stoic manner – to gardens (Marvell), to a "rude and . . . dark Retreat" (Philips), and to "retired silence" (Milton) – each of these writers makes, to use Seneca's language, "a secure retreat" with "ensignes displaied," and thus gives to "vertue" – carrying on the characteristic military metaphor – "a more spacious field to shew her self in." Stoic literature of the 1640s and 1650s is best understood, then, not simply as a response to the Civil War, but as a crucial part of the discursive history that prepared for and structured that conflict from beginning to end. The properly vigilant Stoic lays "Gardens out in sport / In the just Figure of a Fort," as Marvell, the subject of chapter 2, writes in "Upon Appleton House." In that poem, and in "The Garden" and elsewhere, Marvell's gardens figure conflicts between intellectual and military fortitude on the one hand and weakness, vanity, and corruption on the other. They are compact with the history of civil conflict, and the latter pages of chapter 2 and chapters 3, 4, and 5 follow that history through the Restoration and beyond.

In a century so dominated by "fears and jealousies," Stoic rhetoric was available and attractive to the "winners" and "losers" alike – a fact that bound many writers together who might otherwise have been strangers. Maren-Sofie Røstvig's still-valuable *The Happy Man* and fine studies by Earl Miner and Raymond A. Anselment have, for the most part, stressed the conservative and reactionary phases of English Neo-stoicism.[15] We have been shown that Seneca, Cicero, and Boethius consoled displaced royalists during the 1640s and 1650s, providing them with philosophical warmth during their long "Cavalier winter." But while Miner and Anselment have been convincing in regard to their chosen writers, they have not come close to exhausting the topic. Indeed, the Stoicism of the Cavaliers should not be limited to the war years and interregnum. Notable in this regard are Sir Roger L'Estrange's popular *Seneca's Morals by Way of Abstract* (1678), a work whose appeals for Senecan "gratitude" were intended in part to shore up the Stuarts amid the Exclusion Crisis. Nor, of course, was there any monopoly on "offices," those actions which are for the Stoic, as Thomas Stanley writes in *The History of Philosophy* (1655–62), "whatsoever reason requireth to be done, as, to honour our Brethren, Parents, Country, to relieve our friends."[16] It is not surprising that "reason" required different things to be done by different writers at different times. For Philips as she wrote *Pompey*, the subject of chapter 3, her proper "office" as a "man," so to speak, was Stoic criticism of Stoic clemency as a means of monarchical control. For Marvell in the 1670s, the subject of chapter 4, the best "office" was "to relieve our friends" by surrounding the beleaguered Milton with a protective aura of "retired silence" in *The Second Part* of *The Rehearsal Transpros'd* and by placing him in the Stoic-republican tradition of Lucan, Jonson, and Thomas May in "On *Paradise Lost*". Marvell had his own reasons for understanding Milton's career in this way, of course, but they are to my mind definitive: the Stoic casuistries that do so often mark his career, and an extended comparative reading of *Paradise Regain'd* and Lucan's *Pharsalia*, are the topics of chapter 5. In Milton we reach one culmination of the Stoic tradition, a tradition in which constancy could imply conflict, peace could imply war, and a translation of *De Constantia* published in the year after *Paradise Regain'd* could be called *War and Peace Reconciled*.

A few things remain to be said about my method. Because so many of the texts that I deal with are not readily available on library shelves or even in rare book collections, I have often quoted from them at considerable length in the pages that follow. This has been necessary sometimes to lend credibility to particularly troublesome arguments; but it is always necessary, in my opinion, to read even the lesser writers of the seventeenth century carefully and at length in order to acquire a just appreciation of their styles and outlooks. Readers will also notice the liberal use that I have made of sixteenth- and seventeenth-century translations of Lipsius and the ancient writers – Cicero, Lucan, Seneca, and Epictetus, among others – who play important roles in this study. Although scholarly translations from our own century are easier to find and would in most cases provide the most reliable texts, I have desired on every page to give the reader a feel, not for what Stoicism supposedly *is*, but for what it could *mean* to seventeenth-century readers and writers. The two are not always the same, although we should ourselves be careful not to assume that we know in any objective sense what Stoicism is. In some cases, as in Marvell's relatively well-known use in the "Horatian Ode" of Thomas May's translation of Lucan, we are dealing with writers who almost certainly used popular translations rather than originals. But my reasons for relying on the labors of May, Sir John Stradling, Thomas North, Thomas Lodge, and other translators are really more broadly based than that. I have been concerned throughout to understand the "Silver Age" of the English Renaissance as a hermeneutic project – or a series of hermeneutic crises – caught, as it were, between the demands of its own rigorous scholarship and the natural desires of writers to respond meaningfully to contemporary political and commercial situations and even to create new ones. The typical seventeenth-century translation of Seneca or Lucan, however difficult it may be to find and read, poses those exciting crises for us again.

CHAPTER I

Conflict and constancy in seventeenth-century England

When civil war broke out in England in 1642 Stoic constancy was a moral ideal embraced by both sides. Tears and outrage had a place with the vulgar, but the heroic norm is stated in Sir John Denham's *The Sophy*, the most celebrated play of that climacteric year. The youthful and brilliantly militaristic Prince Mirza, cruelly blinded at the command of the king his father, would somehow find greater victories and a better kingdom within himself:

> 'Tis something sure within us, not subjected
> To sense or sight, only to be discern'd
> By reason, my soul's eye, and that still sees
> Clearly, and clearer for the want of these;
> For gazing through these windows of the body,
> It met such several, such distracting objects;
> But now confin'd within it self, it sees
> A strange, and unknown world, and there discovers
> Torrents of Anger, Mountains of Ambition;
> Gulfes of Desire, and Towers of Hope, huge Giants,
> Monsters, and savage Beasts; to vanquish these,
> Will be a braver conquest than the old
> Or the new world.[1]

The modern reader may tend at this point to think of the prince as an escapist, as having abandoned his political will as well as the public virtues that had made him such a promising heir to the throne. Yet Mirza's "braver conquest" over "Torrents of Anger" and "Mountains of Ambition" is not, one soon realizes, an escape from anything but fear and regret. Indeed, it brings to him a distinctly anti-monarchical perspective:

9

> Man to himself
> Is a large prospect, rays'd above the level
> Of his low creeping thoughts; if then I have
> A world within my self, that world shall be
> My Empire; there I'le raign, commanding freely,
> And willingly obey'd, secure from fear
> Of forraign forces, or domestick treasons,
> And hold a Monarchy more free, more absolute
> Than in my Fathers seat; and looking down
> With scorn or pity, on the slippery state
> Of Kings, will tread upon the neck of fate.[2]

This is one variety of Stoicism, which for Prince Mirza is an inwardly directed philosophy with public consequences. It is an attack on himself – the "Towers," "Giants," "Monsters," and "savage Beasts" of his emotions – that is also an attack on kings and their counselors, and he is willing to pay the highest price for his victories. Concerned primarily with "tactics of selfhood" in desperate moral and political contexts, such Stoicism, says Braden, "engages powerful psychic drives that are in themselves preethical and have potentially anarchic implications."[3] This is eccentric from the usual philosophical perspectives, but it has pointed Braden's readers to a better understanding of the Senecan dramatic tradition of which Denham's Mirza is a part; as I shall be arguing throughout this chapter and book, the idea that Stoicism amounts to a rhetorical mediation of anger rather than an elimination of it can help us to a better understanding of Stoicism as a cultural and political fact in seventeenth-century England.

England was overcome in the 1640s, 1650s, and 1660s by anger on a national scale, and during those decades men and women sought like Mirza better, "more absolute" kingdoms and often expected to be killed or jailed for doing so. They were angry – angry at the vices of monarchs and their inability or unwillingness to recognize honor and merit, angry at those who they felt trod on the "ancient rights" of the English people, angry at those who denied the fullest reformation of religion, angry when their hopes and plans failed utterly – and when they chose Stoically to resist the tide this was rightly interpreted by their enemies as an especially dangerous kind of anger. Such is the judgment of Haly, the king's vicious counselor in *The Sophy*: Mirza's "constancy" is perceived as a threat to his designs, and he has him poisoned for it. The virtuous Mirza dies an anti-monarch in 1642. While this may seem strange to say of a character conceived by so highly reputed a royalist as Denham, Mirza embodies a tradition that has been passed over as escapist or, on the basis of the "passive" Stoicism of certain Cavaliers, misinterpreted as faithfully royalist. Denham was sensitive enough to the fate that we all tread on to know that Stoicism could present some persons with dramatic and honorable reasons, not to avoid conflict, but to proceed with it whatever the cost to body and soul. Conflict is in any case the great theme of the writers to be studied here, and for them Stoicism can be both its remedy and its cause.

"PRESSING TO WINNE HONOR"

In order to understand the attractiveness of Stoicism in the seventeenth century, one must consider the central role of war in European society at the time. Most striking is the independent nature of the armies themselves. "In 1600 war was within the means of individuals," writes D. H. Pennington. "A large landowner could raise and maintain an army that was virtually his own. It was nearly always said to be for the service of the monarch; but everyone knew that it might be used against him."[4] Although states did, of course, eventually come to dominate armies, the most obvious fact about seventeenth-century war is that it was not "ideal" by any modern, Clausewitzian standards: war most definitely was not an extension of policy by other means. "War created policy rather than continued it," writes Sir George Clark.[5] Even at the end of the century and in the most centralized of European states – the France of Louis XIV – war with its ancient rituals and privileges, not policy *per se*, was the most important force in international and intranational relations. During the Thirty Years War – indeed during the century of religious and political conflict from the beginning of the Dutch Revolt in 1566 through the march of General George Monck into London in early 1660 – it became clear that "professional commanders of armed forces like[d] to use them, to increase them, and to control policy."[6] The mercenary and financier Albrecht Wallenstein became something of a cosmopolitan prince on the Continent; in England Thomas Fairfax, Oliver Cromwell, and their New Model Army shaped Parliamentary policy decisively during war as well as during the troubled peace that followed. "War was not a mere succession of occurrences but an institution, a regular and settled mode of action, for which provision was made throughout the ordering of social life," Clark writes; "the structure of society implied that it would occur."[7] The prominence of standing – and wandering – armies in political and diplomatic equations discouraged any clear separation between states of war and peace. After all, the same army that secured the peace could turn to plunder when its commanders ran out of funds. Nor could there be any sure distinction between civil wars and external ones. Civil wars were the more dreaded; but civil and external wars tended to follow one upon the other, and "even civil war was not merely an aberration but part of the regular institution of war."[8] War – and this is one of Clark's strongest points – was generally regarded by the political elite as a "positive" state of human affairs while the rhetoric of their treaties implied "a negative view of peace as the absence of war."[9] Those not among the elite had little choice but to live their lives as best they could by war's awful rules. "The victims of devastation could survive by joining the armies that had caused it," Pennington writes. "Wars, in fact, helped to create the conditions in which people were willing to take part in them."[10]

The conditions of war involved everything from the plunder of crops and towns to the patronage of much of what we call secular high culture. Certainly, we should not expect our cultural heroes to be immune to war's necessities, nor their texts to be untouched by the physical and rhetorical violence that always surrounded them. "Despite the devastation of the Thirty Years War, there was no surge of popular demand for an end to warfare," writes Robert Fallon; "it was generally accepted, sometimes with stoic resignation, that war was a tragic but unavoidable feature of the human condition."[11] Perhaps "tragic" is too strong a word, however, for war could be regarded in a fully positive light. "Truth" in Milton's *Areopagitica* (1644) is, among so many other things it is, a warrior who may with "Falsehood grapple" with no worry of being "put to the wors, in a free and open encounter."[12] "The wars of Truth in Milton's age," writes David Loewenstein, "generate the conditions of energetic social conflict necessary to realize his dynamic vision."[13] In an imaginative study of *Milton and the Culture of Violence*, Michael Lieb describes the "sparagmatic sensibility" of Milton's greatest works: "the body is portrayed as a phenomenon beset by a world of violence in which it must sustain itself, assert itself, maintain its integrity lest it be torn asunder, violated, and destroyed."[14] One should also keep in mind the curious recollections found in the *Defensio Secunda* (1654) and the old biographies of a happy Milton wrestling and practicing with the long-sword he was in the habit of wearing in London streets. The "institution of breeding" that he describes in *Of Education* (1644), published just a few weeks before the battle of Marston Moor, was to be "equally good for Peace and warre":

The exercise which I commend first, is the exact use of their weapon; to guard and to strike safely with edge, or point; this will keep them healthy, nimble, strong, and well in breath, is also the likeliest means to make them grow large, and tall, and to inspire them with a gallant and fearlesse courage, which being temper'd with seasonable lectures and precepts to them of true fortitude, and patience, will turn into a native and heroick valor, and make them hate the cowardise of doing wrong. They must be also practiz'd in all the locks and gripes of wrastling, wherein English men were wont to excell, as need may often be in fight to tugge, to grapple, and to close . . . [Youths must train in the arts of war so that] having in sport, but with much exactnesse, and dayly muster, serv'd out the rudiments of their Souldiership in all skill of embattailing, marching, encamping, fortifying, beseiging and battering, with all the helps of ancient and modern strategems, *Tactiks* and warlike maxims, they may as it were out of a long warre come forth renowned and perfect Commanders in the service of their country. (*CPW* II, 409, 411–12)

Milton's fascination with the martial arts is typical of men of his class and of men who pretended to his education. Typical, too, is the belief that the Stoic virtues of "true fortitude and patience" can and should be combined with martial virtuosity, a virtuosity that Milton, in concert with military theorists of the time, knew must be strongly technical and technological in character. Moreover, while such virtues and skills were in unusual demand in the England of 1644, it is also true that "Milton would have considered preparation for war an important part of his educational plan at any time" (*CPW* II, 408n). Indeed, Milton was very much a man of his time when it came to what J. R. Hale calls that "novel, classically derived ethic of grin-and-bear-it positive pessimism" – Neostoicism – which "taught how men should adapt to the strains of a world war of their own creation."[15]

War and civil war had been common experiences, not only in the Low Countries and Germany for eight decades, but also in England throughout the fifteenth century and, in the form of local revolts, throughout much of the sixteenth century. Caroline and Protectorate nostalgia for the Elizabethan and Jacobean periods was driven, not simply by the fact that they had not been seriously threatened by civil wars or more limited rebellions, but by the fact that so few other recorded periods in English history had not been utterly dominated by them. But if civil war had been only a memory under Elizabeth and James, it had been a vivid one. Robert Burton might as well be referring to yesterday when in *The Anatomy of Melancholy* (1621) he laments "our late Pharsalian fields, in the time of Henry the Sixth, between the houses of Lancaster and York, an hundred thousand men slain . . . ten thousand families . . . rooted out."[16] The Essex conspiracy and rebellion are exceptions to the history of a reign, not the history of the nation. If there was peace in England when Sir John Stradling was translating Justus Lipsius's popular Stoic dialogue, *De Constantia Libri Duo* (1584), it may well have been because God had seen fit after "continuall warres and slaughters," as the wise Langius says, to entrust it to the "government of a peaceable sex."[17] As the reigns of James and Charles I wore on, the most remarkable thing about England from a European perspective was that it was still enjoying some measure of internal peace.

But if England was peaceful in fact during the late sixteenth and early seventeenth centuries it was not peaceful in its fancies. Numerous literary representations of civil war appear in the decade of Stradling's version of *De Constantia*, *Two Bookes of Constancie* (1594), some occasioned no doubt by the troubles of Queen Elizabeth's "second reign" but others concerned, somewhat clairvoyantly, with unseen turbulences of the future.[18] To cite only a few notable examples: Samuel Daniel's verse-and-prose history of the Wars of Roses, *The Civile Wars* (1595–1609); Thomas Lodge's *The Wounds of Civill War* (1594); Christopher Marlowe's fine blank verse translation of the first book of Lucan's *Pharsalia* (1600); Shakespeare's Roman plays and, of course, the Henriad, in which Machiavellian fraud of the sort practiced by Prince John of Lancaster in the Forest of Gaultree (*2 Henry IV* 4.2) is found to be the only way to combat the native English tendency toward civil war; Jonson's *Sejanus his Fall* (1605), whose Stoic patricians sometimes seem nostalgic for civil war; Sir Arthur Gorges's translation of the *Pharsalia* in octosyllabic couplets (1614); Thomas May's popular translation of *Lucan's Pharsalia* (1627) in heroic couplets; and May's original seven-book *Continuation* (1630) of the same epic. "The very subject of [*Lucan's Pharsalia*] and the interest it excited suggest an undercurrent of anxiety running through the reign, and a doubt about the political stability of the nation," argues Graham Parry in an essay on Caroline literary culture. "The possibility of civil war was not unimaginable, and the prevalence of May's Lucan fed such speculations."[19] May's works ran through several editions, the last appearing in 1659 as full-scale civil war seemed quite likely to erupt again. These texts and many, many others feature heroes and heroines who face down outrageous fortune with severe Stoic constancy, who confront tyrants and their base multitudes with unbending faith that, as the wise Langius says in *De Constantia*, "such things as bee pure, everlasting, and of fierie nature, set nought by all external & violent handling" (*TBC* 196).

In an important though hard to document sense, civil war and a "native" Stoicism had been linked in England from the immemorial beginnings of the "honor culture" of the landed nobles. This, of course, is the honor dramatized in the character of Shakespeare's Hotspur, an aristocratic willfulness which Mervyn James has shown was a major motivation for dissidence before the Tudors succeeded in redefining and moralizing honor for their own ends.[20] But their success in this moralization was only temporary, honor having more heirs than the Tudors. "Among the manifold origins of the English Revolution," writes Pennington, summarizing the findings of a number of historians, "the Bishops' Wars were at least in part a Scottish baronial revolt; and in the leadership of both the Royalist and the Parliamentary sides there were clear vestiges of the old-style wars of the nobility."[21] Stoicism, to borrow again from Braden, had always been a matter of "guts."[22] Combined at times with providentialist fervor – even *De Constantia*, as we shall see, aligns the self with a violent Christian destiny – Stoicism remained an important rhetorical means for noble English malcontents and their intellectual retainers to reclaim honor over and against institutional authorities at a time when the moorings of honor to royal authority and the royal church, so strong during the Tudor reigns, were steadily unraveling.[23]

The values of the traditional honor culture – not least of which was an appreciation of the bloody excitements of the battlefield – spark even such scholarly works of Stoic doctrine as *De Constantia*. Such texts "contributed to the emergent strength of Stoic influences at the turn of the century," writes James; moreover, they "strengthened the honour culture, confirming its basic attitudes but giving them new subtlety and sophistication."[24] War and civil war constituted the political and the cultural contexts of early modern Stoicism both in England and on the Continent; they account for its emotional appeal and may even be said to provide its philosophical basis. The peripatetic intellectual everyman of *De Constantia* – Lipsius "himself" – asks in the first paragraph: "Who is of so hard and flinty a heart that he can anie longer endure these evils? Wee are tossed, as you see, these manie yeares with the tempest of civill warres: and like Sea-faring men wee are beaten with sundrie blastes of troubles and sedition" (*TBC* 72). But the "tempest of civill warres," his teacher Langius insists, is a situation – *the* situation in this widely translated book – in which one must be truly Stoic. Lipsius writes of constancy *in publicis malis*, and for him there appears to be no other kind of constancy worth considering philosophically. The connection between conflict and constancy asserted by Lipsius's title is deeply motivated by philosophical tradition and political situations, and, as Gerhard Oestreich has argued in *Neostoicism and the Early Modern State*, it is not enough to think of Stoic constancy as only a *response* to military conflict. "The ideal individual in the political world, as portrayed by Lipsius," Oestreich writes, "is the citizen who acts according to reason, is answerable to himself, controls his emotions, *and is ready to fight*."[25] As Oestreich tells the story, Lipsian Stoicism was an instrumental and causal force in the rise of centralized states and, crucially, in the waging of their wars. What he forgets and what Lipsius could not forget – for the detractors of this notorious "chameleon" would not let him – is that a citizen may doubt his or her *true* citizenship during civil wars and wars fought over shifting boundaries. Being ready to fight means being ready to fight *for* someone or something, of course, but being "answerable to himself" alone could become all-important to the Neostoic. "Nor is he moov'd," writes Samuel Daniel in his epistle to the Countess of Cumberland (1603), "with all the thunder cracks / Of Tyrants threats, or with the surly brow / Of power"; for he – and *she*, as we shall find in chapter 3 – "hath no side at all / But of himself."[26] Milton's ideal student practices "true fortitude and patience" and "hate[s] the cowardise of doing wrong"; he is ready "to tugge, to grapple, and to close" – come what may. As they tested the fetters of what Etienne La Boétie called voluntary servitude, readers of Seneca and Lipsius could find that Stoicism prescribed, not passivity, but violence against others and perhaps violence against oneself.

Given this long literary and political history, it does not seem plausible to speak of a Stoic "response" to the English Civil War as if there were, first, war and, second, philosophical and literary reactions to it. For many English intellectuals, Stoic philosophy and civil war were two sides of the same coin, and in particular cases the philosophy would seem to have prepared the way for actual battles. There was more at work here than the tradition by which war and peace, with their characteristic virtues and vices, were thought to follow one upon the other in an interminable cycle.[27] The good Stoic was supposed to be willing to accept events as they happened, of course, but if in theory he saw war and peace as positions in a Polybian cycle, in practice he was willing to see them as identical, as forming a paradoxical identity understood only by the truly virtuous. If the Stoic was more willing than others to "set open" the "Temple of *Janus*," as Milton "not insignificantly" proposed in *Areopagitica* (*CPW* II, 561), it was because he tended to think that true reconciliation and reformation occurred not after but amid the bloodletting. If the work of Worden, Norbrook, Patterson, and others on seventeenth-century republicanism has made Hobbes's claim that the Civil War was brought on by the teaching of ancient republican history in the universities seem more plausible, then it is time to take some of the basic assumptions and propositions of early modern Stoicism more seriously. One of these assumptions, one hardly out of place in the society that the historians describe, is that violence and war are inevitable facts of life. One of these propositions is that persons of "fierie nature" are, as Lipsius's Langius puts it, quite indifferent to "violent handling" – indeed, that they welcome it.

The central cultural place of violence and its traditions explains some part of the attraction of Seneca to the age. A moralist who sought to pacify his readers' inner conflicts – he could be read as Christian "comfort" – Seneca also acknowledged the ritualistic attractiveness of violence in all its glorious bloodiness.[28] His texts are saturated with images of athletics and the martial arts that are never fully contained by the moral argument that one should think of honor as a thing to be won in an inward rather than outward context. "Our life (my *Lucilius*) is but a warfare," he states in *Epistulae Morales*; "They therefore who are tossed, that mount and descend from rockes and high places, that execute dangerous Commissions, ought to be reputed valiant men and chiefest in the Armie" (*WS* 412; 96.5). He argues in *De Providentia* that the "spectacle" of Cato battling against fortune presents a "couple of combatants worthie the presence of God: that is to say, a generous man planted before adverse Fortune, challenging her hand to hand. I see not, say I, what thing *Jupiter* hath more admirable upon the earth . . . than to behold *Cato* remaining firme and resolute, after his confederates had been more than once defeated; and invincible amidst his countries ruines" (*WS* 500; 2.9). Seneca's Stoic virtue loves violence no less than anger does: "Vertue gapeth after danger, and thinketh on that which she intendeth, not that which she is to suffer, because that which she is to suffer is a part of her glory. Valiant Souldiers glory in their wounds, & joyfully shew the bloud that runneth from them, if it be spent in a good cause" (*WS* 504; *De Prov.* 4.4). Violence, as the frontispiece to the 1620 edition of Lodge's translation of the *Workes* makes clear, is not only a subject of Senecan Stoicism but also, in the end, its final *modus operandi* (see fig. 1). Overseen by figures of Vertue and "THE STOICKS," and flanked by Nero and Temperance, Seneca sits in his bath while the blood flows freely from his arms and "JOVI LIBERATORI" flows from his lips. "VERTUE BRED HIM," "TYRANNY SLEW HIM," "CONSTANCY BURIED HIM": metaphors do not kill, of course, but they can provide reasons to kill and reasons to die.

Cicero was less gory, but no less seriously Stoic, when he compared the trials of body and soul in *Tusculan Disputations* 2.3:

> For as it falls out in Battle, that the Coward and timorous Souldier, as soon as he sees the Face of an Enemy, flingeth away his Shield, and sets on running as fast as he can; and for that very reason, sometimes is lost before he had receiv'd any wound . . . So they who cannot abide the appearance of Pain, cast away themselves, and so grown heartless, sink under Affliction; whereas they who have resisted it, most commonly come off with Victory. Now there are certain resemblances of the Soul with the Body. As burdens are more easily borne, whilst Bodies bear upright, if these give way, they overwhelm them: Just in like manner, *the Soul, by putting forth its utmost Efforts, doth bear off all the pressure of those grievances which burthen it; but, upon shrinking, is so follow'd, that it can never raise it self up.* And so to speak the truth, an intention of the whole mind, is to be used in the Prosecution of all Offices of Life, for it is the sole guard of Duty.[29]

The full range of Cicero's "Offices of Life" was proven when his head, tongue, and hands were posted in the Forum. Indeed, there are few useful distinctions to be made between physical and intellectual fortitude in the Stoic tradition that Seneca had inherited from Cicero, Cato the Younger, and the other fallen heroes of the Republic. "He lived more hardly than before," writes Plutarch of Cato in a characteristic passage, when

> he fell into acquaintence with *Antipater* TYRIAN, a Stoicke Philosopher, and gave himself chiefly unto the study of Morall and Civill Philosophy, imbracing all exercise of vertue with such an earnest desire, that it seemed he was pluckt forward by some god . . . He studied also to be eloquent, that he might speake openly before the people, *because he would there should be certaine warlike Forces entertained in civill Philosophy, as also in a great City.*[30]

Plutarch was critical of Stoicism elsewhere, but here he shows Cato grounding his admirable political stances on Stoic principles. Moreover, Cato is praised for seeking to make philosophy itself a matter of public debate and, indeed, public *strife*.

If the idea that Stoicism could countenance and even encourage strife, violence, and war seems strange to us, it did not seem at all strange to its sixteenth- and seventeenth-century critics. Stoic bogeymen were routinely attacked on the grounds that they were prideful, discontented, and divisive.[31] Again, the type of Stoicism displayed by Denham's

Figure 1   Seneca, *Workes*, trans. Lodge (London, 1620).

Prince Mirza was not thought to be a retreat from conflict but rather a cause of it. The Stoics' paradoxical beliefs, their aggressively dialectical manner of philosophical dispute, and even their curt prose style were thought to sow the seeds of cultural and national division. If Stoics ever in fact withdrew from the world it would be a good thing, their critics thought, because they were dangerous to its routines and institutions. The unusual style of the Stoics, we are often told by these critics, is a sign of their unusual beliefs. Although I am not trying here to resurrect arguments for an "organic" connection between style and belief, to miss the basic if thoroughly conventional associations of Stoic style with certain political attitudes is to miss the political volatility of Neostoic writing, a volatility that was not missed at the time.

These associations of Stoic style and politics were ancient, reaching back before Seneca to the Roman civil wars if not before, and a brief look at some of their cultural roots and branches will be worthwhile. Cicero writes in *Paradoxa Stoicorum* that the Stoics' "high and abstruse pointes of Philosophie" – I quote from a sixteenth-century translation – deliberately flout linguistic and political conventions: "because they bee mervaylous sentences, and such as are contrary to the opynion of all men, they are by them termed Paradoxa, whyche signifyeth, things mervaylous and inopinable."[32] Cicero's goal, as he explains to Brutus in the preface, is to make these Stoic arguments palatable to a general readership. It is not an easy task. Cato, whom Cicero calls "a ryght and perfect Stoike," thinks "thinges which the vulgare people allowe not." Moreover, Cato and the rest of the Stoics "care not for elegancie of speache and floures of eloquence"; they "neither dilate nor amplifie their argumentes, but with breafe questions and Interrogatories (as it were with certaine prickes or points) prosecute their reasons and dispatch their purposed intentes."[33] But Cicero thought that the terrible times, times of continual civil war and proscriptions, required strong medicine, and so he found time to write "this smale woorke . . . compiled by Candlelighte these short nightes."[34] He chose six "mervaylous and inopinable" arguments for study: "that nothinge is good and laudable but only that which is honeste and vertuous"; "that in whomesoever vertue is, there lacketh nothing els to bring him to lead a happy life"; that "all faultes . . . bee equall"; "that all fooles and brainsicke persons be distraught and alienated from their right mindes"; that "all wise men . . . be free, and all fooles . . . be Slaves and bondemen" (directed specifically, or so the translator insists, against "the insolencye and voluptuous lyvinge of Marcus Antonius"); and "that noone are ryche, but onelye wyse and vertuous men" ("privaylye nippynge Marcus Crassus whoe sayde that none was to be named rich, unlesse with his revenues he were able to furnishe and mayntaine an armye").35 The paradoxes could be argued seriously by dedicated Stoics and Neostoics – far more seriously than Cicero meant to bother in the *Paradoxa Stoicorum* – but the tendency displayed in this catalogue toward "privaylye nippynge" satire, sometimes intended by Cicero and sometimes invented by the translator, is very much to the point in considering their significance to sixteenth- and seventeenth-century readers. Indeed, "Stoical opinions" still seemed dangerous to John Bramhall in 1658 when he wrote in his *Castigations of Mr. Hobbes* that "a Paradox, is a private opinion of one man, or a few factious men, assumed or maintained sometimes out of errour of judgement, but commonly out of pride and vainglorious affectation of singularity."36

Cicero was an extremely important source of Stoic ideas in the sixteenth and seventeenth centuries, but in *Paradoxa Stoicorum* he can be seen straddling a philosophical and emotional fence sided by Zeno and Cato on one hand and by his own oratorical and normative predilections on the other. The essayist Robert Johnson was following the normative Ciceronian tradition in 1638 when he referred to "proud inconstant Stoickes" and called them "busie-headed and turbulent."37 So, too, was a much more powerful commentator, King James VI and I, when in *Basilikon Doron* (1599, 1603) he advised Prince Henry to "Keepe true Constancie, not onely in your kindenesse towards honest men; but beeing also *invicti animi* against all adversities: not with that Stoick insensible stupiditie [that proud inconstant LIPSIUS perswadeth in his Constantia], wherewith many in our dayes, pressing to winne honor, in imitating that auncient sect, by their inconstant behaviour in their owne lives, belie their profession."38 The essayist and the King may have been inspired by the great English pedagogue Roger Ascham, whose attack on those who "care not for words, but for matter" in *The Scholemaster* (1570) associated Stoics with religious schismatics and also pointed to their stylistic theory as a cause of schism in general:

All writers, either in Religion, or any sect of Philosophy, who so ever be found fond in judgment of matter, be commonly found as rude in uttering their mind. For Stoics, Anabaptists, and Friars, with Epicures, Libertines, and Monks, being most like in learning and life, are no fonder and pernicious in their opinions, than they be rude and barbarous in their writings. They be not wise therefore, that say, "What care I for a man's words and utterance, if his matter and reasons be good?" Such men say so, not so much of ignorance, as either of some singular pride in themselves, or some special malice of other, or for some private and partial matter, either in Religion or other kind of learning . . . Ye know not, what hurt ye do to learning, that care not for words, but for matter; and so make a divorce betwixt the tongue and the heart. For mark all ages: look upon the whole course of both the Greek and Latin tongue, and ye shall surely find that, when apt and good words began to be neglected . . . then also began ill deeds to spring, strange manners to oppress good orders, new and fond opinions to strive with old and true doctrine, first in Philosophy, and after in Religion.[39]

Ascham combines an attack on the Stoics' "learning and life" with an attack on their style, one known for its extreme clausal brevity and paradoxical obscurity. These were crucial issues for Ascham, a man professionally "concerned with an emerging language and how to teach it."[40] By advocating a style antipathetic to Ciceronian style – apparently antipathetic to any notion of *public* style at all – Stoic writers could not help but threaten pedagogues and other institutional conservatives with political and religious anarchy. Their identification of "matter," or *res*, with the writer's sense or purpose and *verba* with whatever got in the way of that sense or purpose, as well as their stress on one's personal relationship with *res*, together worked against the very thing that Ascham and his colleagues were in the business of conserving: *verba* taught through rigorous imitative drills in the schools. Wesley Trimpi writes that "any emphasis upon *res*, in contrast to *verba*, would tend, so far as style was concerned, to weaken any doctrine of imitation, which must be, in the long run, concerned with words." The so-called "styleless" Stoic style "gradually threatened to destroy any program for stylistic improvement" and "encouraged intellectual and political independence."[41]

Ascham's attack on those "that care not for words, but for matter" is itself closely modeled on Cicero's *De Oratore* 3.16.60–61, in which Crassus attacks the Socratic dialectic and its "absurd" legacy: a "severance between the tongue and the brain [*cordus*]" that had led to a philosophical chaos peopled by "families at discord with one another and widely separated and unlike."[42] It should be stressed that Ciceronianism – the version of Cicero, that is, that was of most interest to Ascham – was not simply a stylistic program, not simply a way of writing sentences that end, syntactically, where they begin. Cicero and Ascham shared a tradition of thinking about tradition itself, about attacks upon tradition, and about the need to maintain a traditional stock of expressive forms for public use. Normative Ciceronianism provided a style to be conserved as well as a rationale for a particular mode of conservatism. The Stoics – the most troublesome of the "families at discord" – stood in the way of any such *paidiea*, and Crassus attacks them in *De Oratore* 3.18.65–66 on both stylistic and political grounds:

Clearly there is something in them that is quite out of keeping with the orator whom we are depicting: in the first place their assertion that all those who are not wise are slaves, brigands, enemies, madmen, and that all the same nobody is wise – yet it would be the height of folly to place a public meeting or the Senate or any assembly of people under the direction of a person who holds the view that not one of those present is sane, or a citizen, or a free man. There is the further point that even the style of their discourse, though possibly subtle and undoubtedly penetrating, yet for the orator is bald, unfamiliar, jarring on the ear of the public, devoid of clarity, fullness and spirit, while at the same time of a character that makes it impossible to employ it in public speaking; for the Stoics hold a different view of good and bad from all their fellow-citizens or rather from all other nations, and give a different meaning to "honor," "disgrace," "privilege," "punishment" – whether correctly or otherwise does not concern us now, but if we were to adopt their terminology, we should never be able to express our meaning intelligibly about anything.[43]

Stoics such as Seneca and Lipsius were interested in a different sort of style from that of Cicero's ideal orator, one meant not to join groups together but to separate them and keep them so. This style – often explicitly an epistolary style – was appropriate to the politics of dissidence rather than the politics of the forum or court.[44] To distrust a traditional style in the name of one's own honesty is, of course, to suggest that most other writers are dishonest. And indeed, to its enemies Stoic style appeared to issue, not from honesty, but from pride. We have seen that Ascham sensed in the Stoics' bias against "words" a "singular pride in themselves, or some special malice of other, or for some private and partial matter, either in Religion or other kind of learning." For Robert Johnson they were "busie-headed and turbulent." For King James the self-professed Stoics of his court were under the spell of "proud inconstant LIPSIUS" and were in fact "pressing to winne honor." These critics had a point, however misinformed they may have been about the finer points of Stoic philosophy. Pride and the guarding of the self's boundaries *are* recurring themes of Stoic writing, perhaps most strikingly in its republican and oppositional phases. Fulke Greville stated the problem well in "Fame and Honour" (1622) when he reflected on the political consequences of one who trusts only in a "self-constellation" and "makes himself his end": "Selfnesse [is] even apt to teare it self asunder: / All governments, like man himself within / Being restlesse compositions of the sinne."[45] No matter how indifferent to the world he claimed to be, the Stoic was held to be a dangerous political animal. After all, those who hold, as Cicero thought, "a different view of good and bad from all their fellow-citizens" and who give "a different meaning to 'honor,' 'disgrace,' 'privilege,' 'punishment' " will be likely to present at least a tacit challenge to the status quo. Moreover, they will tend to challenge those monarchs engaged in finding their own new meanings for "honor," "disgrace," "privilege," and "punishment" – meanings based, not on absolute personal integrity, but absolute political power.[46]

"INTO GOOD LIKING WITH GOD AGAINE"

James's "proud inconstant LIPSIUS," author of *De Constantia, Politicorum sive Civilis Doctrinae Libri Sex*, and celebrated editor of Tacitus (1574) and Seneca (1605), is the central figure here.[47] Lipsius was dead only a few years into the reign of James I, but Lipsian themes sound the direst strains of that reign and the one following. His influence runs from the broadest political concepts to the subtlest political implications of literary style. And again, his critics allowed their political motivations to be bound up with stylistic concepts. One convenient example is John Earle's characterization of "The Selfe-Conceited Man" in *Micro-Cosmographie* (1628) as one who prefers "whosoever with most Paradox is commended and *Lipsius* his hopping style, before either *Tully* or *Quintilian*."[48] The signs of "selfe-conceit" are for Earle at once stylistic and political. They are mutually reinforcing. The idiosyncratic obscurity of the "hopping" style was analogous to the moral and political shiftiness of the Stoic paradox; and to prefer commendation by paradox meant, of course, that anyone at all might be preferred. Read with sufficient attention, such texts as Sir William Cornwallis's "Prayse of King Richard the Third" (1616) have the effect, if nothing else, of making praise of good kings seem like little more than a special form of nonsense.[49] And again, this critic was close to his target. Earle, like Ascham and James I, was quite justified, I think, in sensing in the Lipsian style an anti-authoritarian and anti-monarchical turn. Although the point will not be allowed by all judges, I suspect that Lipsius encoded a subtle political allegory in the stylistic program of *Epistolica Institutio* (1591). In chapter 11, the central chapter on imitation, he accuses "a few Italians" of needlessly restricting imitation to the texts of Cicero. He proposes instead a multi-staged imitative program meant to encourage a style appropriate for the *adult*:

Oh vain and snobbish! Not only contrary to the thought of the ancient teachers, but contrary to reason and contrary to custom . . . Take your stand with me, reading and imitating all; not, however, all at once or at the same age. There is some distinction among levels of maturity, which I shall set down in practical terms.

There is a certain elementary imitation for *children*, there is *youthful* imitation, and there is *adult* imitation. In the first phase, the sect of the Italians satisfies me: and for some time Cicero should not only be chiefly read, but solely read. To what end? So that, it is evident, the structure and coherence of the prose may at first be strictly formed according to one certain habit, and in a consistent line of discourse . . . Now for youthful and maturing imitation, I admit others, but still gradually, so that you do not proceed by leaps but, as it were, by degrees [through Quintius Curtius, Livy, Caesar, Plautus, Terence, Pliny the Younger, and others]. Let there be this two-year period of recruit-training, as it were, in which there is a hand restraining the style somewhat within a plain toga. Now in due order, in *adult* imitation, I permit him to go forth freely and wander through every type of writer. Read, examine, and gather flowers from every meadow for this garland of eloquence. But especially I would urge the reading of Sallust, Seneca, Tacitus and that kind of concise and subtle writer by whose sharp pruning hook the luxuriance is cut back for a little while, and the discourse is made terse, strong, and truly masculine.[50]

The Ciceronians, if not Cicero himself, are said to be the teachers of children. Yet Lipsius's intention is not to abandon rhetorical imitation for unmediated expression but rather to expand rhetoric's traditional range. The writer must grow, through imitative means, from rhetorical and intellectual dependence to rhetorical and intellectual independence. This is anything but "natural," of course, and Lipsius the consummate rhetorician understood this as well as anyone. Indeed, his program is riven by consciously held paradoxes; he prescribes, as Morris Croll wrote long ago, "les modes de l'expression individuelle, une routine qui assure l'originalité, un système pour produire la nouveauté."[51] Stylistic novelty alone was enough to alarm such peda-gogical conservatives as Roger Ascham, but the important thing to notice here is that Lipsius would have the student reenact, in terms of the history of his own stylistic development, the political history of ancient Rome's turn from open republicanism and military prowess to a closed politics of tyranny and Stoic resistance to tyranny. He inscribes a political and historical allegory within a stylistic pedagogy. Cicero will always be "usefully read and re-read" by adults, "especially in the evening hours and, if occasion permits, just at the time of retiring";[52] but Sallust, Seneca, and Tacitus are good for those who do not want to sleep through a world in violent conflict around them. It does not matter to Lipsius in this context that Cicero died in the name of the Republic. Seneca and Tacitus are for those writers who have gone through their "period of recruit-training" and who want to be "terse, strong, and truly masculine." They are for those writers, Lipsius suggests, who do not have masters or do not want to have them anymore.

In Lipsius's epistolary theory and in his letters themselves, *res* – from the most serious religious and political issues to his gardens and dogs – are always accompanied by a concern with historical and political change. Trimpi has argued that the shift from the Ciceronian to the Senecan model lead to the "cultivation, the analysis, the expression, and even to the dramatization of the individual mind and personality."[53] It did all of these things and more. The shift to the Senecan model was also significant because that model provided a dramatization of the problem of choosing models itself. To follow Seneca was to be deeply involved in the problem of imitation, and to sense as Seneca does in *Epistulae Morales* that reading and writing themselves are best conceived as competitive operations of an individual's "strength" (*WS* 346; 84.1–2). To choose Seneca's letters over Cicero's speeches as models for literary imitation was, as we have seen, to choose a model that represented the virtuous Stoic life as a matter of combat and the acts of writing and reading as subtle and often unsubtle forms of violence. For Lipsius, to follow Seneca was to conceive literary imitation as a problem with historical and political causes and ramifications, and as part of an effort to make a "disciplined, strong, and truly virile" response to real political situations.

Nobody who distrusted the paradoxes and self-proclaimed honesty of the Stoics could find much comfort in Lipsius's *De Constantia*. Lipsius, as Croll demonstrated so well, was the most important, most creative exponent of Senecan style in his time; but *De Constantia* fuses, as none of his other texts do, his favorite stylistic *desiderata* with challenging ethical and political concepts. Indeed, style is not the central issue in *De Constantia*. Langius's one departure from the "craggie hill of philosophy" into what he calls "the pleasant fieldes of philology" and "historicall and delectable matters" features appalling stories of murderous tyrants, plagues, famines, natural calamities, and a long casualty list of ancient battles (*TBC* 177–78, 184–94). Renaissance philology had seldom been less "pleasant." Lipsius is concerned with the proper way of living for persons surrounded by civil war, persons whose lives are structured and even fulfilled by war, persons who are even said to have war *inside* themselves. He wrote *De Constantia* during his years in Leiden, the center of learning in the new Dutch republic. Its Stoic heroes are most often republicans caught in losing battles with the vices of monarchs. Their virtue does not save them from failure, but it does save them from despair:

Doth it grieve thee that Pompey should be overthrowne in Pharsalia, and his army almost consisting of Senatours? That the Tyrant shoulde take his pleasure and pastime awhiles in the bloud of citizens? I blame thee not much, considering that Cato himselfe here lost the helme of sound Judgment, & from his heart uttered this doubtful voice, *Divine matters are full of obscurity.* Notwithstanding thou Lipsius, thou Cato, cast your eies a little aside, you shall see one thing that will bringe you into good liking with God againe. Behold that Cesar, statly, a conquerour, in his own and some other folks opinion, a very god; Slaine in, and of the Senate. And that not with one simple death, but wounded with three and twenty severall thrusts, and rouling in his own bloud like a beast. And (what more could you wishe?) this was donne even in the courte of Pompei, the Image of Pompei standing there on high, celebrating a greate sacrifice to the ghost of that Greate one. (*TBC* 167–68)

This is typical of *De Constantia* both in argument and image. To confront "you" with histories of violence and yet to then "bringe you into good liking with God againe" is Lipsius's aim throughout. But what, morally and politically speaking, does being "in good liking with God" entail? The crucial thing is that one must believe that God's plans are *not* "full of obscurity" at all. Lipsius does not ask readers to blindly accept a fate they cannot understand. Virtue is and always has been under attack in the world, but he insists that we have no cause to abandon it. For Julius Caesar, as Langius reminds his friend, *was* killed under Pompey's statue. Of Mark Antony he asks: "Where art thou now that of late wast Lord of all the east? Leader of the Romaine Armies? Persecuter of Pompei and the common-wealth? Loe thou hangest in a rope by thy bloudy hands!" (*TBC* 168). God, insofar as He was involved in Roman history, was a republican at heart.

Divine justice is always at work in Lipsius's violent world, and in *De Constantia* it is always at work against tyranny. It has even worked, it should be noted, against such "happy" princes as Augustus: "Let him be happy and mighty Caesar, and truly *Augustus*: But with all . . . let him live with his *Livia* unhonestlie married, unhonestlie kepte: And upon whom he doted with unlawfull love, let him die a shamefull death by her meanes" (*TBC* 168–69). Princes "happy" and unhappy are the great scourges to be faced in *De Constantia*. Stoically conceiving them and their threats as beneath one's care does not necessarily make one a republican, of course, but republicans were likely to be the best models of such behavior for the editor of Tacitus's *Opera* (1574) and the many readers whose historical, political, and philosophical judgments were influenced by that great edition. Lipsius wrote in his preface – here quoted in Degory Wheare's *De Ratione et Methodo Legendi Historias* (1623) – that Tacitus is a

usefull and a great writer, and who ought to be in their hands, who have the steering of the Common-wealth and Government . . . Let every one in him consider the Courts of Princes, their private Lives, Counsels, Commands, Actions, and from the apparent Similitude that is betwixt those times and ours, let them expect the like Events; you shall find under Tyranny, Flattery and Informers, Evils too well known in our times, nothing simple and sincere, and no true fidelity even amongst Friends; frequent accusations of Treason, the onely fault of those who had no fault; the Destruction of great men in heaps, and a Peace more cruel than any War. I confess the greatest part of his History is full of unpleasant and sorrowfull Accidents, but then let us suppose what was spoken by the dying *Thrasea*, spoken to every one of us; *Young man, consider well, and though I implore the Gods to avert the* Omen, *yet you are born in those times that require the well fixing your mind by examples of Constancy*.[34]

To say that "Courts of Princes" are typically corrupt is to suggest, whether one wants to or not, that there must be some better way of governing a commonwealth. For Tacitus a better way had been republican government, although it was fast becoming a distant memory and heroes like Thrasea were seeming more and more unreal. Lipsius had no substantive political platform to offer either – we cannot ignore the fact that he ended his career in Louvain under the watchful eyes of the Jesuits and Spanish Habsburgs – but the proposition that "Courts of Princes" enforce "a Peace more cruel than any War" is matched in *De Constantia* by the implication that war itself may actually be a reasonable alternative to such a vicious peace.

Indeed, Lipsius's Stoic argument is structured on the analogy of campaign strategy and battle tactics. For instance, Langius opens chapter 13 of book 1 with this rhetorical enfilade:

I come nowe from skirmishes to handie-gripes, and from light bickerings, to the maine battell. I will leade forth all my souldiers in order under their Ensignes, dividing them into fower troupes . . . These troupes if they discharge their partes each one in his place, can the whole armie of your SORROW make anie resistance, or once open the mouth against me? No trulie, I must have the victorie. In token whereof sound the Trumpets, and strike up the drummes. (*TBC* 101)

Constancy can be quite exciting to the man of honor familiar with the arts of modern war. Oestreich has judged that "the famous Lipsian style, with its terse, laconic, peremptory language and its abundance of military similes and metaphors, was bound to captivate the select circle of officers educated in the classics, a class which was so important in this warlike age."[55]

But Lipsius's military rhetoric also has a basis in Stoic tradition. It is an early-modern equivalent of the eloquence which Plutarch tells us Cato "studied . . . because he would there should be certaine warlike Forces entertained in civill Philosophy." There is also a basis for Lipsius's images and concepts, as we have seen, in Seneca's moral *acies*. Violence functions more than rhetorically in *De Constantia*: it characterizes the very essence of the self – the same sort of self seen by the blind Prince Mirza in *The Sophy* – that must be attacked, divided, and conquered. This fact is not clear at first to the ingenuous Lipsius: "If I love quietnesse and rest," he complains to Langius, "the Trumpets and ratling of armour interrupt mee. If I take solace in my countrey gardens and farmes, the souldiers and murtherers force mee into the Towne." If we suppose that Stoics love "quietnesse and rest," Langius teaches us otherwise: the goal, rather, is to make our minds "so confirmed and conformed, that we may bee at rest in troubles, and have peace even in the midst of warre" (*TBC* 72). To Lipsius's desire to leave "this infortunate and unhappie *Belgica*" and "chaunge *Land* for *land*, and to flie into some other part of the world" (*TBC* 72), Langius responds:

This thy wandering into other countries shall not availe thee, it shall nothing boot thee . . . For thou shalt still finde an enemie about thee, yea even in that closet of thine. (And therewithall hee stroke me on the breast) what good will it do thee to be setled in a peaceable place? Thou cariest warre with thee. What can a quiet habitation benefit thee? Troubles are ever about thee, yea in thee. For this distracted mind of thine warreth, and ever will be at warre with it selfe, in coveting, in flying, in hoping, in despairing. And as they that for fear turne their backes to their enemies, are in the greater danger, having their face from their foe, and their backes unarmed. So fareth it with these ignorant novices, who never have made any resistance against their affections: but by flight yeelded unto them. (*TBC* 77–78)

If the Stoic can have "peace even in the midst of warre," he is also aware that one must always battle against a mind that "warreth, and ever will be at warre with it selfe," regardless of the physical surroundings.[56] The Stoic is indeed, as Robert Johnson put it, "busie-headed and turbulent." The metaphors of Senecan and Lipsian Stoicism carry war from a world at war to the self and thence to a warlike world again. Where the circuit starts – inside or outside the pickets, as it were – is less important than the fact that this rhetoric of violence is never interrupted by philosophy or treaty. Moral success and moral failure are both defined in martial terms in *De Constantia*. Combat of one sort or another – life in the *acies* or "warre" – is the primary Stoic experience. There is only one form of violence that Lipsius will not countenance. At the close of book 1, the culmination of the chapters on destiny, Langius tells Lipsius: "If thou see by certain and infallible tokens that the fatall alteration of the State is come, with mee this saying shall prevaile, *Not to fight against God*" (*TBC* 127). In *De Constantia* it is never a matter of refusing to go to war, but rather of choosing one's wars wisely. If fighting *against* God is the greatest failure in this world, fighting *for* God is the greatest victory.

"WAR AND PEACE RECONCILED"

Much like Seneca, then, Lipsius emphasized the violence focused and manipulated in the Stoic attitude. Moreover, whereas Seneca wrote one treatise *De Ira* – facing down anger like a lion trainer, as he might say – Lipsius wrote numerous lengthy and exacting works chronicling and rationalizing the forms and uses of violence in the ancient world: from the Greek phalanx and Roman maniple to the amphitheater, from siege engines to all the varieties of crucifixion.[57] Beyond his gargantuan philological efforts, Lipsius's wider project amounted to an effort to tell the history of violence in all its classical cultural forms. Seneca's philosophical *acies* is historicized and even literalized in Lipsius's humanist scholarship; while in Seneca the philosophical life is a kind of war, in Lipsius war is the kind of life most interesting to the philosopher. In *De Ampitheatro Liber* (1584) and *Saturnalium Sermonum Libri Duo, qui de Gladiatoribus* (1585), for instance, Lipsius discusses the "reason" of amphitheaters and arenas, and explores with scholarly relish the practices of gladiatorial spectacles from the communicating perspectives of both audience and combatant. Swords are thrust amid the gamesters and literati, while philosophy and letters serve in turn as handmaidens to the history of violence. Indeed, it is not simply that Lipsius advises constancy in the face of a violent world: he is evidently fascinated by violence itself. Whether this thematization of violence had a definite political purpose for Lipsius is debatable. Oestreich has argued not only that the ideal readers of *De Constantia* were military officers trained in the classics, but that Lipsian Stoicism in general was an "activism" totally in the service of bureaucratic absolutism. "The Lipsian view of man and the world," he writes, "entails rationalization of the state and its apparatus of government, autocratic rule by the prince, the imposition of discipline on his subjects, and strong military defence."[58] The problem with this argument is that it has virtually no applicability to sixteenth- and seventeenth-century England. We have seen that Seneca, Lipsius, and Stoicism generally were not liked by English authorities. Certainly, they did not realize – if French, Spanish, and Dutch authorities ever did – that Lipsian Stoicism "constituted the theory behind the powerful military and administrative structure of the centralized state of the seventeenth century."[59] King James is famous for his heartfelt if somewhat sporadic absolutism, but he put no trust in "that Stoick insensible stupiditie [that proud inconstant LIPSIUS perswadeth in his Constantia]." The reasons for this difference are not entirely clear. J. H. M. Salmon has pointed to a special English "blend" of Senecan Stoicism and Tacitean realism: "Tacitus politicized Senecan philosophy and gave it a cynical bent, while Seneca strengthened the lessons, already suggested in Tacitus's history of Roman tyranny and civil war, that private prudence and withdrawal were the best policies."[60] But the English "blend" was hardly unique: Lipsius himself presents Tacitus in Senecan terms and vice versa in the pages of *De Constantia*. The King's animosity was crucial in the political formation of English Stoicism, as Salmon points out, but it appears to have been aroused less by a dislike of cynicism or withdrawal than by an unwillingness to compete for honor with those who thought that honor was not a thing dispensed by a monarch – those who, as Cicero's Crassus says in *De Oratore*, "give a different meaning to 'honor,' 'disgrace,' 'privilege,' 'punishment.'" James's focus on honor when denouncing the Stoics in *Basilikon Doron* seems deeply motivated when we consider the cultural links between Stoicism and conflict discussed above. To speak of honor in courtly contexts was to speak in metaphors drawn from the traditions of war, metaphors still quick with malice. "Pressing to winne honor" meant looking for a fight in a court and country that did not have enough honors to go around.

James was responding to some essential themes in Stoic thought. He was, after all, dealing with writers who liked to say that "vertue gapeth after danger," that "Souldiers [of virtue] glory in their wounds, &

joyfully shew the bloud that runneth from them, if it be spent in a good cause" (Seneca); and that "such things as bee pure, everlasting, and of fierie nature, set nought by all external & violent handling" (Lipsius). This is not the language of docile subjects. "And when the time shall come, that the world shall cease, to the end it may be renewed againe," says Seneca in one of his many alarming excursions into Stoic physics, all "things will beat and break one another, and all things set on fire . . . We also that are blessed soules and partakers of eternitie, when it shall seeme good unto God to warpe these things once againe . . . shall returne into our ancient elements" (*WS* 738; *Cons. ad Marciam* 26.6). In *De Constantia* Lipsius defends "the Stoickes my friendes . . . who were the authors of VIOLENT FATE, which with Seneca I define to be, *A necessitie of all thinges and actions, which no force can withstande or breake*" (*TBC* 115).

"VIOLENT FATE" is here, of course, a technical term; but fate really *is* violent for Lipsius, and the better part of book 2 would justify the ways of a violent God to violent men. "I say these publike calamities which we suffer are profitable unto us accompanied with an inward fruit and commoditie. Do we call them EVILS? Nay rather they are good . . . The original of these miseries . . . is of God" (*TBC* 142–43). Calamities "do moreover prove and trie us. Else how could any man be assured of his own proceeding and firmnesse in vertue?" (*TBC* 149). The afflictions of good men make for good examples: "so many notable citizens we see to be violently & injuriously either banished or murthered: but out of the rivers of their blood we do (as it were) drink vertue & constancy every day" (*TBC* 150). Such attitudes amount, as Braden has suggested, both to a death wish and to drama.[61] The afflictions of good and bad men together make for excellent theater:

Nowe then in this Tragedy of the World, why art not thou so favourable towards God, as to a poore Poet? This wicked man prospereth. That Tyrant liveth. Let be awhiles. Remember it is but the first Act, and consider aforehand in thy minde, that sobs and sorrowes will ensue uppon their sollace. This Scene will anon swimme in bloud, then these purple and golden garments shall be rowled therein. For that Poet of ours is singular cunning in his art, and will not lightly transgresse the lawes of his Tragedie. (*TBC* 163)

Violence for the Stoic is at once inevitable and universal. It is also, as we have seen, wholly characteristic of the individual self: "Troubles are ever about thee, yea in thee." There is war in peace and peace in war. Stoics draw no hard distinction between them, just as they draw no hard distinction between physical reward and physical punishment. Such distinctions are either erased entirely or interpreted in the manner of the Stoic paradoxes. "Warre," writes Cornwallis in his grim *Discourses upon Seneca the Tragedian* (1601), "is the remedy for a State surfeited with peace, it is a medicine for Commonwealths sick of too much ease and tranquil-itie."[62] Although not classed by Seneca, Calvin, or Hooker with food, drink, clothing, and the other *adiaphora*, war and peace may be said to be things indifferent within Stoic and, for that matter, Puritan thought. War is given to us by God for our use; like this or that meat or drink, it is good or bad only with regard to how one uses it or how one thinks about it.[63] When one turns misfortunes to benefits and makes virtues of war's necessities, war is no worse – and it is quite possibly better – than being at peace; and, when one uses peace virtuously, it is much the same as fighting a war. It is fitting that the last English translation of *De Constantia* to appear in the seventeenth century is entitled *War and Peace Reconciled* (1672).[64] To "reconcile" war and peace in the Stoic manner is not to beat swords into ploughshares but to commit oneself to a life in which war and peace are political and psychological equivalents.

Such views were offensive to English kings. Oestreich may well be correct to argue that the metaphorical militarism of *De Constantia* was attractive to authorities on the Continent, where religious and dynastic wars were presently ongoing features of political life and where rulers needed populaces that were always "ready to fight." These were wars, however, that both James and his son Charles, after 1630, made it their prime foreign policy goals to avoid. James began his reign as the *Rex Pacificus* and did his best to remain such. He was a king who marched in triumphs not of war but of peace. As Jonathan Goldberg has shown, his coronation entrance to London in 1603 "was a triumph in the high Roman style," complete with arches bearing "a strong meaning, since they . . . situate James's entrance in the context of the absolutist revival of classicism."[65] The entertainments of the London entrance and many of the masques of the following years represent James as Augustus Caesar – but whether he was Augustus or Julius mattered less than that he triumphed in all things including peace. In the King's coronation entertainment at Temple Bar, Ben Jonson made "Irene, or Peace" triumph over "Mars, groveling, his armour scattered upon him in several pieces, and sundry sorts of weapons broken about him"; Jonson explains: "Her word to all was UNA TRIUMPHIS INNUMERIS POTIOR . . . Signifying that peace alone was better, and more to be coveted than innumerable triumphs."[66] Or, as Goldberg puts it, "peace is more powerful than innumerable triumphs, because it is triumph itself."[67] A peace policy became synonymous with Stuart rule. Apologists for Charles's personal rule could defend it in the name of the peace it preserved, and a "Caroline Myth of Peace" energized the praise and laments of many royalist writers in the 1630s and 1640s.[68]

For some Englishmen, however, the long Jacobean and Caroline *pax* was specious at best, dishonest at worst. A Stoical protestant militarism had been espoused by Sir Philip Sidney in the 1580s; later Essex and his intellectuals – the "Senecan and Tacitean cults" – combined a warlike protestantism with Senecan and Tacitean critiques of the late-Elizabethan court. This tradition was carried on during the reigns of James and Charles by those who refused to take the royal peace at face value. They saw peace as vicious when used viciously and war as virtuous when used virtuously – and a virtuous war was more likely, they thought, when fought by a citizen militia under Parliamentary control.[69] Fulke Greville, sometimes the Seneca and sometimes the Jeremiah of the Jacobean and Caroline world, condemns war as "the perfect type of Hell" in "A Treatie of Warres" (1622). But what begins as a praise of peace soon becomes praise of war's characteristic virtues. In war one finds "much more politicke celerity, / Diligence, courage, constancy . . . / Than in good arts of Peace or piety"; and, of course, one can see "the hand of God . . . / In all these sufferings of our guiltinesse."[70] Many watched for the divine signs of "violent fate." To advocates of an aggressive protestant foreign policy, the blessed Jacobean and Caroline peace was purchased at the cost of the slow loss of the protestant cause in Europe. The ineptly managed feints by the Duke of Buckingham at Cadiz (1625) and La Rochelle (1627) were embarrassing failures; but even if successful they would not have given Frederick of Bohemia and his English queen, Elizabeth, the help that the Earl of Bristol and others thought was deserved. "In all our enterprises lately," Bristol declared in the House of Lords, "we have been as he that shoots against marble, whose arrow rebounds back upon himself . . . The distress of our friends lies before us, the power and malice of our enemies."[71]

A philosophy that argued that there was no important difference between peace and war for the virtuous person, that argued that God was not necessarily interested in peace – that God may well want us to be embroiled in war and civil war for our eventual correction and benefit – could not help but be subversive of royal policy at a time when royal policy was synonymous with peace and diplomatic evasiveness. After the war that eventually did break out had been concluded, it was natural for Milton to look back on Cromwell's pre-war private life and see seamless relationships between Stoic control of the self and masterful control of the means, tactics, and strategies of organized violence:

When war broke out . . . he soon surpassed well-nigh the greatest generals both in the magnitude of his accomplishments and in the speed with which he achieved them. Nor was this remarkable, for he was a soldier well-versed in self-knowledge, and whatever enemy lay within – vain hopes, fears, desires – he had either previously destroyed within himself or had long since reduced to subjection. Commander first over himself, victor over himself, he had learned to achieve over himself the most effective triumph, and so, on the very first day that he took service against an external foe, he entered camp a veteran and past-master in all that concerned the soldier's life. (*CPW* IV, 667–68)

Cromwell, Milton insists in the *Defensio Secunda*, had been fighting a war against his passions all through the Caroline *pax* – a "Peace," he no doubt thought, "more cruel than any War." The Protector had been much like the valiant Prince Mirza conquering "Torrents of Anger, Mountains of Ambition; / Gulfes of Desire, and Towers of Hope." Unlike Mirza, however, he lived to fight his external enemies as well.

In the sixth chapter of the first book of *De Constantia*, "The praise of Constancie: And an earnest exhortation thereunto," Langius asks Lipsius, "Hast thou not seene in the armes and targets of some men of our time, that lofty poesie? *Neither with hope, nor with feare*" (*TBC* 83). Langius is speaking of a nobleman's coat-of-arms or *impresa*, which John Florio defined in *Queen Anna's New World of Words* (1611) as "An attempt, an enterprise, an undertaking. Also an impresse, a word, a mot or embleme. Also a jewell worne in ones hat, with some devise in it."[72] The "lofty poesie" of this defiant Stoicism is figured in the actions, words, clothes, and even bodies of its noble exemplars. This is a "lofty" kind of existential "poesie" indeed – so high, so sublime that Plutarch, who usually would have none of it, wrote famously in his *Moralia* that "the fables of Poets [are] devised with more probability and likelihood of reason" than "this Lapith of the Stoicks, to wit, their imagined wise man."[73] Any poet worth the name in the seventeenth century would have taken this comment as a challenge to represent the Stoic loftiness poetically. "*Neither with hope, nor with feare*" may not strike us as probable, reasonable, or especially poetical, but in the following chapter we shall see that Andrew Marvell found just such "lofty poesie" in the example of the Lord General Thomas Fairfax.

CHAPTER 2

Andrew Marvell: the Stoicism
of nature, war, and work

Likewise, according to his custome, [Zeno] concludeth his argument with a similitude: If out of an Olive-tree should come har-
monious Pipes, that made Musick, you would not doubt, but that
the science of Musick were in the Olive-tree. What if a Plain-tree
should bear Musicall instruments, you would think there were
Musick in those Plain-trees: Why then should we not judge the
world to be animate and wise, that produceth out of it selfe animate
and wise creatures?

Thomas Stanley, *The History of Philosophy*, paraphrasing Cicero,
De Natura Deorum 2.22.[1]

When Andrew Marvell entered Lord Fairfax's service in 1650, both men
were faced with the problem of what to do with the retired life that
Fairfax had just so surprisingly chosen. Peace had been a more provoca-
tive and in some ways more dangerous choice than war. Indeed, the
poems that Marvell wrote while living at Nunappleton suggest that he
felt that peace, or peace as obtained by Fairfax at least, needed to be
defended to those who had gotten accustomed to the ongoing victories
of the Saints on the battlefield – victories for which Fairfax himself, as
commander-in-chief of the Parliamentary army, had been directly or
indirectly responsible. Although its horrors were not to be denied, war
had seldom been a more normal, more expected state of affairs in
England than during the summer of 1651 as Marvell was writing "Upon
Appleton House" and Fairfax was testing the political limits of a peaceful life.[2] Even after their astounding victory at Dunbar, "Cromwell's
forces were tied down in a war of attrition through the spring of 1651.
English pamphlets, newsbooks and diaries remained full of war and the
rumor of war . . . Scottish forces moved towards the border in late July.
Should they take the eastern road into England they would pass within a
few miles of Fairfax's estate."[3] Marvell and Fairfax may well have felt as

Lipsius does when, near the beginning of *De Constantia*, he laments "the many years . . . we have been expos'd to the Rage of Civill Warres" and asks: "Is't *Quiet*, and *Retirednesse* that I would enjoy? The *Trumpet* interrupts it. Is't the pleasure of *Gardens*, or the *Country*? The Barbarous Souldier forces me to this *City*."[4] If the integrity of Fairfax's retirement – not to mention his property lines – was to be honored in 1651, it would need to present a strong front to the "Barbarous Souldier" and his leaders. Moreover, it was not enough for Marvell to defend his master's turn from the warlike *past*: he needed also to defend his turn from the nation's warlike *future*.

Marvell's solution in "Upon Appleton House" was in part, as John Wallace argued many years ago in *Destiny His Choice*, to make Fairfax's retirement seem "more active in a Christian sense than many superficially more heroic deeds in the active life."[5] The solution was also, as I shall argue here, to encourage Fairfax and his detractors to understand his Stoicism in the most vigilant and politically dangerous senses imaginable. For Marvell's poetic defenses of Fairfax follow the spirit and sometimes even the letter of the Stoic lessons that Langius gives Lipsius in *De Constantia* – lessons that would preserve peace, not by eradicating war, but by erasing the lines that inconstant "opinion" draws between war and peace, retirement and action. Indeed, the philosophical and rhetorical designs of *De Constantia* are present in the purlieus of Marvell's two most warlike retirement poems, "Upon Appleton House" and "Upon the Hill and Grove at Bill-Borow," and even in that Neoplatonic, Epicurean, Libertine, and meta-critical poem on "The Garden." "To what purpose . . . will it be," asks Langius, "to come to where *Peace* is, when you have a *Warre* within you" (*DC* 9)? It would be to no purpose at all, replies Marvell, as he puts before Fairfax images of a highly vigilant Stoic retirement – a retirement by no means incompatible with future action – focused on *winning* the battles of what Milton would soon call in *Defensio Secunda* "the warfare of peace."

At times it is as if the poet is reading *De Constantia* in Fairfax's gardens, writing a noble Stoic's "lofty poesie" (*TBC* 83) and "envi'd *Motto*" in them (*DC* 16), and thereby putting into practice Langius's advice concerning the "*true* use, and End of Gardens" (*DC* 81). Seneca, Lipsius, and the Stoic tradition were meaningful throughout the period, and during his lifetime Marvell could have read *De Constantia* in Stradling's spirited translation from 1594, in a verse rendering published in 1653, in fine prose versions by Richard Goodridge (1654) and Nathaniel Wanley

(1670), and, of course, in Lipsius's still-fashionable Latin. In "Upon the Hill and Grove at Bill-Borow" and "Upon Appleton House" Marvell follows Seneca and Lipsius in representing inner battles as outer ones and vice versa, thus expressing the moral indifference of war and peace for the Stoic, and offering for the nation's approval Fairfax's retreat as an occasion for newfound religious, political, and even military achievement. The conflict posed in "The Garden" is less between action and retirement than between two modes of retirement, Epicurean and Stoic, which may have signified political choices for Marvell before and perhaps especially after the Restoration. Siding with the active, performative Stoicism of Seneca and Lipsius, he teaches us that writing in a garden can also be a productive way of living in the public world – a thesis perhaps inspired in part by the Stoic understanding of nature itself as being, as Zeno observes by way of his "similitude" of musical trees, "animate and wise."

This is not to say that Lipsius's *De Constantia*, Seneca's *Epistulae Morales*, or any other philosophical text can provide a key to these eclectic and notoriously difficult poems. Marvell was not that kind of poet, not a versifier of doctrine in the manner of, for example, Fulke Greville. Stoicism was traditional, but Marvell figures tradition not as *dictum* but as dialogue among various competing texts. Moreover, we must keep in mind that *De Constantia* is itself a work of literary art, not a philosophical system, and that like other humanist dialogues it is not a simple work of literature. I shall argue rather that Marvell was fascinated by the Senecan and Lipsian visions, and that he saw they were founded on figures and a sense of paradox not unfamiliar to the poetic motions of his mind. But since the manner of this poetic fascination is as much dialectical and critical as it is sympathetic, we shall need to work through the contextual relationships carefully in order to recover what was once implicit in some of Marvell's finest poems.

"ARMES . . . LAID UP IN A *MAGAZINE*": *DE CONSTANTIA*, "UPON THE HILL AND GROVE AT BILL-BOROW," AND "UPON APPLETON HOUSE"

Perhaps the most familiar passages of *De Constantia* to modern eyes are found in the first three chapters of book 2 concerning Langius's garden. At the close of the third of these chapters Langius asks: "Do you think it troubles Me, what the *French*, or *Spaniards* are plotting? who *keepes*, or who *loses* the Scepter of *Belgia*? . . . None of these. Guarded, and secur'd against any thing *External*, I am *bounded* with *My selfe*; Carelesse of all Things, but this *One*; That I may submit this my Mind, tam'd, and broken, to *Right Reason*, and *God*; and all other Humane Things to my *Mind*" (*DC* 81–82). Richard Goodridge, whose *Discourse of Constancy* I shall use when quoting from *De Constantia* in this chapter, echoes Langius in his lengthy summary poem:

> And what is't that can harm Me now? I'm free;
> Yet by no *Monstrous, taynted* Liberty,
> Above all *Humane pow'r*, secure and High
> I *quietly* attend *All misery*.   (*DC* 159)

If such language is familiar it is not, I suppose, because Lipsius is often read these days but because Goodridge seems to confirm what we already believe about Stoicism: that it advocates withdrawal to a place "Above all *Humane pow'r*" where one can be unconcerned with one's actual surroundings, responsibilities, and possibilities. But "uncon-cerned" is not quite the correct word for the attitude expressed in *De Constantia*. To be "Guarded, and secur'd against any thing *External*" is, after all, to consider oneself as living under siege, as *needing* to live as if under siege even when one is in a quiet garden. Within the fortress mentality of *De Constantia* there is a garden, but within this garden there is, as Langius puts it in book 2, chapter 3, a metaphorical *"Magazine"*: "There I either satisfie my Mind with *Reading*, or plant it with the seedes of good *Meditations*. And as Armes are laid up in a *Magazine*; so doe I, from them, store up Precepts in my Mind, which are alwaies ready by mee, against every *impression*, and *Danger* of For-tune" (*DC* 81). The vivid militaristic rhetoric of book 1 of *De Constantia* leads in book 2, not to anything resembling untroubled philosophical peace, but rather to images of the mind as a fortress, images that replace one set of military tactics, as it were, with another set more appropriate to a life involving, as Langius stresses, *"Meditation, Reading, Writing"* (*DC* 81).

Langius's imagery may suggest to some of us a defensive, even regressive attitude, but it should be emphasized that the fortress did not signify at this time failure, hopelessness, or even separation from the world. Neither the experience of the siege nor the hope for security against sieges were uncommon for persons living in the Netherlands in the fourth quarter of the sixteenth century. During this time through-out Europe, writes a historian of fortress warfare, "most people in a theatre of war considered themselves lucky to have walls and a garrison as protection against marauding bands."[6] The fortress town, that basic fact of so much early modern life, expresses in its orderly streets, public greens and markets, and ingeniously engineered bastions, moats, and counterscarps the dependency of arts, sciences, and commerce on the most advanced, "secure" technologies of violence. Indeed, it was a city's lack of such defenses that could suggest isolation from wider political, economic, and cultural communities. "In fact the whole urban area" of the fortress "represented a subtle compromise between the two concepts of the city as a place for people to live in and a place for soldiers to defend," and *De Constantia* instructs its readers to make similar compromises in their own psychological and political architectures.[7] If Langius prefers reading and writing in his gardens over a more active life in the world, it is because Lipsius was pragmatic enough to model the good life on the basic military means by which the Dutch republicans were then maintaining their novel political integrity: the fortress and the tortoise-like methods of fortress warfare.[8] Langius's "Armes . . . laid up in a *Magazine*" remind us that there is no important distance between his garden, his "Mind," and the fiery conflicts that surround both. The pleasures of *remissio* and *lusus*, the "Recreation . . . and Release" that Langius finds in his garden (*DC* 81), are never more than temporary and perhaps are only names for *turbae* in a major key. Here one writes about violence from a central, strategic place within that violence. There is a "*Magazine*" within the green "Arbour" (*DC* 81).

A natural place to begin considering Marvell, civil war, and the Lipsian garden would seem to be "The Garden." Nevertheless, it will be best, given the evidence (discussed in the following section) that the poem was not finished until well after the Restoration, to walk first through "Upon the Hill and Grove at Bill-Borow" and "Upon Appleton House." These poems, which were almost certainly begun and finished in the early 1650s, are both more violent in their imagery and more vigilant in their Stoicism than "The Garden." Although there is no Lipsian "*Magazine*" in "The Garden," there are many such things in these earlier garden spaces. As in "The Garden," however, Marvell represents these gardens, groves, and woods as essays or studies, as it were, rather than finished canvasses. The reality of Fairfax and his estate in "Upon the Hill and Grove at Bill-Borow" is so perfect that it cannot truly, so Marvell informs us, be pictured at all: not even the "softest Pensel" could "draw a Brow / So equal as this Hill does bow" (lines 5–6).[9] The decorum of this remarkable poem would not only balance imperfect representations of perfection but also the extremes of private virtue and public violence. Indeed, the final couplet – "Nor he the Hills without the Groves, / Nor Height but with Retirement loves" (lines 79–80) – summarizes the poem's larger argument so neatly that we may forget the troubling messages of the "Groves" themselves. Grounding Fairfax's rights in force, not law, these "aged Trees" are said to frighten away any "hostile hand" who "durst ere invade / With impious Steel the sacred Shade":

> For something alwaies did appear
> Of the *great Masters* terrour there:
> And Men could hear his Armour still
> Ratling through all the grove and Hill.   (lines 35–40)

Fairfax's "*Oracles* in Oak" (line 74) are as "animate and wise" as Zeno's olive and plane trees. They have "sense, / As We, of Love and Reverence" (lines 49–50). Yet when they speak for themselves in their "modest Whispers," they choose to call attention to their own representational inadequacy. They feel humbled by the "other Groves" and "Mountains" of Fairfax's former wars:

> Much other Groves, say they, than these
> And other Hills him once did please.
> Through Groves of Pikes he thunder'd then,
> And Mountains rais'd of dying Men.
> For all the *Civic Garlands* due
> To him our Branches are but few.
> Nor are our trunks enow to bear
> The *Trophees* of one fertile Year.   (lines 65–72)

The "Groves of Pikes" and "Mountains . . . of dying Men" impress the trees beyond their capacity to contain, reward, or "bear" the "fertile" past as finished once and for all. But their humility is a kind of praise, of course, and their self-professed failure to represent the past as a finished monument – to "bear / The *Trophees* of one fertile Year" – is integral to the poem's political strategy. If their "Branches are but few" to "all the *Civic Garlands* due" to Fairfax, it is because Fairfax has indeed been responsible for the slaughter of larger "Groves" and raised great "Mountains" – not mere "Hills" – "of dying Men." The figurative failure of the "*Oracles* in Oak" produces a kind of hammer-and-anvil sublimity not inappropriate to martial panegyric. The trees are good self-critics, "certain *Oracles*," says the poet:

'Tis true, yee Trees nor ever spoke
More certain *Oracles* in Oak.
But Peace (if you his favour prize)
That Courage its own Praises flies.
Therefore to your obscurer Seats
From his own Brightness he retreats:
Nor he the Hills without the Groves,
Nor Height but with Retirement loves.   (lines 73–80)

The poem withholds a threat at the same time that it makes one; in the act of asserting the Fairfacian political motto of "Height . . . with Retirement," Marvell also dissolves distinctions between action and stasis, war and peace, past and present, and even the dead and "dying." We should "notice," writes Donald Friedman, that this final stanza "contains no suggestion that Fairfax has rejected the arts of warfare and public policy *per se.*"[10] The "Groves" and "Mountains" of dead men are pointedly left unmourned by the poet and the "*Oracles* in oak," for to mourn them would be to admit that they are done "dying" and that Fairfax is done winning.

But why does Fairfax need "Height" now that he has chosen "Retirement"? Who, exactly, are the enemies of this man who no longer has enemies? Marvell's "*Oracles* in oak" are again suggestive, perhaps more suggestive than Fairfax himself might have wished. To have oak trees praise a general in such warlike terms was itself a curious move given what we know about Marvell's reading in the early 1650s. It is often said that the Cromwellian "three-fork'd Lightning" that "blast[s]" "*Caesars* head" in the "Horatian Ode" (lines 21–24) alludes to *Pharsalia* 1.143–57, where Caesar is compared to the terrifying and irresistible *flamma* and *ignes* of the heavens. It is somewhat less well-known, however, that Pompey the Great, who "in years was grown, / And long accustomed to a peaceful gown," has just been compared by Lucan to an old oak:

> now strength he sought not out,
> Relying on his ancient fortunes fame,
> And stood the shadow of a glorious name.
> As an old Lofty Oak, that heretofore
> Great Conquerours spoils, and sacred Trophies bore,
> Stands firm by his own weight, his root now dead,
> And through the air his naked boughs does spread,
> And with his trunk, not leaves, a shadow makes:
> He, though each blast of Eastern winds him shake,
> And round about well rooted trees do grow,
> Is onely honour'd; but in *Caesar* now

Remains not onely a great Generals name,
But restless valour, and in war a shame
Not to be Conquerour.[11]

Marvell turns Lucan's epic simile of lost power into allegorical geography: it is not that Fairfax is like an old oak tree but rather that he has Fairfacian oaks on his property. Having thus distanced the trees somewhat from the man, Marvell rewrites the meaning of the trees against Lucan's model:

> Yet now no further strive to shoot,
> Contented if they fix their Root.
> Nor to the winds uncertain gust,
> Their prudent Heads too far intrust.
> Onely sometimes a flutt'ring Breez
> Discourses with the breathing Trees;
> Which in their modest Whispers name
> Those Acts that swell'd the Cheek of Fame. (lines 57–64)

Fairfax was, after all, one of those unsuspecting men who had "nurst," as Marvell writes in the "Horatian Ode," "the three-fork'd Lightning" that "Did thorough his own Side / His fiery way divide" (lines 13–16). Putting complex historical events into the poetic shorthand of the *Pharsalia*, "Upon the Hill and Grove at Bill-Borow," and the "Horatian Ode," one could say that Cromwell burned many groves of oaks before finally blasting the royal "Laurels" (line 24) at Whitehall. Parallels between the Lord General and Pompey the Great may have seemed quite obvious to Marvell's readers – not least in their parallel ironies. Generals who enjoyed tremendous success in fighting against established order, they both came to represent the last hope of political traditionalists. Nevertheless, if the Fairfacian "*Oracles* in Oak" are being compared with the old Pompeian oak laden with *veteres exuviae* and *sacrata dona*, the comparison is supposed to be negative. Although they are "aged Trees," although they "now no further strive to shoot," although their "Branches are but few," and although their "trunks [are not] enow to bear" the Lord General's many trophies, they are entirely "prudent" trees. Indeed, their prudence is now their strength, and they are as "safe" as the laurel tree that crowns Goodridge's poem on *De Constantia*:

> plac'd *on High*
> (*As our Defence is*) when the *stormes passe by*,
> The wild impatient Stormes, *beneath* us, we,
> As the *safe Lawrell* . . .
> Shall still be *Green*, and flourish like that *Bay*.   (*DC* 164)

By laying aside the trophies and by being careful not to "intrust" themselves to anything more than a "flutt'ring Breez," Fairfax's trees can survive the "winds uncertain gust" and any future Cromwellian lightning-strikes.

The "uncertain gust[s]" of "Upon the Hill and Grove at Bill-Borow" could usher in the "three-fork'd Lightning" of the "Horatian Ode" at any time, of course, and some measure of security against the vagaries of military and political fortune was a sophisticated strategic goal, not only for Fairfax, but for many other important actors on the national scene in the early 1650s. To procure "Height . . . with Retirement" was a good trick – perhaps the best one of all – if one could pull it off. Height with activity was something that only Cromwell and the young Charles II could "Love" at this time, and Charles would soon give up his affections at Worcester. It cannot be stressed enough that retirement – and especially "Height . . . with Retirement" – was a strategic thing in 1651, not capitulative. One retired in order to come out of retirement. Even Cromwell, so Marvell tells us in the "Horatian Ode," had once lived "reserved and austere" in "his private Gardens" – lived, writes Marvell with a twinkle in his eye, "As if his highest plot" had been "To plant the Bergamot" (lines 29–36). Marvell's puns and our knowledge that the bergamot was thought to be "the prince's pear" have the effect of turning a paradox (a retired life in "private Gardens" can somehow issue in "industrious Valour" that "climbe[s] / To ruine the great Work of Time" [lines 33–34]) into a rather straightforward, consequential statement. The pun on "plot" is sewn into a ready-made metaphorical fabric in which retreating to "private Gardens" is the same as taking the Stoic "middle path" of alternative "offices": agitation through letters, controversial prose, poetry, and histories. In retirement one could, as Langius advises in *De Constantia*, "store up Precepts" as "Armes are laid up in a *Magazine*." In this culture retirement naturally issues, not only in plots, but great military success. As Milton would soon stress in *Defensio Secunda*, the earlier, private victories of Fairfax's great rival over "whatever enemy lay within" meant that when Cromwell "took service against an external foe, he entered camp a veteran and past-master in all that concerned the soldier's life" (*CPW* IV, 667–68). It was quite possible that Fairfax was not yet done raising "Mountains . . . of dying Men."

The "prudent Heads" of "Upon the Hill and Grove at Bill-Borow" have cousins both more and less fortunate in Fairfax's more famous estate, Nunappleton. One tree, which Don Cameron Allen did not hesitate to call "the Royal Oak," is also said "to speak" in "Upon

Appleton House" – not voluntarily, however, but rather by the "tink-ling" of a hewel's "Beak" in stanza 69. The poet's bitter surprise that "the *tallest Oak* / Should fall by such a *feeble Stroke*" is palliated in stanza 70 by knowledge that the "*Traitor-worm*" that made it weak now "serves to feed the *Hewels young*" and that "the Oake seems to fall content, / Viewing the Treason's Punishment." This bird, Allen informs us, was associated by "the Latins . . . with the God of War," and he draws from the episode a grim allegory of historical process worthy of Seneca or Lipsius: "As Nature restores itself through death, so the state is revivified by the forces of war, that are also those of religion and justice."[12] More fortunate than "the Royal Oak" but no less involved in the Stoics' "violent fate" is "the *Fairfacian Oak*" of stanza 93. The Fairfaxes' only child, Maria, grows from it "like a *sprig of Misleto*," but necessity dictates that this pretty sprig will someday need to be grafted to another dynastic tree "for some universal good." Whatever happens, we are told, the "*glad Parents*" will "make their *Destiny* their *Choice*."

All this, as Wallace pointed out with reference to Cicero, Seneca, and Lipsius, is deeply Stoic.[13] Moreover, the poem is Stoic in the active and violent senses that I have been exploring in the foregoing pages of this study. Marvell's rhetorical problem as he praised Fairfax was, as I have suggested above, not war but peace, not the painful legacies of Fairfax's past violence but his unexpected, unpopular, and perhaps inexplicable future of personal peace. As Michael Wilding suggests, the "theme of retirement was obviously an appropriate one" for royalists "out of political office and influence," and Marvell needed to "discriminate [Fairfax's good retirement] from the false retirements, the corrupt retirements."[14] The solution offered in "Upon Appleton House" is to make Fairfax's peace a matter of personal and public wars, just as war had been thought by Lipsius and many of his English readers to be a matter of peace for those willing to practice Stoic constancy within that war. The site of Fairfax's retirement is itself infused with a "*Discipline severe*" (line 723) at once military and Stoic, and the poem reads in many stanzas like a faithful if utterly unexpected development of Lan-gius's advice in *De Constantia* upon learning that Lipsius plans to run from the "Rage of Civill Warres" and "*change Land for Land*":

Change not your *Aire*, or your *Country*, but your *Mind*, which you have subjected to your *Affections*, and withdrawn from its lawfull Commander, *Reason* . . . You desire now to see fertile *Panonia*; faithful, and strong *Vienna*, and the chief of Rivers, *Danubius*; and those *New Wonders*, which suspend the Hearers. But how much better it would be if this desire of yours pointed at *Wisdome*; that you

might penetrate her fruitfull, and abundant Fields; to enquire out the Fountaines, and Originalls of *Humane Passions*; if you would raise up Fortresses, to
resist the Assaults of your *Affections*. (*DC* 8–9)

The "fruitfull, and abundant Fields" of wisdom are found by the
poet–teacher in the gardens, fields, streams, and woods of Nunappleton
itself. Lipsius's moral allegory is converted by Marvell into metaphors,
similes, and metonymies drawn from the phenomena of this large estate.
Its garden is a fortress, its fields are like battlefields, and all "seemeth" to
stand for things that require Stoic constancy to build, use, fight, resist, or
overcome. The "lawfull Commander" of this remarkable land is Fairfax, of course, and his genesis is traced through memories, at once
romanticized and ideologically loaded, of religious violence. This violence, like much of the violence in the poem, is presented as inevitable
and providential. The nuns resist Sir William Fairfax when he seizes
Isabella Thwaites, but

> Is not this he whose Offspring fierce
> Shall fight through all the *Universe*;
> And with successive Valour try
> *France, Poland*, either *Germany*;
> Till one, as long since prophecy'd,
> His Horse through conquer'd *Britain* ride?
>
> (lines 241–46)

The nuns stand "against Fate" (line 247). A brief mock-heroic battle
ensues at the "Breach" of the nunnery. Even if the nuns had better
"Cannon [than] their Lungs" and sharper "Weapons [than] their
Tongues" (lines 255–56), they could not stop the conquests of such
"successive Valour." William's virtuous violence will be translated under a watchful providence into "Offspring fierce" and finally into the
Lord General himself, who shall "through conquer'd *Britain* ride." The
prophetic mood of this passage recalls the sixth book of the *Aeneid*, to
name only the most respected of several models available to Marvell,
but the pronouncing of the prophecy in an inset historical narrative is
still an unexpected trick. Histories and times – "long since," present,
future – are blurred in an atmosphere of providential inevitability, and
as the poet moves beyond the nunnery's walls there is a sense that the
"fierce Offspring" of William Fairfax do not so much perform deeds or
participate in events as *express* them. The Lord General's "ride" through
the nation is the most explicit reference in the poem to his central,
shaping role in the Civil War; yet within Marvell's temporal fiction this
is not technically a reference to that role but a prediction, a prophecy

"long since" made about events that the poet refuses to acknowledge precisely as having begun at a certain time or as having ended at a certain time. Nor is Fairfax's retirement treated as an event with clear causes, antecedents, and consequences; we are told only that "it pleased him and God" (line 346) that he would not do other things. And although the "warlike Studies" figured in the formal gardens of the estate are practiced by the Lord General, they were not, a careful reading of stanza 36 discloses, *instituted* by him. Their origins are traced by the poet to an unnamed ancestor, probably William's son, Sir Thomas Fairfax:

> From that blest Bed the *Heroe* came,
> Whom *France* and *Poland* yet does fame:
> Who, when retired here to Peace,
> His warlike Studies could not cease;
> But laid these Gardens out in sport
> In the just Figure of a Fort;
> And with five Bastions it did fence,
> As aiming one for ev'ry Sense.   (lines 281–88)

The retirement "here to Peace," the "warlike Studies" that "could not cease," and the gardens in the "Figure of a Fort" are all said, subtly but certainly, to predate Fairfax, Marvell, and the troubles of 1651. Indeed, Marvell's "*Heroe*" prefigures the Lord General so well that the latter is decorously absolved, for the purposes of this poem at least, of the need to make (and even to *have* made) a real *choice* between war and peace in his career.

Here and throughout the poem, the sense of fate or destiny, the "universal good," is masterfully combined with another Stoic concept that seemed important in its own right in 1651: Marvell makes Fairfax's retirement seem *useful*. Of the several instructional "*Squadrons*" that Langius deploys against Lipsius's vanity in *De Constantia*, "*Utility*" is said to be the most "Valiant, and Subtile Power," one that "does *slide* and *insinuate* into our Mindes, and with a *pleasing kind* of Violence, does not force, and *compel*, but *invites ore* the Vanquished" (*DC* 88). Fairfax has already been "Vanquished" by the utility of retirement, of course, but insofar as the poem is also a defense of that retirement Marvell uses this "*pleasing kind* of Violence" to reassure him and others that his retirement will be positively useful, not merely convenient, to the commonwealth as it fights the battles of 1651 and thereafter. The utility of "Upon Appleton House" is a kind prudence by other means, with the "prudent" trees of "Upon the Hill and Grove at Bill-Borow" having been replaced by flowers that stand "as at *Parade*, / Under their *Colours*" (lines 309–10) and meadows of hay that "seemeth" like battlefields "quilted ore with Bodies slain" (lines 419–22). Indeed, to say that "Fairfax's puttering among make-believe forts and flowery bastions at Nunappleton seems a little silly"[15] is to trivialize an important and extremely useful element in this family's "*Magazine*" of dynastic symbols. Gardens "laid . . . out in sport / In the just Figure of a Fort" did not seem silly at all to intellectuals of Marvell's generation. "'Tis withall necessary that [the young prince] learn Fortification," says Diego Saavedra de Fajardo in his *Idea de un Principe Politico Christiano* (1642). This "widely-propagated" educational work advises that "Forts of Clay, or some such material," should be constructed for the prince "with all sorts of Trenches, Breast-works, Pallisadoes, Bastions, Half Moons, and other things necessary for the Defence of them; then he may Assault and play upon them with little Artillery made for that purpose." Then, pointing to "the present Emblem" at the head of his chapter (see fig. 2), Saavedra advises that in order "to fix those Figures of Fortification more firmly in his Memory, 'twould be for his advantage to have the like artificially contrived in Gardens, cut in Myrtle, or any other Greens."[16] We may well imagine – not a great stretch for such an imaginative poem – that Fairfax had played in such fortress-gardens at Nunappleton as a boy and that his great-grandfather, the "*Heroe*," would have seen his successes at the battles of Naseby and Marston Moor as confirmation of sound educational principles. For Marvell's Fairfax, then, the retirement from war is actually a return to the grounds of its first preparation. Retirement is a refreshment of his military "Memory," a useful return to the "Emblem" both of his former victories and – taking Saavedra's assumptions as seriously as Marvell seems to have done – his *potential* victories.

Colie, Turner, Hirst, and Zwicker have made it unnecessary to explore in great detail the various military conceits of "Upon Appleton House." "The garden is," as Colie said, "entirely militarized" and the "war-games theme runs through the poem, recurring in the mowing-triumph and the wood-siege"; and if, as Turner says, the poem "uses military imagery . . . to recommend a process of education through joy," it is also true, as Hirst and Zwicker have observed, stressing the poem's insistent present tense, that these metaphors must have seemed "alarmingly real" at a time when "soldiers with real guns are gathering."[17] What does need to be emphasized here – an extension of a point made by Wallace – is that Fairfax's formal garden is an artfully violent region within a chaotically violent estate, and that by making this artful vio-

DELEITANDO ENSENA

Figure 2   Saavedra, *Idea de un Principe Politico Christiano* (Milan, 1642).

lence the subject of the central stanzas of the poem, Marvell allows his praise and defense of Fairfax to stand or fall on the symbolic bastions of that garden. Each day "naturally" begins with military action: when the sun "Hangs out the Colours of the Day" in the morning, a humming bee beats "the *Dian* with its *Drumms*"; the flowers unfold "Their Silken Ensigns" and each calmly "dries its Pan yet dank with Dew, / And fills his Flask with Odours new" (stanza 37). The violence of this garden is pleasing indeed:

> Well shot ye Firemen! Oh how sweet,
> And round your equal Fires do meet;
> Whose shrill report no Ear can tell,
> But Ecchoes to the Eye and smell.
> See how the Flow'rs, as at *Parade*,
> Under their *Colours* stand displaid:
> Each *Regiment* in order grows,
> That of the Tulip Pinke and Rose.   (lines 305–12)

While the formal garden figures the benefits of neoclassical military drill of the sort made fashionable by Lipsius, the meadow figures the realities of war:

> The Mower now commands the Field;
> In whose new Traverse seemeth wrought
> A Camp of battail newly fought:
> Where, as the Meads with Hay, the Plain
> Lyes quilted ore with Bodies slain:
> The women that with forks it fling,
> Do represent the Pillaging.   (lines 418–24)

But before Marvell takes us into the meadow he pauses to consider the meaning of Fairfax's garden, which provides the terms for a nostalgic vision of England before the Civil War. The point of stanzas 41–44, as surprisingly few critics have been willing to say, is that the "just Figure of a Fort" represents, not a warlike blight on what once had been a pastoral landscape, but the survival of militaristic virtue within a larger landscape blighted by chaotic, vicious violence. The alternative is not between war and peace but between orderly militarism and disorderly militarism. The old pastoral virtues are figured by military metaphors – as if they could not be well figured otherwise. In the garden there is a "sweet *Militia*" that may not be "restore[d]" elsewhere (lines 329–30); here "the only *Magazeen*" is "The Nursery of all things green" (lines 339–40); here, men "Plant" flowers and "sow" seed, not "Ord'nance" and "Powder" (lines 43–44). Fortune reigns beyond the "warlike Studies" expressed in the garden, and the greater estate suffers the general "Wast" of the "luckless Apple" (lines 327–28). But Fairfax is content to be a sign of future things, for he stands, as Lipsius would say, in "good liking with God":

> And yet their walks one on the Sod
> Who, had it pleased him and *God*,
> Might once have made our Gardens spring
> Fresh as his own and flourishing.
> But he preferr'd to the *Cinque Ports*
> These five imaginary Forts:
> And, in those half-dry Trenches, spann'd
> Pow'r which the Ocean might command. (lines 345–52)

Both God and Fairfax are "pleased" that he has retired to Nunappleton, that he has "spann'd" (restrained) his great "Pow'r" for the time being within the "half-dry Trenches" and moats that accompany his "imaginary Forts." Outside there is vicious war; inside there is military order, artfulness, *constancy*.

The poem's insistent combination of military and horticultural metaphors is inspired, not only by actual "military gardens" and the rhetoric of military drill, as Turner has shown, but by a philosophical tradition that considered combat its primary existential fact. Thus, although the meanings of activity and contemplation are at issue in the poem, critics have drawn false dichotomies when trying to make Marvell favor one way of life over the other. Marvell does not in fact make "repeated attempts to show the superiority of the contemplative life" to the active life in "Upon Appleton House"; nor, on the other hand, does he anywhere express "his impatience with the withdrawal and his almost stifled hopes that Fairfax will once again enter the world of action."[18] Nor is it true that Marvell "implies" that this is the time when "men like Fairfax must leave the retired life they rightly prize and enter the lists of war and politics in defence of that life" – as if either Marvell or Fairfax thought that retirement *per se* is worth dying for – or that "retirement and humility cannot, at this moment in history, provide the security which they were traditionally thought to ensure."[19] Although the many critics who have sensed from the poem's warlike images that Fairfax is not happily isolated from conflict at Nunappleton are certainly correct, most have been wrong in their conclusions – whether that Marvell failed as a poet, that he failed as a rhetorician in his effort to make Fairfax seem isolated from conflict, or that he intended subtle or unsubtle criticisms of Fairfax's retirement. Marvell's goal was to show that Fairfax had not become isolated from conflict at all, that he had found crucial and "ultimate" conflicts to wage, and that these could finally issue in astounding victories. Violence had always been a feature of the Fairfacian "garden" and always would be: Fairfax's gardens are "just Figure[s]" not only for the distant and immediate past, but also for a violent and perhaps apocalyptic future. In Lipsian terms, the "Armes" in the Fairfacian "*Magazine*" are preserved across the generations.

One of the many remarkable things about "Upon Appleton House" is that there is no place whatsoever given to political activity in it: if war is the continuation of politics by other means (it is not), then Marvell does not say so. Nor, for that matter, does he admit the possibility that *politics* is the continuation of *war* by other means. There is no mediating activity between war and retirement in "Upon Appleton House" because they are the same thing. Fairfax, his forebears, and his heirs are defined totally in terms of war; and so also is the nation in gory tableaux where "The Mower now commands the Field" and a "Plain/Lyes quilted ore with Bodies slain." This, of course, was to accept honestly much of the record of English history to that point. But the thoroughness of Marvell's acceptance is not to be expected in a retirement poem. The identity of war and peace, retirement and violence, has seldom been so strong in a work of humane literature, and Marvell pushes the old Stoic trope to its limits in a decorous apocalypse with dynastic, political, and religious ramifications. Perhaps Milton, who had his own views on Fairfax, had somehow taken note of Marvell's poem before he wrote these sentences from the latter pages of the *Defensio Secunda*:

Many men has war made great whom peace makes small. If, having done with war, you neglect the arts of peace, if warfare is your peace and liberty, war your only virtue, your supreme glory, you will find, believe me, that peace itself is your greatest enemy. Peace itself will be by far your hardest war, and what you thought liberty will prove to be your servitude . . . Unless you expel avarice, ambition, and luxury from your minds, yes, and extravagance from your families as well, you will find at home and within that tyrant who, you believed, was to be sought abroad and in the field – now even more stubborn. In fact, many tyrants, impossible to endure, will from day to day hatch out from your very vitals. Conquer them first. This is the warfare of peace, these are its victories, hard indeed, but bloodless, and far more noble than the gory victories of war. Unless you be victors here as well, that enemy and tyrant whom you have just defeated in the field has either not been conquered at all or has been conquered in vain. (*CPW* IV, 680–81)

The bloodless "warfare of peace" that Milton would have citizens fight in the 1650s recalls the private battles of the spirit that Cromwell had supposedly fought before the 1640s. Milton is teaching a lesson in civics for 1654, trying to use the metaphors of centuries of outrageous self-reliance in the interests of the Protectorate. But if England actually lived out its national life in a cycle of real and metaphorical wars, there was no reason to suppose that this cycle would end in metaphors of the spirit rather than blows to the head.[20] No doubt Fairfax thought that he was putting his own "warlike Studies" into good practice when in 1659 he raised arms against Lambert, provided decisive aid to Monck, and secured the return of Charles II.[21] If Marvell thought Fairfax misunderstood the purpose of retirement he left no record of it.

"THE *TRUE* USE, AND END OF GARDENS"

"Do not those various Prospects of *Fields, Rivers*, and *Mountaines*, take up our *Thoughts*" – asks Langius rhetorically early in *De Constantia* – "& so *cousen*, and *betray* away our *Griefs?*" His answer – that such pleasant sights may help a person "but neither *surely*, nor *long*" (*DC* 7–8) – is, as we have seen, built into Marvell's approach to the landscapes of retirement in "Upon Appleton House" and "Upon the Hill and Grove at Bill-Borow." The alternative posed in these poems is not between action and quietism but between chaotic violence and a violence ordered by God's providence and, crucially, by study. When Maria appears near the end of "Upon Appleton House," after so much metamorphic chaos in the meadow and wood, we are told to

> See how loose Nature, in respect
> To her, it self doth recollect;
> And every thing so wisht and fine,
> Starts forth with to its *Bonne Mine*.   (lines 657–60)

The trees and flowers stand at attention, while teacher and student begin their own kind of drills. Lipsius uses similar bait in *De Constantia*: "as the *Heliotropium*, and other Flowers, do Naturally turn to the *Sun*; so *Reason* alwaies beholds *God*, and Its *Original*; steddy, and unmov'd in that which is Good" (*DC* 13). For all his poem's fancies, Marvell asks finally that we be very reasonable about the future: if Maria is the dynasty's only hope, then she must be taught well for "the universal good." Part of the wit of "Upon Appleton House" is, of course, that neither Fairfax nor Maria have any real need of the poet's Stoic lessons. Fairfax is by nature a man of "*Discipline* severe," a seventeenth-century sage (a piously Christian one, to be sure) whose garden is and always has been an elaborate and beautiful kind of fortress. But how do these "warlike Studies" and "just Figure[s]" from the 1650s relate to Marvell's most famous literary garden, "The Garden"? Is it not a poem that teaches us to "lye still" in "some secret Nest" – to quote Marvell's translation of the second chorus of Seneca's *Thyestes* (lines 3–4)?

That "The Garden" teaches nothing of the sort begins to become more clear once we consider seriously two propositions – one quite persuasive, the other virtually undeniable – about context. The first of these, which was put forward several years ago by Allan Pritchard but which still has not gained the currency it deserves, is that "The Garden" "bears marks of the influence of Katherine Philips's *Poems* (1667) and Abraham Cowley's *Several Discourses by Way of Essays, in Verse and Prose*, first published in his *Works* (1668)."[22] It is possible that Marvell could have read some of the poems in question earlier in manuscript, but regardless of the chronological conclusions to be drawn the point remains that he was probably *reading* at least two well-known poets of gardens and retirement as he wrote "The Garden." This poem about "delicious Solitude" (line 16) was certainly not written in cultural solitude, and it is only a small step to see "marks of . . . influence" as allusions, as Marvell's strategic efforts to publicly correct respected models and rewrite the meaning of gardens in his own terms.

The second proposition is that the most important contextual fact about "The Garden" is that it was written during years when a civil war was either being fought or being remembered with punishing bitterness. Pritchard's later dating may seem to provide a less warlike context for "The Garden" than the early 1650s, but Marvell's own satirical and controversial works show that divisions similar to those that had stood in the way of stable government in the 1640s and 1650s also troubled government in the late 1660s and 1670s. Meanwhile, the destabilization of rhetorical and generic forms that had begun in the early 1640s was bearing unexpected fruit in such works as Cowley's *Essays* and, of course, Milton's *Paradise Lost*.[23] "The Garden" registers these tensions in playful allusions to admired literary works and genres, and in its distinctively unstable lyric voice.[24] Indeed, the amusing, sometimes rather irritating instability of the poet's character, the uncertainty in his voice, and the uncertainties he voices all suggest a poem in dialogue with itself and other texts. Although we have come to think of such dialogism as a typical Marvellian trait, its motives and direction in "The Garden" become much clearer when the poem is compared with the dialogue of *De Constantia*, especially with the heated exchanges between the Stoic Langius and the Epicurean Lipsius on "the *true* use, and End of Gardens" in the memorable early chapters of book 2, and with some advice about reading and writing that Seneca gives his friend Lucilius in the *Epistulae Morales*. Although a subtle debate between Epicureanism and Stoicism does not in itself make for a companion piece to Marvell's "Last Instructions to a Painter" (1667) or *The Rehearsal Transpros'd* (1672–73), the Stoic simplicity discovered in "The Garden" is not far removed from the militaristic Stoicism of "Upon Appleton House," and the imagery of both of these garden poems informs the great political satires that Marvell wrote in the 1660s and 1670s.

A poem which begins by rejecting action altogether – even the pursuit of the poet's "Bayes" – concludes by identifying the life of the poet with a productive life lived in accordance with nature and "th'industrious Bee." But while "The Garden" is indeed situated on "Stoic Ground,"[25] we should not expect Marvell's language to be any more univocal than

Lipsius's dialogue nor his "ground" to be any more stable than Lipsius's chaotic Netherlands. We have seen that Langius considers that his *own* garden needs to be an intellectual fortress and that his "Mind" while in his garden needs to be a "*Magazine*" of "Precepts . . . against every *impression*, and *Danger* of Fortune." This is not the attitude of someone at ease. Now we need to see how he persuades Lipsius to accept these severe attitudes and how he separates them from others that Lipsius associates with gardens. The persuasion is not easy, and it is only in contrast with these other attitudes that the meaning of Langius's garden can be fully understood. In book 2, chapter 1, Langius calls Lipsius from his chamber and takes him to his "Gardens by the waters side":

Being entred the Garden, and casting my Eyes round about it, wondring at the curious Elegance of it; My Father, (said I) what *pleasantnesse*, what *lustre* have you here? 'Tis a *Heaven, Langius*, not a *Garden*; Nor do those *Fires* above shine out *fairer*, in a cleare, open Night, then do these (as they) *bright*, and *darting Flowers*. Let none any more remember the Gardens of *Alcinous, Adonis*, so far *beneath*, and *after* These. And with this being come somewhat nearer, and *looking* on, and *smelling* some of them; which should I rather wish, (said I) to be *All Eye*, with *Argus*; or all *Nose*, with *Catullus*? the delight so *equally engaging*, and *dividing* both Senses? Hence all yee *Arabian Odours*, which *distast* onely, and *urge the Sense*, when compar'd with this perfect, and truly *Heavenly Breath*. The *Elysian Fields* are *lesse so*, then these *Your Gardens*. For, see what a *Comelinesse*, and *Proportion* there is every where; how fitly all things are *dispos'd* in their *own Beds*, and Borders, like the exact Checquerings, and Inlayings of a Pavement! What *plenty* of Herbs and Flowers! What *Rarity*, and Strangeness of them! that Nature may seem to have call'd hither into this little place, whatsoever this *Our* World hath excellent, or the *Other*. (*DC* 74–75)

Langius's garden is an unexpected sight in a world at war, and one recalls that *De Constantia* begins with Lipsius lamenting that "The Barbarous Souldier" has forced him from "the pleasure of *Gardens*." The poet in the early stanzas of "The Garden" is less loquacious than Lipsius but no less pleased to find in his garden such "*Comelinesse*, and *Proportion*," and such "*plenty* of Herbs and Flowers":

> How vainly men themselves amaze
> To win the Palm, the Oke, or Bayes;
> And their uncessant Labours see
> Crown'd from some single Herb or Tree.
> Whose short and narrow verged Shade
> Does prudently their Toyles upbraid;
> While all Flow'rs and all Trees do close
> To weave the Garlands of repose.   (lines 1–8)

Although "the Palm, the Oke, or Bayes" are, for men who "vainly" wander through the maze of worldly pursuits, powerful *metaphors* of those pursuits, they are, for the poet, only *plants*. The poet has literally left such figures behind, having happened upon a place where "all Flow'rs and all Trees" – and nothing else – "do close / To weave the Garlands of repose." Both Marvell's poet and Lipsius's naive alter-ego eschew the moral significances traditionally seen in gardens, and both celebrate sense impressions and the senses. Indeed, the only question for Lipsius upon seeing Langius's new "*Heaven*" is whether "to be *All Eye*, with *Argus*; or all *Nose*, with *Catullus*." His sophisticated praise of "*Gardens in generall*," the "*Kings* and other *Famous Men* addicted to them," and "The Pleasures of them" in chapter 2 is explicit in its recommendation of "this *Lower World*":

And as none look upon the *Heavens*, and those *Eternall Fires*, without an inward kind of *Horrour*, and *Religion*; no more do any behold these *Sacred Treasures* of the *Earth*, nor the *beautifull wealth* of this *Lower World*, without a secret Sense, and Evidence of Delight. Ask your *Soul*, and your *Mind*; 'twill tell you, that it is *taken*, nay *cherished*, and *fed* with this Beauty . . . Look about, and observe the severall *Growths* and *Ages* of the Flowers! . . . Observe in . . . them the beauty, Forme, and appearance, a thousand wayes *diverse*, and *the same* . . . Let the curious *Eye* be admitted, and dwell a while upon those bright, *daz'ling Colours*, and even *Glances* of the *Flower*; look upon this Native *Purple*, this *Blood*, that *Ivory*, that *Snow*, this *Flame*, that *Gold*; and so many Colours, which the pencill may *emulate*, but nere *expresse*. To conclude, what a subtile *Odour* and *Spirit* exhales there! and (I know not what) Part of the heavenly Air, breath'd down from Above! So that not in vain our Poets have fain'd, that Flowers are born from the Juice, and Bloud of the *Immortal Gods*. O the *true fountain* of Joy, and perfect Pleasure! O the *only* seat of *Venus*, and the *Graces*! May my time ever pass away amongst your *Shades*! May it be lawfull for Me, being deliver'd from the *Wild*, *endless* Tumults of the People, with a free, satisfy'd Eye, to wander among these Flowers, of the knowne, and unknowne World! Sometimes to behold This *beginning*, and the Other *fading*; and, with a wandring kind of deceipt, to be depriv'd and cousen'd of all my Cares, and Labours. (*DC* 76–77)

Just as Marvell's "Flow'rs and . . . Trees" are desirable precisely because they are nothing more than flowers and trees, Lipsius's "*true fountain* of Joy" is, I think, quite simply a fountain. And, just as Lipsius escapes "the *Wild*, *endless* Tumults of the People" by circulating only among flowers, sees "*Venus*, and the *Graces*" in fine statues, and wishes "to be depriv'd and cousen'd of all my Cares, and Labours" in a garden tilled by another man, so the sensually literalistic poet finds that the "sacred

Plants" of "Fair quiet" and "Innocence" are nothing more – nor less –
than "Plants":

> Fair quiet, have I found thee here,
> And Innocence thy Sister dear!
> Mistaken long, I sought you then
> In busie Companies of Men.
> Your sacred Plants, if here below,
> Only among the Plants will grow.
> Society is all but rude,
> To this delicious Solitude.   (lines 9–16)

This "Solitude" is "delicious," as we learn in stanza 5, because it tastes
good. In stanza 3 the sensations of color and smell lend themselves
naturally to the language of love:

> No white nor red was ever seen
> So am'rous as this lovely green.
> Fond Lovers, cruel as their Flame,
> Cut in these Trees their Mistress name.
> Little, Alas, they know, or heed,
> How far these Beauties Hers exceed!
> Fair Trees! where s'eer your barkes I wound,
> No Name shall but your own be found.   (lines 17–24)

One recalls Lipsius's sensual ardor when he looks on "those bright,
daz'ling Colours, and even *Glances* of the *Flower*." Indeed, the thoroughly
Epicurean views expressed by Marvell in these stanzas are views that
Lipsius, still regarded as the greatest Stoic of the age, had expressed at
artful length in *De Constantia*. "Ask your *Soul*, and your *Mind*," says
Lipsius to Langius, and it will "tell you, that it is *taken*, nay *cherished*,
and *fed* with this Beauty." Marvell's poet is hungry for such beauty in
stanza 5:

> What wond'rous Life is this I lead!
> Ripe Apples drop about my head;
> The Luscious Clusters of the Vine
> Upon my Mouth do crush their Wine;
> The Nectaren, and curious Peach,
> Into my hands themselves do reach;
> Stumbling on Melons, as I pass,
> Insnar'd with Flow'rs, I fall on Grass.   (lines 33–40)

Langius would disapprove, of course, as would practically every grave
commentator on *otium* since Cicero. "The *persona* in 'The Garden,'"

writes Brian Vickers, "is guilty of hedonism, selfishness, and the arrogant rejection of God's will."[26] The problem is not with the garden itself, of course, but with attitude. Both Stoics and Epicureans, says Seneca in *De Otio*, "send a man to his repose, but the truth is that the ways are different. The Epicure saith, *That a wise man shall not have accesse to the Common-weale, except some accident happens that driveth him thereunto*. And *Zeno* saith, *That he shall have accesse to the Common-weale, except there be somewhat that retayneth him*" (*WS* 907; 3.2–3). Fine as the garden of *De Constantia* surely is, Langius is at pains to rebuke the sensual and formal delight that Lipsius takes in it. He observes in chapter 3 that "you stay upon, and admire onely some *vain* and *external* pleasure," that "you look greedily on the *Colours* only, and seem to be fully satisfied, and *Happy* among the *Knots* and *Borders*" (*DC* 78). Lipsius, he says, is an Epicurean, "one of the Sect of those idly curious people" who "onely *sit, walke, gape,* and *sleep*; as if they intended their Gardens . . . for a *Sepulcher* of their *Sloth*" (*DC* 78–79). Langius esteems "things at their own *Inward Rates*" (*DC* 79). *His* garden is "intended for the *Mind*, not the *Body*," and he goes there not to relax but to *perform*: "in this *Retirement*, and *Secession*, I finde *Business*; and my Mind is rais'd to something, which it may *performe*, without *Action*; and *finish*, without *Labour*" (*DC* 80). The Stoic garden, traditionally a place not of *otium* but of *negotium animi* "from which the philosopher would return to the *vita activa* refreshed and inspired by the Stoic attributes of wisdom and reason," is in *De Constantia* modernized into a writer's study, even something of a publishing house.[27] "The *Old Sages*," Langius points out, "dwelt in *Gardens*," and "the Learned, and Knowing Spirits of *Our Times*" use gardens as places for literary composition: "To this green *Lyceum* we owe so many Disputations about *Nature*; to this Shady, retir'd *Academy*, those *Dissertations* about *Manners*: And from out of the Recesses of these Gardens, those abundant Fountaines of *Wisdome* . . . whose rich Inundations have fill'd the World" (*DC* 80). When Langius speaks of performing "without *Action*" he is speaking of reading and writing. If he is less sure than we are today about the *active* character of literature, he is more sure of its "performative" value in a world at war.

There is no such reading and writing going on in Marvell's fifth stanza, of course. The poet's "head" is lost, as it were, in thoughts of "Ripe Apples"; his mouth and hands are occupied with wine and fruit. Just how far we are from Langian doctrine may be measured against one of Goodridge's poetic variations on *De Constantia*:

For who enjoyes the *falne* flowre? Who can tell
Where th' Rose has hid its *Colour*, left its *Smell*;
Whither its faire, its untaught *Blush* did stray,
Or what rude *winde* stole its last *Breath* away,
That can *new dresse* the *Scatter'd Flower*, can *ty*
The *Leaves* into their *knot* agen, which fly
The vain winds scorn?   (*DC* 163)

But why worry about such depressing questions when one is "Insnar'd with Flow'rs" and can "fall" quite easily, as the poet does in "The Garden," "on Grass"? Here one may always "behold This [flower] *beginning*, and the Other *fading*," as Lipsius says. In a sense, Marvell has separated Lipsius's Epicurean character from *De Constantia* and preserved him, freed from the influence of his Stoic interlocutor, in the amber of his memorable poetry. And yet, although there is no Langius in "The Garden" to teach the poet the hard facts of constancy, there is a strong sense in which Langius's allusion to Cicero's *De Officiis* 3.1 and *De Republica* 1.17 – "I am never *lesse* alone, then *when* alone; Never *lesse* at leasure, then *when so*" (*DC* 80) – holds true for this poet as well. Just when it seems that he is truly alone in his garden to enjoy a "wond'rous Life" of the senses, his words begin to echo Langius's strongest exhortations to Stoic wisdom. By the end of his sojourn, indeed, he has come to read the garden in correct if rather slippery and allusive Stoic terms, terms that through a subtle translation of prose dialogue into verse monologue are made to seem imminent in the garden *itself*. "Philosophical content is apparent but not actually mentioned," writes Colie; "we are (literally) given phenomenal hints, in terms of appearances, adumbrations, shadows, rather than actualities making up this garden's green shade."[28] A literary performance, not a treatise, "The Garden" makes its philosophical case through an internalized exchange, a concentrated poetic replay of the dialogue of *De Constantia* in which an "idly curious" man first praises gardens from a sensual, Epicurean perspective and then is asked to reread them, as it were, from his interlocutor's writerly, Stoic, universalizing one. This movement marks "The Garden" from beginning to end, but perhaps the shift is most clear in stanzas 5 through 7, the central stanzas of the poem beginning with a man "Insnar'd with Flow'rs" and "fall[ing] on Grass" and concluding with the same man's "Soul," having cast "the Bodies Vest aside," singing "like a Bird," and "comb[ing] its silver Wings" in preparation for some "longer flight." The crucial stanza of this central group is, of course, the famous sixth:

> Mean while the Mind, from pleasure less,
> Withdraws into its happiness:
> The Mind, that Ocean where each kind
> Does streight its own resemblance find;
> Yet it creates, transcending these,
> Far other Worlds, and other Seas;
> Annihilating all that's made
> To a green Thought in a green Shade.   (lines 41–48)

Here, as many critics have sensed, is the poem's argument in one "green Thought." With *De Constantia* in mind, however, it is possible to see two distinct arguments at work in this stanza, for in fact Marvell begins in the manner of Lipsius on gardens and ends in the manner of Langius. For my purposes, then, the stanza organizes two relationships of structure and allusion. Its first four lines conclude the argument of the first half of "The Garden" and allude to the highest reaches of Lipsius's Epicurean praise of gardens in *De Constantia* 2.1–2. And then, with an immense "Yet," the second four lines announce the issues of the second half of the poem and allude to the culmination of Langius's exhortation to Stoic wisdom in *De Constantia* 2.3. We have already noticed Lipsius's praise of Langius's garden, but we have only begun to notice the literary importance that Langius accords this "green *Lyceum*." Having patiently listened to Lipsius speak of the Epicurean mind's "*soft*, lovely Meditation" amid flowers, Langius counters with his own description of the mind's proper activity while in "the recesses of these Gardens." Here one is able to *read* and *write*, he says, and when one does so,

the Mind does raise, and advance itself, to *Higher*, and *Farther* Endeavors, when *free*, and at *large*, She beholds *her owne* Heaven, then when she is *enclos'd*, and *hindred* within the Prison of a *House*, or *City*. Here, you Poets frame an Enduring Verse. Here, let the Learned *meditate*, and *write*. Here you Philosophers talke of *Tranquillity*, of *Constancy*, of *Life*, and *Death*. See, *Lipsius*, the *true* use, and End of Gardens; *Rest*, *Secession*, *Meditation*, *Reading*, *Writing*; and all these by way of Recreation onely, and Release. As Painters, who by a long intention have *dimm'd* and *wearied* their Sight, do renewe againe, and quicken it, by calling it off to some kind of *Glasses*, and *green Objects*; so do Wee, our Mind, when either *tyr'd*, or *affected*. And why should I conceale my Custome from you? Doe you see that Arbour, set out with *Topiary* Worke? 'Tis the place I have consecrated to the *Muses*; 'tis my *School* of *Wisdome*. (*DC* 80–81)

There had always been the "flowers of rhetoric," of course, but the Lipsian garden is really an allegory of literacy. When in the 1590s Sir John Stradling wrote in his "Epistle to the Reader" of the "good ground, watered with the fruitfull streames flowing in goulden and silver cesterns from the sweete fountaine of Lipsius," he felt obliged to note in the margin, "I meane the Greeke and latin phrases" (*TBC* 69). This was a gloss that Goodridge did not need to add in the more rhetorically sophisticated 1650s. Lipsius gradually learns that the garden is less important as a pleasant place than as an opportunity for literary and intellectual performance. Meanwhile, we learn that the garden is not only an occasion for reading and writing but a figure for rhetorical contestation in general. Langius's garden is a centrally placed emblem of the wider textuality that surrounds it. It pools together the text's "abundant Fountaines" and it figures in flowers and trees the numerous centos out of Epictetus and Seneca that decorate the text's pages. The garden of *De Constantia* is thus a place of safe retirement, but it is also a figure of texts and the conflicts that texts such as *De Constantia* itself symbolically mediate.

Returning now to "The Garden," we can see that Marvell's first four lines turn Lipsius's rhetorical question from chapter 2 – "What Mind is so rigid, which will not here *return* a while upon *Itself*, and *withdraw* into some *soft*, lovely Meditation" – into a more confident declaration. Something similar to Lipsius's answer – "Let the curious *Eye* be admitted, and dwell a while upon those bright, *daz'ling Colours*" – has already been provided by Marvell in the lines on "am'rous" white, red, and "lovely green" in stanza 3. *De Constantia* and "The Garden" first describe the pleasures of the mind at play with the senses and with itself, as it turns sensations into other sensations and comes to terms with its ability, when it "from pleasure less, / Withdraws into its happiness" or into "some *soft*, lovely Meditation," to convert "less" pleasurable effects into more pleasurable ones. Lipsius's "curious *Eye*" and "Mind" are quite satisfied to match colors with concepts; colorful flowers evoke things outside the garden – "look upon this Native *Purple*, this *Blood*, that *Ivory*, that *Snow*, this *Flame*, that *Gold*" – which happen to share their colors and which, by clever metonymical displacements, are used to name those same flowers. Similarly, Marvell's "Mind" is an "Ocean" in which each "kind" of flower. "Does streight its own resemblance find." But neither flowers alone, nor thoughts of flowers alone, can make a life lived amid war and threats of war substantially better. The games played by an unrigid "Mind" are only part of the attraction of the garden in *De Constantia*. What the garden can do well, as Langius stresses again and again in the third chapter of book 2, is encourage one to think and write about one's proper role in the world – to allow "the Mind" to "raise, and advance itself, to *Higher*, and *Farther* Endeavors" and to "*her owne* Heaven."

This, of course, is precisely the argument of the second half of Marvell's sixth stanza. For "The Mind" hovers only momentarily on one side of a semicolon before giving up the rhetorical play of "resemblance" in favor of an entirely new response to its *otium*: "Yet it creates, transcending these" figures of speech and thought, the poet insists, "Far other Worlds, and other Seas." "Annihilating all that's made / To a green Thought in a green Shade" is not obviously the same as "*Meditation, Reading, Writing*," but it would seem that Marvell is reading Lipsius in these very lines, meditating on his meaning, and rewriting his dialogue in the form of a dialogical poem. Like Lipsius, the poet first enjoys the happiness of "resemblance" whereby sense impressions are found to have mental analogues. Next, like Langius, the poet enjoys the greater happiness of mental creation and "Annihilat[ion]" whereby the mind itself is discovered to govern the significance of its physical surroundings. The latter idea is deeply Stoic and, moreover, the language that Marvell uses to express it is remarkably close to Langius's words on the benefits of the garden for the "*tyr'd*, or *affected*" mind. In *De Constantia* green associates a green place of "Recreation[al]" reading and writing with a painter's restorative "*Glasses*, and *green Objects*" – surely a clever use of the commonplace analogy of vision and knowledge.[29] Similarly, in "The Garden" the color green associates a "green Shade," a place of "sweet and wholsome Hours," with a poet's own "green Thought" and poetic *silva* – what Colie wonderfully called "the mixed garden of his making."[30] Marvell's equivalent for Lipsius's "renew[ed]" and "quicken[ed]" "Mind" is a "green Thought"; instead of the "*Glasses*, and *green Objects*" he provides a "green Shade." It is as if he has taken Lipsius's colorful simile – a green garden is to a Stoic's mind as "*Glasses*, and *green Objects*" are to a painter's eyes – and collapsed the tenor and vehicle into a single line and single "green Thought in a green Shade."

Art held a mirror to nature in the Renaissance, of course, but it was a glass on which the varied light, shade, and colors of nature commingled with the artist's thoughts in ways governed, quite literally, by his perspective. In the most widely disseminated theoretical work on painting in the seventeenth century, *Della Pittura* (1540), Leon Battista Alberti advises painters to consider their canvasses as glass panes and to understand that when they "fill the circumscribed places with colours, they should only seek to present the forms of things seen on this plane as if it were of transparent glass"; the color of objects is always influenced by the "rays [that] carry with themselves the colour they find on the plane," a plane chosen by the "natural instinct" of the painter. "You may have noticed," remarks Alberti, as if to Marvellians, "that anyone who walks through a meadow in the sun appears greenish in the face."[31] The point here is *not* to adduce more "sources" for Marvell's lines but, on the contrary, to suggest that too much has been said about the *content* of his "green Thought" and not enough about the *function* of such thought in the philosophical progress described in the poem.[32] Like Alberti's dedicated artists with their imaginary glass panes and Lipsius's tired-eyed *pictores* with their useful if somewhat mysterious *specula* and *virores*, the poet may be less interested in "green Thought in a green Shade" as a final product or experience than as a necessary step in a process or progression.

This is obscured by one of Marvell's characteristic rhetorical inversions. What comes first in the poem – "Yet it creates, transcending these, / Far other Worlds, and other Seas" – should be understood to come second in the process being described; and what comes second in the poem – "Annihilating all that's made / To a green Thought in a green Shade" – actually comes first in that process. The same sort of inversion – the goal stated first, the means second – happens to be used by Langius when describing the Stoic's progress in *De Constantia*. First we are told that in the garden "the Mind does raise, and advance itself, to *Higher*, and *Farther* Endeavors," that it "beholds *her owne* Heaven," that there "you Poets frame an Enduring Verse," and that there "Philosophers talke of *Tranquillity*, of *Constancy*, of *Life*, and *Death*." Such works and activities serve the community or commonwealth of mankind and constitute for the Stoics, who like to praise labor more than any of the ancients, the best work of all for humans *qua* humans. This work, as Langius says, is "the *true* use, and End of Gardens." Meanwhile, the colorful simile that follows on a painter's "*Glasses*, and *green Objects*" is simply a way to visualize how gardens can prepare "our Mind, when either *tyr'd*, or *affected*" for these greater activities. Similarly, in "The Garden" one must first "Annihilat[e] all that's made / To a green Thought in a green Shade" *in order to* turn away from vain personal pleasures, reject religious and political constraints, and create "Far other Worlds, and other Seas." These are places that a poet might create or that a philosopher might reason about in their enduring works. Certainly, we should not expect them to be green, shady, or annihilated.

The poet likes his "green Shade," to be sure, but to consider "Annihilating *all* that's made" *except* that shade is to be rather far along in the practice of Stoic indifference whereby "all that's made" *outside* the self is held to be of no intrinsic value. Paradoxically enough, however, as one pares down reliance on particular things of the world – things that one had mistakenly thought were one's *own* – one becomes more free, creative, and *reasonable* about the world(s). "Far other Worlds" begin to open themselves up to discourse, worlds that for the Stoic are not, it should be emphasized, *fantastic* worlds. "Let us imagine two Commonweales," writes Seneca in *De Otio*:

> The one great and truely publique . . . wherein we cannot confine our eye within this or that limit, but wee measure the extent of the same with the Sunne: and the other, that where Nature hath caused us to be borne . . . We may in repose serve this greater Common-weale, & I know not whether better in contemplation then in action, as if we enquire what vertue is, or if there be but one or divers; whether it be nature or studie that maketh men vertuous: whether there be but one world that comprehendeth the seas, the firme lands, and that which is inclosed within them: or if God hath created divers worlds, if the matter whereof all things are made, is continuate and compleate, or in parcels: if there be void intermixed amongst those things that are solid: if God onely beholdeth his worke, or if he manage and governeth it: if he be spred about the same, and not inclosed, or if he be infused into all creatures. (*WS* 908; 4.1–2)

Here Seneca borrows from Posidonius a progressive, exploratory optimism that had been latent in Stoicism since Zeno.[33] Such optimism infuses "The Garden" even at its most quiet, withdrawn, shady moment. The paradoxical freedom of stanza 6 could open, some day, into the "longer flight" imagined in stanza 7:

> Here at the Fountains sliding foot,
> Or at some Fruit-trees mossy root,
> Casting the Bodies Vest aside,
> My Soul into the boughs does glide:
> There like a Bird it sits, and sings,
> Then whets, and combs its silver Wings;
> And, till prepar'd for longer flight,
> Waves in its Plumes the various Light. (lines 49–56)

The traditional generic setting of this stanza, it seems to me, is the Stoic's "Arbour, set out with *Topiary* Worke," a "place . . . consecrated to the *Muses*" which is "alwaies ready . . . against every *impression*, and *Danger* of Fortune" (*DC* 81). To be always ready against fortune is, of course, to be never quite ready enough: the sage Langius does not claim to be a sage. Similarly, the "Bird"-like "Soul" that "whets, and combs its silver Wings" is at ease precisely because it has made a virtue of the necessity of constant preparation. Such preparation is not to be confused with the "uncessant Labours" of stanza 1 – attempts "Crown'd" by fame, but always more or less vain, to claim the things of the world as one's own, to unify rather than accept the "various Light" of experience, and to escape one's timely duties. Such constancy may seem merely custodial and hygenic at times, but Seneca, Lipsius, and Marvell would agree with Milton's judgment in Sonnet 19 that often "They also serve who only stand and wait."34 "What service doth he to God," asks Seneca, "that beholdeth and considereth these things? It is to that end, that the workes of God should have such a man for a witnesse" (*WS* 908; *De Otio* 4.2). If the poet's "Soul" had Platonic hopes at the beginning of its flight, he ends with the intention simply of being "prepar'd": "brought back from the threshold of presumption," the poet "is folded again into the providential scheme, a scheme shared by Puritanism and Stoicism."35

After comparing the garden briefly and negatively to the "happy Garden-state, / While Man there walk'd without a Mate" (lines 57–58), Marvell continues exploring the theme of constant preparation and settles finally in stanza 9 on the example of "th'industrious Bee" which "Computes its time as well as we":

> How well the skilful Gardner drew
> Of flow'rs and herbes this Dial new;
> Where from above the milder Sun
> Does through a fragrant Zodiack run;
> And, as it workes, th'industrious Bee
> Computes its time as well as we.
> How could such sweet and wholsome Hours
> Be reckon'd but with herbs and flow'rs!   (lines 65–72)

As the bee gathers its nectar, as it moves from flower to flower in a sundial composed "Of flow'rs and herbes" and "Computes its time" by making thyme, it causes the poet to check *his* time on the "Dial new": *tempus fugit*, as so many sundials remind us. Yet if the bee calls the poet to timely activity, to the responsible use of his time in a fallen, time-bound world quite unlike the "happy Garden-state," these lines "of praise and thankful acceptance" also invite comparison between poets and bees as both being good workers, good gatherers.36 Marvell's bee is not only an example *for* the poet but *of* the poet. As Colie has shown so well, the "flowers in the garden are emblematic of the traditions the poet inherit-ed; the poet, like the bee, has gathered from the literary kinds, accom-modating what he gathered to his own structure, to the mixed garden of his making . . . gathered into a poem that is, among so much else that it is, also an illustration of the root-meaning of 'anthology.' "[37] An admir-able openness to the "mixed" character of Marvell's gathering may in this case leave too little room for the ethical concerns informing the resulting "structure," however, for within Stoic tradition the bee signi-fied much more than anthological virtuosity. While there are no bees in the garden of *De Constantia*, they play an important role in what one imagines was one of Langius's favorite texts: *Epistulae Morales* 84, Seneca's famous letter on literary imitation which advises writers, as they choose their models, "to imitate Bees, which wander up and downe, and picke fit Flowres to make Honey" (*WS* 346; 84.3). In this "central text for all later discussions of imitation,"[38] Seneca forges the strongest bonds between reading, writing, and living the life of Stoic constancy – a life "whereunto fortune submitteth itself":

We also ought to imitate Bees, and to separate what things soever we have heaped together from divers reading; for distinct things are the better kept. Then using the abilitie and care of our wit, to mingle divers liquors into one taste . . . Such would I have our minde to be, that there be many arts therein, many precepts, examples of many ages, but conspiring in one. How, saiest thou, may this be done? By continuall taking of heed; if we shall doe nothing but by the perswasion of reason: this if thou wilt heare, it will say unto thee; Leave these things even alreadie now, whereunto men doe runne; leave riches . . . leave the pleasures of the bodie and of the minde, they mollifie and make weake; leave suing for offices . . . Hither rather unto wisdom direct thy course, and seeke to attaine the most quiet and therewithall most ample things . . . Unto the height of dignitie there is a broken way. But if thou wilt climbe unto this top, whereunto fortune submitteth itself, thou shalt beholde indeed all things under thee, which are accounted exceeding high; but notwithstanding thou shalt come unto highest things by that which is plaine. (*WS* 346–48; 84.5–13)

Seneca's letter is digressive, speculative, and concerned to find just the right analogy for the imitative process. Indeed, the bee is only his favorite among several possibilities. Yet in these final sentences Seneca is less concerned with compositional technique *per se* than with its *moral* significance, its use as a means of pointing his friend Lucilius to a better life lived in accord with Stoic principles – lived, that is to say, in accord with nature. Bees can teach us about literary imitation, and literary imitation teaches us in turn about the building and control of our character – of a "selfe" that Seneca represents as the site of an interminable battle between *reading* and *writing* for possession of one's physical "strength." Bees are like good writers and they are also, as Seneca knew with Homer, Vergil, and Lucan, like good soldiers.[39] Reading the texts of others, Seneca assumes, "is necessarie . . . that I may not be content with my selfe alone," but reading will "dissolve and dissipate" the strength if not "exchanged" with writing; writing is equally necessary to the maintenance of the self, but will "make sad, and . . . consume the strength" if not "moderated" with reading (*WS* 346; 84.1–2). A perfectly unified work of imitative art is for Seneca a fine thing, of course, but most importantly it is evidence of a strong and constant "minde" in which "there be many arts therein, many precepts, examples of many ages, but conspiring in one." Only by "continuall taking of heed" – only by sheer effort of the will – can we hope to do with our texts and lives what the bees do naturally with nectar and honey.[40] Even "the pleasures . . . of the minde" must be left behind on the long "climbe" to a life beyond the reach of fortune. For although these pleasures may well be of a rather serious, retired character – one thinks of the mature Epicurean who finds that "the pleasures of the mind are the greatest he can have"[41] and the "happiness" which Marvell's "Mind" finds while withdrawn from "pleasure less" – they can have little to do with a "climbe" whose path to "highest things" is so surprisingly "plaine."

Perhaps the challenge of literary imitation would not seem so great to Seneca, so ethically charged and even dangerous, if the most important "reading" in his *Epistulae Morales*, the philosophical model that he is most concerned to convert, like a bee, into his own Stoic honey, were not the great Epicurus. Langius demands a similar conversion from Lipsius in *De Constantia*; and while Marvell is not nearly so severe in his engagement with Epicurean thought in "The Garden," its final stanza makes literary closure coincide with a philosophical, disciplined plainness of the sort desired by Seneca. One might also recall here Fairfax's "just Figure of a Fort" in "Upon Appleton House" – the imagery of which, as Friedman points out, Marvell had developed "in a style closely related to" this stanza – and especially the happily militaristic bee which through its "known Allies hums, / Beating the *Dian* with its *Drumms*." As in "Upon Appleton House" where Marvell "elaborates the initial military metaphor so that the garden becomes less a static, formal symbol of a military stronghold than a living model of the life and discipline Fairfax had supposedly left," so in "The Garden" he transforms the garden from a collection of beautiful *things* to a setting for *activities* and *performances* at once natural and disciplined.[42] The drawing of the "skilful Gardner," the running of the "milder Sun," the working and reckoning of "sweet and wholsome Hours" by bee and poet all express a quiet, purposeful simplicity that the poet has been moving towards, dialectically and allusively, from the first stanza. For the Stoics such simplicity entailed the perception of the universal *taxis*, or organizing principle, in all things and persons. For them, as for the poet in "The Garden," this principle is a matter both of order and, crucially, of internally generated dynamism, change, possibility, and action in time; it is, in a word, *nature*, which is "made up of parts that hang together, cooperate, and are bound to one another by sympathy, by organic cooperation as it is found . . . in the growing of plants, in the working of the human body, in the seasons of the year."[43] Seneca stresses in *Epistulae Morales* 84 that each person has the opportunity to be so wise and so natural before death. And yet, as he stresses again and again elsewhere, any progress is always shadowed by lost opportunities, wasted time. In *Epistulae Morales* 1 he warns that there are some days that

are taken away from us, some other which are stolne from us, and other some which slip away from us . . . What man . . . hath put any price upon time, that esteemeth of a day, and that understandeth that he daily dieth? For herein we are deceived, because wee suppose death to be farre off from us, and yet . . . the greater part thereof is alreadie over-passed, & all our years that are behind death holdeth in his possession . . . Embrace and lay hold of each houre . . . While life is deferred it fleeteth. All other things, my *Lucilius*, are forren to us: time only is our owne. Nature hath put us in possession of this fraile and fleeting thing, from which we may be expelled by any man. (*WS* 163; 1.1–3)

And in *De Otio* he writes:

Consider how small a time man hath received, although he employ himselfe wholly herein, although he permit no man to distract him, and were carefull to husband well every minute of an houre, without losing one: although he lived longer then any other, without touch of any crosse or disaster whatsoever, yet he is . . . of too small continuance to attaine unto the knowledge of eternall things. So then I live according to Nature, if I addict my selfe wholly unto her, and admire and reverance her. But her will is that I should intend to contemplation and action. I do both the one and the other, for contemplation is not without action. (*WS* 909; 5.7–8)

Marvell's ninth stanza takes time for what Seneca held it to be: a "fraile and fleeting" opportunity for "sweet and wholsome Hours," nature's best gift to us, and our chance to follow nature by studying and revering nature. The time of the individual bee or poet in Stoic thought is also the time of the universe; all are ticking together, and while things, persons, and thoughts generate themselves, they are also "movements or aspects of one and the same being, the divine fire, of which the changes in time and space or the 'history' is the history of the world."[44] Although "The Garden" does not sponsor explicitly Seneca's rejection of the selfish "pleasures of the bodie and of the minde," the poet leaves many of them behind on his way towards an understanding of work and pleasure, time and poetry, as unified within the design of a "skilful Gardner" whom Zeno, Seneca, and Lipsius's Langius would have called God. Not content with himself alone, the poet has read widely and well, and united disparate texts in one poem indicative of a writer's and a reader's time well spent – "for contemplation is not without action."

Such allusive interplay with its lack of clear-cut philosophical state-ment may seem to separate Marvell from Lipsius and Seneca. In fact it is a point of contact: the Stoicism of these writers is inseparable from their artful texts, and all figure integrity as a life lived at some risk to the self amid texts. In "The Garden" the words of a Stoic are folded upon those of an Epicurean, thus continuing their prose dialogue as poetry in a work more memorable than Lipsius produced. To speak roundly against fortune was not, after all, the best way to follow Langius's advice. Reading and writing carefully in one's "Arbour" and stocking one's preceptual "*Magazine*" was a better constancy: it was more honest and also more brave to turn texts back on themselves as things indiffer-ent, to turn back on one's self and one's reading since to rest too readily at ease is to be open to vanity and "opinion." By imitating and revising *De Constantia* and so many other admired texts of his culture, Marvell masters in practice what was held by Lipsius to be "the *true* use, and End of Gardens" for the Stoics. He sees Langius's garden for what it really is: an allegory of the strenuous reading and writing of texts within a world of strife. The further one walks into "The Garden" the further one enters into dialogue with a dialogue named *De Constantia* and with all the other dialogues and disputes which one may have thought one was escaping from by reading the poem. The poet re-mains in his garden in the last stanza, but there is a strong sense that its inside and outside have reversed or that inside and outside have be-come the same.[45] Indeed, "The Garden" plays out in a compact, figuratively intensified form the basic paradox of the garden of *De Constantia*. If such gardens are retreats at all, they are retreats to intensi-fied discourse.

"AN OLD HONEST COUNTRY MAN"

A close to this chapter, and a transition from Marvell's garden retirements to what Katherine Philips calls her "rude and . . . dark Retreat," may be found by returning briefly to Pritchard's observation that "The Garden" "bears marks of the influence of" several poems and essays by Philips and Cowley published in the late 1660s on gardens and the virtues of rural retirement. While these "marks" suggest to me not so much "influence" on Marvell as common traditions that had become interesting to all three writers at this time, I am more interested in trying to understand what the political stakes of "The Garden" could have been for Marvell *circa* 1670. Pritchard has suggested only that the poem may respond to the horticultural interests of Cowley and John Evelyn, and that it may express "a light and witty dissent from some aspects of the Royal Society, with which both Evelyn and Cowley were closely associated."[46] But Marvell was always more interested in the morals of flowers than the flowers themselves. If a "later date widens rather than narrows the context of this remarkably comprehensive poem," we should consider more profound and lasting concerns.[47] Cowley's volume of *Poems* from 1656, with its "Pindarique Odes" – notably "Brutus" and "Destiny" – must have seemed worthy to Marvell as a poet, and perhaps Cowley's rejection by the Earl of Clarendon in 1660 lent him something of a dissident's honor. Philips, on first face an even more surprising source of inspiration for this "notable English Italo-Machiavellian," may have been interesting to him not only for such poems as "A Countrey Life" and "La Solitude de St. Amant" but also for her celebrated play on the politics of Caesarism and Stoic resistance, *Pompey* (1663), the theme of the next chapter. Although "The Garden" may well have had its origins at Nunappleton, it does not seek to record some early, unrecoverable experience of innocence but rather bridges historical change by means of a studied and quite strategic Stoic constancy. Retirement to the garden is an act of the experienced soul. A successful retirement ends with return to the world of action on one's own terms, and these terms may refer back through many years and travels and texts. Earlier and later texts merge usefully in one's "*Magazine*" which is "alwaies ready . . . against every *impression*, and *Danger* of Fortune."

If my Lipsian interpretation has disclosed similarities between "The Garden" and "Upon Appleton House" that run deeper than a common concern with flowers and trees, it should also help us to read them better in relation to the great political satires that Marvell wrote in the

1660s and 1670s. If virtue lives anywhere after the death of "brave *Douglas*" in "The Last Instructions to a Painter" (lines 649–96), it lives in the country, perhaps in the poet's own out-of-the-way neighborhood, and Charles II is told that some of the wisest "Kings in the Country oft have gone astray, / Nor of a Peasant scorn'd to learn the way" (lines 959–60). Of course, the praise of country simplicity, especially when filed to a sharp Stoical point, could amount to dispraise of sophisticated and powerful persons. *Contemptus mundi* could mean contempt for kings, courtiers, and ministers. A case in point is "Senec. Traged. ex Thyeste Chor. 2," Marvell's deft translation of thirteen lines from the second chorus of Seneca's *Thyestes* into fourteen lines of English tetrameter:

> Climb at *Court* for me that will
> Tottering favors Pinacle;
> All I seek is to lye still.
> Settled in some secret Nest
> In calm Leisure let me rest;
> And far of the publick Stage
> Pass away my silent Age.
> Thus when without noise, unknown,
> I have liv'd out all my span,
> I shall dye, without a groan,
> An old honest Country man.
> Who expos'd to others Ey's,
> Into his own Heart ne'r pry's,
> Death to him's a Strange surprise.

Pritchard would date this poem, as he dates "The Garden," from the late 1660s or 1670s. It compares very well with Cowley's much longer version in the *Essays, in Verse and Prose,* and for most readers it has seemed to express a Cowleyan renunciation of political action with a lyrical economy that Cowley could never quite match. Nevertheless, two seemingly innocuous terms, *"Court"* and *"Country,"* should mark this as a political and, indeed, a polemical poem for us if we take it, with Pritchard, as having been written in the same decade as *An Account of the Growth of Popery and Arbitrary Government* (1677). The political context is not mysterious. Against the Earl of Danby's attempt to manage the House of Commons through "patronage, places, and pensions," writes J. G. A. Pocock in *The Machiavellian Moment,* Shaftesbury's "polemical counterattack... restated the old antithesis of 'Court' and 'Country' in a new form, one based on employment of the civic and republican concept of 'corruption' . . .

Patronage, it was argued by the pioneers of the 'Country' ideology, rendered representatives of the people, who ought to be as independent as those they represented, dependent on the Court and the ministers from whom they received it."[48] If the ideological force of "Climb at *Court*" – its attack on "Tottering favors Pinacle" and praise of independent, "honest" men of the "Country" – seems compromised by the stated desire to "lye still," Marvell's poem is no more contradictory than the ideology itself. As shaped by Shaftesbury and Marvell among others, the politics of the "Country" provided an effective opposition to the Crown for many years – even though, as Pockock observes, "it was to be the recurrent problem of all Country parties that they could not take office without falsifying their own ostensible values."[49]

Marvell was willing to be more explicit. Some of the most memorable if also least amusing passages of *The Rehearsal Transpros'd* recall with a surprising normative force the kind of Stoic discipline that Marvell had witnessed at Nunappleton some twenty years earlier. Such personal and public virtue has been thoroughly overridden by what he calls "*Debauchery Tolerated*," the fourth of Samuel Parker's – or rather Mr. Bayes's – "six Playes."[50] Having quoted Parker's proposals that it is "*safer to give a Toleration to mens Debaucheries than to their Religious Perswasions*," and that "*greater severity ought to be exercised over mens Consciences than over their Vices and Immoralities*," Marvell observes that it "were easie here to shew a man's reading, and to discourse out of History the causes of the decay and ruine of Mr. *Bayes* his *Roman empire*, when as the Moralist has it, *saevior armis / Luxuria incubuit, victumque ulciscitur / orbem*."[51] The "Moralist" is Juvenal at a moment in the sixth *Satire* when his lament for the lost ethos of "Roman poverty" is combined with lament for Rome's lost military virtue:

> Long peace undoes us. Lust, than War more fierce,
> Revenges now the conquer'd Universe.
> When poverty left Rome, no horrid sin
> But entred; then to our sev'n hills flow'd in
> Rhodes, Malta, Sibaris; Tarentum crown'd
> With flowers, and still in wine and women drown'd.[52]

The same applies to England in 1672, Marvell complains. The effects upon the nation of this "Corruption of Manners, and always fatal Debauchery" are broad and complex:

It exhausts the Estates of private persons, and makes them fit for nothing but the High-way or an Army. It debases the spirits and weakens the vigor of any

Nation; at once indisposing them for War, and rendring them uncapable of Peace. For if they escape intestine troubles . . . then they must either, to get a maintenance, pick a quarrel with some other Nation, wherein they are sure to be worsted; or else (which more frequently happens) some neighboring Prince that understands Government takes them at the advantage, and, if they do not like ripe Fruit fall into his lap, 'tis but shaking the Tree once or twice, and he is sure of them. Where the Horses are, like those of the *Sybarites*, taught to dance, the Enemy need only learn the Tune and bring the Fiddles.[53]

England is becoming again, but now in a most ironic and unpleasant sense, "The Garden of the World" whose ruin Marvell had lamented some twenty years earlier in "Upon Appleton House" (line 322). "What luckless Apple did we tast," he had asked in that poem, "To make us Mortal, and The Wast?" (lines 327–28); if the answer in 1651 was "intestine troubles," the answer in 1672 is ease, sloth, and Mr. Bayes's "*Debauchery Tolerated.*" While the nation may seem to have escaped the "intestine troubles" of the 1640s and 1650s, it is now ripe for the plucking because its leaders no longer encourage "warlike Studies," "*Discipline* severe," or anyone like the Fairfax of "Upon Appleton House" who might make "our Gardens spring / Fresh as his own and flourishing" (lines 347–48). England has itself become a "ripe Fruit" like one of the "Ripe Apples" that drop about the pleasure-loving poet's head early in "The Garden": a pleasant, tasty thing devoid of any moral value enjoyed by those who are not willing to tell the difference between debauchery and true freedom. No Juvenalian himself, Marvell had usually found that wit and dialogue were the best corrections to public vices. But the issues, one gathers, were very serious for him: "And therefore, till I meet with something more serious, I will take a walk in the Garden and gather some of *Mr. Bayes* his Flowers. Or I might more properly have said I will go see *Bedlam*, and pick straws with our Madman."[54]

In all the gardens explored in this chapter, whether designed by Lipsius or by Marvell, readers are encouraged to make their "*Destiny* their *Choice.*" But the *right* choices are always understood to be the hardest, plainest, and most rigorous ones. A recurrent theme of the first two chapters of this book about Stoic responses to conflict has been the tendency to see the hardest choices as being those posed in times of public or personal peace – in times when we are likely to be "crown'd / With flowers." This is the attitude of Seneca writing under Nero, of Langius discoursing with Lipsius in *De Constantia*, of Milton in *Defensio Secunda*, and of Marvell in "Upon the Hill and Grove at Bill-Borow,"

"Upon Appleton House," *The Rehearsal Transpros'd*, and also, I think, in "The Garden." The *"Warre* with you" that the Stoic senses so acutely is not for any of these writers something that can be solved by external peace. Indeed, they are less troubled by war than by peace – and troubled especially, as we shall see in Katherine Philips's *Pompey*, when rulers attempt to impose peace by *fiat* and force the Stoic, literally, to *enjoy herself.*

CHAPTER 3

Katherine Philips: the Stoicism of hatred and forgiveness

I may well say (my *Serenus*) that there is as much difference betwixt the *Stoickes* and other Philosophers, as betweene Females and Males, whereas both the one and the other are equally assistant to the good of humane society; but the sect of the Stoicks is borne to command, and the other are made to obey.

Seneca, *De Constantia Sapientis* 1.1 (*WS* 656).

If we are surprised that Marvell, panegyrist of Fairfax and Cromwell, may have been attracted to the poetry of Katherine Philips when writing "The Garden," it is probably because we have not considered Philips's writings as seriously as they demand. Taking Philips seriously reveals, on the one hand, that the links between her work and Marvell's run much deeper than a few poetic echoes and, on the other hand, that there is much more to her work than its appeal to Marvell, Cowley, and other famous male contemporaries. Indeed, while Marvell was sitting on the back bench of the Cavalier Parliament and Cowley was prostrating himself before an unfriendly court, Philips herself was busy at work translating Pierre Corneille's *La Mort de Pompeé* (1644) for the Dublin and London stages. Philips approached translation, observes a historian of seventeenth-century women's writing, as a "restrictive format" that could "be used, however, to vindicate her own expertise."[1] Through *Pompey* she vindicated not only her writerly "expertise" but also republican ideals and Stoic modes of preserving those ideals. "Made to obey" because she was a woman and the wife of a former Cromwellian, Philips chose to work within a philosophical tradition whose members, as Seneca says, were "borne to command." Her memorable Stoic heroine, Cornelia, walks forth from Philips's "rude and dark . . . Retreat" to defend republican virtue in a world of force, fraud, and *friendship*.

"TO KILL THEIR HATE, AND FORCE THEM TO BE KIND"

Cowley wrote in tribute that Philips "Turn'd upon Love himself his own Artillery" – and I am sure that he meant it.[2] Presumably he was thinking of her numerous love poems to women "friends"; but as he develops his metaphor, drawn from the tactics of seventeenth-century siege warfare, he strains eros of every kind to the breaking point and impresses on us the truth of Achsah Guibbory's contention that "the intimacies of the private world and the social orders of the public world are complexly intertwined in this period in ways that have yet to be fully understood."[3] It is time to shift our perspective on Philips's "love" and "friendship" from the domestic sphere, however interestingly that sphere is conceived,[4] to a noisy public one. The best way to do so is to consider *Pompey* and its immediate political and intellectual contexts, for when Philips "Turn'd upon Love himself his own Artillery" in her celebrated play, "Love" was quite definitely political in character.

Pompey was the cause of most of the fame that Philips was able to enjoy in her short life. Although we now know a good deal about its genesis and its claim to be one of the very first "heroic" dramas performed in English,[5] the play has received little comment of value. While the fact that *Pompey* is a translation need no longer stand in the way – most critics and historians would agree with Stephen Greenblatt that "there is no translation that is not at the same time an interpretation"[6] – the play's unfamiliar mixture of historical allusiveness and moral and political casuistry may remain as a barrier. If they were to read the play at all, most moderns would echo what Dryden's Neander says of Corneille's *Cinna* and *La Mort de Pompée*: "they are not so properly to be called plays, as long discourses of reason of State."[7] The cast list of *Pompey* includes Julius Caesar, Cleopatra, Ptolemy, Pompey's blessed ghost (who, although he does not appear in Corneille's text, is given crucial prominence in one of Philips's original entr'actes), and Pompey's widow, Cornelia. But *Pompey* is less "about" a character or characters than a virtue, namely the virtue of clemency. Clemency was a major political problem in the 1660s, the years immediately following the restoration of Charles II that involved the grim process of deciding who should die, lose property, be excluded from public activity, or be otherwise harassed given the previous twenty years of war and experimental government. Clemency had an august intellectual heritage, fashionably Neostoic in orientation: the classical texts include a treatise that Seneca addressed to Nero, *De Clementia*, and his seven dense books on giving and returning favors, *De Beneficiis*; but to mention the Senecan texts is only to scratch the surface, for the textual universe of seventeenth-century clemency includes lengthy casuistical manuals, broadside appeals by Charles I from the 1640s, and, not least, popular productions such as *Pompey* itself. Always regarded as a virtue, clemency was nevertheless seldom a happy solution in the seventeenth century. At best it was a political device, underwritten by admired writers both ancient and modern, that presented rulers, politicians, and subjects with difficult problems. Philips's *Pompey* intervened in one crucial phase of those problems.

The theoretical and practical complexities of clemency have not been understood by those who have discussed the play and Philips's motivations for writing it. Philips's most dedicated biographer argues that she meant to only please her patron, Roger Boyle, Earl of Orrery, "who had an enthusiasm for French literature."[8] More recently, critics have focused on the situation of James Philips, Katherine's husband, who had been a loyal servant of the Protectorate regime but who was now out of work. Katherine had gone to Dublin on legal business in 1662 and left him "home in Wales in a nearly suicidal depression over the loss of his political position"; this led her to *La Mort de Pompée*, we are told, because act 3, the first act that she translated, "contains several long speeches pleading for political magnanimity and mercy as well as other passages that might seem complimentary when applied to the royal family."[9] While this explanation may sound plausible, in fact it has little if anything to do with the play that Philips actually wrote: certainly her play does *not* contain "several long speeches pleading for political magnanimity and mercy." By my reckoning, *Pompey* contains only one "pleading" speech: in act 4, scene 3, Cleopatra tries unsuccessfully to get Caesar to "forgive" two Egyptians "that have Guilty been" (4.3.103); after thirteen lines she is cut off first by Caesar and then by news that they have planned yet another conspiracy. Nor is it true that *Pompey* as a whole "depicts not only the just punishment of treachery but pleads for kingly mercy."[10] In any case, to say that James Philips, who lost his tenuous position in the Cavalier Parliament in March 1662, may have desired the King's favor in 1663 does not require that one believe that Katherine Philips wrote a play that "pleads for kingly mercy." Philips does engage with the problem of clemency in *Pompey*, and she does so as deeply as any controversialist of her age, but to other ends than her modern admirers have supposed. Indeed, *Pompey* repeatedly calls the motives and ends of "kingly mercy" into question, as it does all relationships that would ignore or smooth over the problem of the self as an autonomous political agent resistant to the persuasive and coercive powers of governments.

As Cornelia says to her more fortunate enemy, Cleopatra, "Our thoughts are, as our Int'rests, different" (5.2.18). To identify the interests of Philips with those of her husband in the name of a political interpretation is in fact to misunderstand the politics of the play. For *Pompey* gives us good reason to move beyond the usual labeling of Philips as a "royalist" poet and distinguish, not only between her interests and those of her husband, but also between her interests and those of Charles II. The first play "written by a woman to be produced in the professional British theater,"[11] *Pompey* emphasizes the character of Cornelia, whose Stoic integrity is expressed in her lasting hatred for the clement Caesar, who claims that, in destroying his republican enemies, his "Ambition only this Design'd, / To Kill their Hate, and force them to be kind" (3.2.113–14). This emphasis on Cornelia is not found in *Pompey the Great* (1664), a rival version written by Edmund Waller and Charles Sackville, Lord Buckhurst, among others; nor do these fashionable "Persons of Honour" give any weight to the problem of Stoic indifference to a ruler's Stoic clemency. Not surprisingly, their version seems to have been more favorably received at court than Philips's *Pompey*.[12] Moreover, an objective, critical representation of clemency would have been likely to carry special force for readers and theatergoers in the early 1660s, including those not especially concerned with the daily lives of the Philipses: *Pompey* dramatized issues and emotions touching on the Act of Indemnity and Oblivion, the basic legal feature of the Restoration "settlement." I shall argue that Caesar's clement rhetoric may be taken as an example of the godlike power that Charles II arrogated in 1660, a power that, in the words of Edward Hyde, Earl of Clarendon, to the Convention Parliament in September 1660, was "able to look into mens hearts" and eliminate discord and competition within the nation.[13] One can be quite specific in placing *Pompey* in its proper historical context, although in this case being specific means not missing the forest for the trees. Philips's primary interest in writing and producing *Pompey* was neither to follow a French fashion nor to help her husband to the benefits of royal clemency. She sought, rather, to engage in the salient political and intellectual controversy of the day by criticizing the notion of royal clemency itself and rethinking and refining the Stoic rhetoric that could support it as an instrument of royal absolutism. Of course, Philips may have felt that such a critique was in her husband's *best* interests; but if so, there is no evidence that he understood what she was doing.

"THERE IS NOTHING OF THE TYRANT IN EXAMPLE"

A brief summary will be helpful in coming to terms with Philips's "reason of State." Act 1 opens with Ptolemy, King of Egypt, having called together his "Councel Board" to debate the question of how to receive Pompey, who "in our Ports chooses his last Retreat" (1.1.21) following his loss to Julius Caesar at the battle of Pharsalia. Photinus, the Machiavellian "Governour," advises murdering Pompey in order to win the favor of Caesar: "They fear no Conquerour," Photinus states, "who the Conquer'd strike" (1.1.116). Achillas, a lieutenant general, advises against such rashness, but offers to do the deed if necessary. And finally, Septimius, a Roman exile who sees a peculiar psycho-political dynamic at work between Caesar and Pompey, also advises murder. For Septimius, however, the purpose in murdering Pompey is to limit the glory of Caesar, "Who must forgive him, to Augment his Fame" (1.1.174). The clever Roman knows that, if Caesar is allowed to bestow clemency on Pompey, Caesar's power will become irresistible. Septimius's argument is the most persuasive, and the remainder of act 2 and much of act 3 develop the dynastic and political ramifications of the Egyptians' decision to murder Pompey, the admirable leader whose "last Gaspe was an Illustrious one" (2.2.80).

Leaving aside, for the moment, the pivotal act 3 in which Pompey's widow, Cornelia, is introduced, act 4 opens with Photinus advising Ptolemy that "In vain you hope [Caesar's] Fury to asswage, / Who now secure, does Politickly rage" (4.1.11–12). For Caesar has proved Septimius's analysis of the Stoic bond between him and Pompey to be all too correct: their bond holds even after Pompey's death. The Egyptians resolve to "surprize him, and act our design, / When he is Drunk with Pleasure, Love, and Wine" (4.1.79–80). Pleasure and love come to Caesar when he and Cleopatra appear together in act 4, scene 3. Caesar presses his suit for her love but refuses her request, made on behalf of her brother, Ptolemy, that Photinus and Achillas be spared. Scene 4 begins with Cornelia's news that "Traytors have against thy Life Combin'd, / And sworn thy Head shall be to *Pompey's* Joyn'd" (4.4.2–3). Caesar soon exits to crush the Epyptians' conspiracy. Act 5 begins with Cornelia meditating on Pompey's funeral urn; continues with discussion between Cornelia and Cleopatra; and reaches its crisis in a report from Achoreus, Cleopatra's "Gentleman Usher," who arrives with the story of Caesar's "usual Fortune" and the death of Ptolemy, who "charg'd, and broke our Ranks, bravely to shew / What Virtue armed by Despair can do" (5.3.44–45). The crowd clamors to see Cleopatra, the reluctant new queen, in scene 4. Caesar has the last word: his lines on Cleopatra and Pompey – "To her a Throne, to him let's Altars Build, / And to them both Immortal Honours yield" (5.4.57–58) – are triumphant and balanced in the manner of his "usual Fortune."

Act 3 and some parts of act 5 will be discussed below, but from what has been covered so far the topical interest of the play to Philips's audiences may seem obvious. Jacqueline Pearson is surely right to point to "its images, a virtuous leader beheaded, a coronation, treason defeated, the restoration of order" as especially suggestive.[14] Certainly, Cleopatra's assertion that "Tyranny [is] ruin'd, and the times are chang'd" (2.2.126) could not fail to interest audiences in the early 1660s, regardless of their political sympathies. But the variety of those political sympathies – and they *were* various, for the realm did not change utterly in 1660, no more than it had in 1642 – enjoins on us the responsibility to avoid pigeon-holing the play. One knowledgeable critic is thus on dangerous ground when he claims that "the word 'restore' runs like a *leitmotif*" through *Pompey*.[15] In fact, the word appears on only a few of Philips's pages and, in any case, it would be a mistake to assume that "restore" had the same meaning for everyone. No doubt some in Philips's audiences were favorable witnesses to any and every restoration of monarchical "order"; but others may have seen other, more profound restorations being lost in vanities. After all, *Cleopatra*, not *Caesar*, is the one whose rights are restored in the play, and to take Cleopatra as an example for Charles II is – and surely was – an interpretive stretch. And, even if *Pompey* were a "tragedy of tyranny, which presents vivid, schematic images of history to heighten the audience's gratitude for Charles's return and its own era,"[16] there would still be the question of who the King "is" in the play. If he "is" Caesar, were audiences supposed to see his Parliamentary and Cromwellian opponents in Pompey and Ptolemy?

In dealing with such questions one is faced with the vexing problem of historical allegory. John Wallace and Alan Roper have discussed historical parallels and the application of historical examples in seventeenth-century literature at length in a number of fine articles,[17] but for my purposes it is sufficient to recall as a privileged example Dryden's judgment in *The Life of Plutarch* (1683) that "there is nothing of the tyrant in example." Dryden also felt, however, that "the more powerful the examples are, they are the more useful also, and by being more known they are more powerful."[18] Thus, although seventeenth-century writers and readers did not expect one-to-one allegories, sorting out the "powerful" from the merely possible must still be a problem. A clue to a fuller, more "powerful" political reading of *Pompey* is provided in Corneille's "Examen" (1660) of *La Mort de Pompée*. There Corneille stresses the connections of his play to books 8–10 of Lucan's *Pharsalia*, the violent, pro-republican historical epic on the final defeat of the Roman republic. The modeling, Corneille points out, is both historical and stylistic.[19] Generally ignored by modern readers, Lucan and his translators – most notably Thomas May, poet and eloquent historian of the Long Parliament – were widely popular in seventeenth-century England.[20] There is no reason to suppose that Philips was immune to Lucan's influence. Indeed, she appears to be thinking of the *Pharsalia* when, in a letter to Sir Charles Cotterell, Master of Ceremonies for Charles II, she attacks the "Persons of Honour." Having read their *Pompey the Great*, she concludes that they have abused both the "Original" and the "History." She is particularly annoyed with a speech in act 4, scene 3, where Cleopatra hopes to see Rome "Bound in the Golden Chains of Monarchy":

I must then tell you, that Mr. WALLER's own act is not free in my poor Opinion from just Exceptions. The Word *Roman Blade* shocks me very much, his frequent double Rhymes in an heroic Poem, his calling POMPEY a Consul, when that was not in the Original, or the History, both the Consuls being with him at *Pharsalia*; *Pharsalian Kites* for *les Vautours de Pharsale*; I cannot relish his englishing *le dernier preuve* [sic] *de leur Amitie, their new Friendship*, and many Additions and Omissions of the Author's Sense. Then in the second and fourth Acts (which are all I have) unless the Parts acted were much reform'd from this Copy, there are as many Faults as ever I saw in a good Poem . . . [They are wrong for calling] JUBA, SCIPIO and POMPEY's Sons, (for a Rhyme too) *daring sprights*, making CLEOPATRA say she *courts* CAESAR, and adding ten or twelve Lines of *Rome's* becoming a Monarchy; for which, as there is no Ground in CORNEILLE, so I see not how it would have been proper for her to say at that time, when CAESAR had just refus'd a Crown, being *pique d'honneur*, not to be thought *Rome's* Sovereign, tho' he was her Master.[21]

Philips's habitual deference does not keep her from making her point. This letter reveals not only a poet's affinity with Corneille but also considerable familiarity with the republican ethos. Although Philips may not have shared Corneille's emotional ties to "mon bon ami Lucain,"[22] it does seem likely that when she translated *La Mort de Pompée* she was also dealing at some near remove with the *Pharsalia*. Moreover, the Lucanic tradition, strongly identified with civil war, republican virtue, and "the experience of defeat," carried with it a whole set of powerful examples, few of them flattering when applied to royalty. Consider the prologue to *Pompey* written by the Earl of Roscommon:

> The mighty Rivals, whose destructive Rage
> Did the whole World in Civil Armes engage:
> Are now agreed, and make it both their Choice,
> To have their Fates determin'd by your Voice.
> *Caesar* from none but You, will hear his Doom,
> He hates th'obsequious Flatteries of *Rome*:
> He scorns, where once he rul'd, now to be try'd,
> And he hath rul'd in all the World beside.
> When he the Thames, the Danube, and the Nile
> Had stain'd with Blood, Peace flourished in this Isle;
> And you alone may Boast, you never saw
> *Caesar* 'till now, and now can give him Law:
> Great *Pompey* too, comes as a suppliant here,
> But sayes He cannot now begin to fear.
> He knowes your equal Justice, and (to tell
> A Roman Truth) He knows himself too well.
> Success, tis true, waited on *Caesar's* side,
> But *Pompey* thinks he conquer'd when he dy'd.
> His fortune when she prov'd the most unkind,
> Chang'd his Condition, but not *Cato's* Mind.
> Then of what Doubt can *Pompey's* Cause admit,
> Since here so many *Catos* Judging sit?
>
> (*CW* III, 3–4; italics reversed)

Philips thought that this prologue was "the best writ that ever I read" (*CW* II, 75). And, beyond the expected compliments, it participates to a considerable extent in the Stoic and republican rhetoric of *Pompey* itself. It flatters the audience, of course, but this is far from the sort of flattery practiced in the prologues and epilogues to *Pompey the Great*, which encourage the King to see himself as a long-suffering Pompey and the Duke of York to see himself as patterned on the valiant Caesar.[23] Indeed, Caesar in Ireland is a tyrannous outsider, one who "stain'd with Blood" the Thames but not, thankfully, the Liffey. Here the crucial exemplary relationship is between the audience and Cato, the most admirable philosophical figure in the Lucanic ethos. *Pompey* may be attacked, as Pompey was attacked by Caesar and the Egyptians, but "what Doubt can *Pompey's* Cause admit, / Since here so many *Catos* Judging sit?" The link drawn between the obstinate Stoic republican and Philips's individual readers and audience members is quite apt, since in the *Pharsalia* Cato becomes a figure for the transfer of the experience of actual freedom to a "fiction of freedom . . . confined to the hearts of individuals."²⁴ Whether fictional or not – and, of course, fictions may well have political meanings – the freedom that Roscommon urges on the audience takes as its model the Stoic and republican *libertas* of Cato.

"HATE SHALL BE MY *POMPEY* NOW"

In *Pompey* the function of Lucan's Cato is performed by Cornelia. As the play proceeds it becomes more and more clear that its actions and characters are being judged from Cornelia's perspective, and that she, like Cato, is uniquely qualified to judge them. At this point one must look closely at act 3, which Philips thought "the most noble and best written in the *French*" (*CW* II, 103) and begin to distinguish more carefully between her play and Corneille's *La Mort de Pompée*. The first scene opens with a remarkable report from Cleopatra's devoted servant, Achoreus, concerning Caesar. Although Caesar at first enjoys some "malignant Pleasure" when given the "Fatal gift" of Pompey's severed head (3.1.36, 56), he gradually *reasons* himself to *tears*:

> That the whole World now in his Power lies,
> Could not but bring some flattering surprize.
> But though a while this conflict he endur'd,
> Yet his great Soul it self soon re-assur'd.
> Though he loves Power, yet he Treason hates,
> Himself he Judges, on himself debates.
> Each Joy and Grief at reasons bar appears,
> At length resolv'd, he first let fall some Tears.
> His Virtues Empire he by force regains,
> And Noblest Thoughts by that weak sign explains.
> The horrid present from his sight expell'd,
> His Eyes and Hands he up to Heaven held.
> In a few words their Insolence repress'd,
> And after did in Pensive silence rest.
> Nor even to his Romans could reply,
> But with a heavy sigh and furious Eye.
> At last with Thirty Cohorts come to Land,
> To seize the Gates and Ports he does command.
> The Guards he set, and secret Orders sent,
> Shew his Distrust, as well as Discontent.
> *Egypt* he speaks of, as a Province won,
> And now calls *Pompey* not a Foe, but Son.
> This I observ'd.   (3.1.58–80)

Here Caesar exhibits a proper Stoic rationalization of "Joy and Grief at reasons bar" which, while slow in coming, is nevertheless total and issues in resolute action against the Egyptians. If in *La Mort de Pompée* this speech is "a highly disturbing account of opportunism masquerading as high principle,"[25] Philips does not choose to exploit it as such. In scene 2 Caesar tells Ptolemy what his true aim in warring with Pompey had been. This explanation confirms Septimius's earlier analysis, but the Egyptians have badly underestimated Caesar's anger at being deprived of his proper "Foe" and "Friend":

> You employ, *Ptolomy*, such Crafty Words,
> And weak Excuses as your Cause affords;
> Your Zeal was false, if 'twere affraid to see
> What all Mankind beg'd of the Gods should be:
> And did to you such subtilties Convey,
> As Stole the Fruit of all my Wars away;
> Where Honour me engag'd, and where the end
> Was of a Foe subdu'd, to make a Friend;
> Where the worst Enemies that I have met,
> When they are conquer'd, I as Brother Treat:
> And my Ambition only this Design'd,
> To Kill their Hate, and force them to be kind;
> How blest a Period of the War't had been,
> If the glad World had in one Chariot seen
> *Pompey* and *Caesar* at once to have sate
> Triumphant over all their former Hate!
> These were the Dangers you fear'd should befall;
> O fear Ridiculous! and Criminal!
> You fear'd my Mercy, but that trouble quit,
> And wish it rather; you have need of it:
> For I am sure strict Justice would consent
> I should appease *Rome* with your punishment. (3.2.103–24)

Caesar's anger rises because a chance for glorious clemency has been lost (see fig. 3). It should be noted that, while he is willing to spare Ptolemy for Cleopatra's sake, he does not consider pardoning the lesser Egyptians. Caesar is precise about who is worth his clemency and who is not. With Pompey dead, the only real political question left for Caesar is whether to extend clemency to Cornelia, and that he readily does in scene 4. Irresistible in war, confident of Cleopatra's love, and contemptuous of the "Dangerous Friendship" of the Egyptians (3.2.43), Caesar at the midpoint of *Pompey* would seem to be an agent of both Machiavellian *virtù* and Stoic virtue.

Figure 3   Lucan, *De Bello Civili* (Amsterdam, 1658).

Cornelia is impressed by Caesar's virtues. But she is careful in scene 3 to define what it means to be, as Antonius says, "within" Caesar's "Power now":

> *Caesar*, that envious Fate which I can brave,
> Makes me thy Prisoner, but not thy Slave:
> Expect not then my Heart should e're afford
> To pay thee Homage, or to call thee Lord.
> . . .
> For never think my Hatred can grow less,
> Since I the Roman Constancy profess;
> And though thy Captive, yet a Heart like mine
> Can never stoop to hope for ought from Thine:
> Command, but think not to subject my Will,
> Remember this, I am *Cornelia* still.   (3.4.6–9, 42–47)

Cornelia's insistence on her integrity and name is reminiscent of an earlier, more tragic claim: "I am Duchesse of *Malfy* still."[26] Her situation comes close also to that of Paulina, the wife of Seneca, as described in Tacitus's *Annals* 15.63–64 and developed for feminist purposes in the French *femmes fortes* tradition. In *The Gallery of Heroick Women* (1652), a book which may well have been congenial to Philips and which mentions Cornelia often, Paulina is "No *Amazon*, unless a Philosophick and long Rob'd *Amazon*," who "became a Stoick in the house of *Seneca*, and resolves to die in his Company, and by his Example."[27] The companionate marriage of Stoic heroes and heroines registers as a political force under Nero's tyranny, one not less powerful when the heroes have begun to die off:

This example is very rare: but it is sad, and cannot instruct the mind, but by wounding the heart . . . The Tyrant advertised of *Paulina's* generous resolution, sends Souldiers to hinder her Death, and inforce her to live. Not that he takes care of the Vertues, or is willing to preserve the Graces, which are ready to dye with her. He is *Nero* in all his actions, and doth no less mischief when he saves, than when he kills. It is because he delights to sever the best united hearts, and to divide the fairest Couples: It is because he takes pleasure in forcing inclinations, and violating sympathies: It is because he hath a desire to exercise upon friendships and souls an interiour and spirituall Tyranny: It is because after the death of *Seneca*, he will have the heart of *Seneca* in his power.[28]

There is no difference between saving and killing under Nero, and even the Stoic reserve of "friendships and souls" may lie open to his "interiour and spirituall Tyranny." But Cornelia's problem is more subtle than either Malfy's or Paulina's because her captor is, apparently, more kind. "O Worthy Widow of a Man so Brave! / Whose Courage,

Wonder, Fate does pity crave" (3.4.48), Caesar exclaims. He senses another opportunity for displaying his largesse, one almost as glorious as forgiving Pompey. He repeats his explanation for warring with Pompey and extends his widening fantasy of clemency to her:

> And I, in spight of all our former strife,
> Would then have beg'd him to accept of Life;
> Forget my Conquest, and that Rival love,
> Who fought, but that I might his Equal prove:
> Then I, with a content entirely great,
> Had Pray'd the Gods to Pardon his Defeat;
> And giving me his friendship to possess,
> He had pray'd *Rome* to Pardon my success.
> But since Fate, so Ambitious to destroy,
> Hath rob'd the World, and Us, of so much Joy,
> *Caesar* must strive t'acquit himself to you,
> Of what was your Illustrious Husbands due:
> Enjoy your self then with all freedom here:
> Only two dayes my Prisoner appear.   (3.4.70–83)

Caesar's order to Cornelia to "Enjoy your self" rings strangely familiar in a modern idiom, but it is a piece of pure Stoicism. He forgives in order to show his indifference to *fortuna* – the noun is feminine and the concept feminized – and, as Septimius says, "to Augment his Fame." Caesar would "Honour" Cornelia "above a Queen" (3.4.91). She is so vexed by this because his actions are, apparently, so *virtuous*: "O Gods! how many Virtues must I hate" (3.4.93).

Thus, while the most interesting conflict in *Pompey* takes place between Caesar and the Stoic Cornelia, it is nevertheless not the case that this is a conflict between Stoic resolve and rampant tyrannical impulses. Philips, as I shall show below, does in fact emphasize and favor Cornelia in comparison with Corneille and the "Persons of Honour"; but she does not do so at the cost of turning Caesar into a man easily satisfied with his "usual Fortune," however smoothly Fortune's Wheel has been turning for him. She was, in any case, dealing with an author who did not encourage simple interpretation. Marc Fumaroli has shown that the Cornelian dramas of clemency and magnanimity respond to an ancient division within magnanimity itself, one reaching back through Lucan, Cicero, Aristotle, and Plato. On the one hand, there is the "magnanimité philosophique" of Socrates and Lysander, "une vertu de résistance" indifferent to the vagaries of fortune; on the other hand, there is the "magnanimité guerrière" of Achilles, Ajax, and Alcibiades, "une vertu offensive" that will not suffer affronts to honor without vengeance. This tension continues in Roman philosophy and politics, and it comes to a head during the civil wars in violent competition between the *magnitudo animi* of Catiline and Caesar and the purer *magnanimitas*, "imprégnée d'éléments stoïciens" and "respectueuse de l'ordre républicain," praised by Cicero and by Lucan in the *Pharsalia*.[29] Lucan admired the Stoic magnanimity of the republicans, of course, but he realized that such philosophical integrity would always be doomed when faced with the violent magnitude of Caesarism.

Although Corneille appreciated this tragic awareness in Lucan, he refused to accept the moral and political implications of divided magnanimity. He solved the problem in *Cinna, ou la Clémence d'Auguste* (1643) through a clever double reversal. "Les rôles sont donc inversés," writes Fumaroli in a subtle analysis: "l'héritier de César est en train de devenir un nouveau Pompée . . . et ce sont les héritiers de Pompée et de son parti qui sont en train de devenir les nouveaux Catilinas et les nouveaux Césars."[30] The proper heirs of Stoic republicanism, Cinna and Emilie, act as selfish factionalists, whereas Auguste practices Stoic magnanimity by granting the conspirators clemency. The Augustan *pax* is played out upon a moral and political paradox; it is a marvel to all, whether republican or Caesarian. The contrast with *La Mort de Pompée* is instructive. Most critics see César as an inveterate Machiavellian, who only seems or tries to behave, as it were, like Auguste; César's magnanimity fails to convince because, unlike the finally divine Auguste, he is locked in history. One witnesses in *La Mort de Pompée* "la retombée de l'intemporel au temporel."[31] Although Fumaroli argues that there is a conflict and resolution concerning magnanimity and clemency "dans le cœur" of César as well,[32] the critical consensus is that César does not finally achieve the *pax* of Auguste. The best that can be said of César is that his moral status is left unresolved and that his words exist within a discourse of "corrosive dramatic irony."[33]

Philips understood such Cornelian subtleties, of course, and much of the originality of her translation lies in her interpretation of César's ambiguous moral stature and Cornélie's predicament in relation to it. On the one hand, Philips does nothing to darken César's character – indeed Caesar's speeches are perhaps more clearly honorable and well-intentioned than César's. The central moral and political contest in *Pompey* is between Cornelia and Caesar, two "Great Hearts" (5.1.101), and for a time it seems as if Caesar will be revealed as the greater one, the true heir, like the Auguste of *Cinna*, to Cato, Pompey, and the republicans. On the other hand, Philips knew that any real union of republican virtue and imperial power was unthinkable within Lucanic historiography. Unlike the "Persons of Honour," who chose to make Cornelia irrelevant within their broad Caesarian masque (in act 5 of *Pompey the Great* Caesar cuts off Cornelia's final speech with, "Nature her Ignorance has here confest / To place this Spirit in a Womans Breast" – a couplet having no basis in Corneille),[34] Philips understood that, at the very least, a moral balance between Caesar and Cornelia had to be maintained if the integrity of the Lucanic historical and political ethos was to be preserved. Having to a degree elevated Caesar's character, her solution was to elevate Cornelia's as well – to emphasize Cornelia's role in the political action of *Pompey* and, in a sense, to make that action follow from her special knowledge of it.

Making the most of her decision to write four original entr'actes and a postlude for the play, Philips enlarges Cornelia's role through a political and religious "vision" found neither in Corneille nor the "Persons of Honour." For, "After the third Act," the stage direction reads, "to *Cornelia* asleep on a Couch, *Pompey's* Ghost sings this in Recitative Air":

> From lasting and unclouded Day,
> From Joyes refin'd above Allay,
> And from a spring without decay.
>
> I come, by *Cynthia's* borrow'd Beams
> To visit my *Cornelia's* Dreams,
> And give them yet sublimer Theams.
>
> Behold the Man, thou lov'dst before,
> Pure streams have wash'd away his Gore,
> And *Pompey* now shall bleed no more.
>
> By Death my Glory I resume;
> For 'twould have been a harsher Doom
> T'outlive the Liberty of *Rome*.
>
> By me her doubtfull fortune try'd,
> Falling, bequeaths my Fame this Pride,
> I for it liv'd, and with it Dy'd.
>
> Nor shall my Vengeance be withstood
> Or unattended with a Flood,
> Of Roman and Egyptian Blood.
>
> *Caesar* himself it shall pursue,
> His dayes shall troubled be, and few,
> And he shall fall by Treason too.
>
> He, by severity Divine
> Shall be an offering at my Shrine;

> As I was his, he must be mine.
>
> Thy stormie Life regret no more,
> For Fate shall waft thee soon a shoar,
> And to thy *Pompey* thee restore.
>
> Where past the fears of sad removes
> We'l entertain our spotless Loves,
> In beauteous, and Immortal Groves.
>
> There none a Guilty Crown shall wear,
> Nor *Caesar* be Dictator there.
> Nor shall *Cornelia* shed a Tear.

After this a Military Dance, as the Continuance of her Dream, and then *Cornelia* starts up, as waken'd in amazement, saying.

> What have I seen? and whether is it gone
> How great the vision! and how quickly done!
> But if in Dreams we future things can see,
> There's still some Joy laid up in Fate for me.

(3.4.94–131; italics reversed in verse)

Philips was quite proud of this and the other entr'actes, calling them "not inferior to any thing I ever writ" (*CW* II, 69). The most striking thing about Cornelia's "vision" is that it is prophetic and providentialist. This means, in a popular seventeenth-century paradox, that it has immediate consequences. Ghosts, of course, usually tell the truth on stage. Pompey's last triplet makes it clear that there is a distinctly republican dispensation to Philips's Elysium, and the "Military Dance" that follows enforces this political aspect. Moreover, Pompey's naming of Caesar as a "Dictator" who will bring about the defeat of the "Liberty of *Rome*" should eliminate any lingering thought that the vile "Egyptian Monsters" (2.2.136) represent the only real political problem in the play.

In the previous section I suggested that Philips shows a special interest in the Lucanic basis of her play in a letter to Cotterell. Indeed, I would argue that this beautiful entr'acte constitutes a Lucanic *revision* of Corneille. For, although it has no basis in *La Mort de Pompée*, it most definitely does recall the once-famous opening lines of *Pharsalia* 9. There Pompey's "great spirit" leaves its headless body and seeks, "with wondring eyes," a better view:

> In Pharian coals his ghost could not remain,
> Nor those few ashes his great spirit contain.
> Out from the grave he issues, and forsakes
> Th'unworthy fire, and half-burnt limbs, and takes
> Up to the convex of the skie his flight,
> Where with black air the starry poles do meet.

> The space betwixt the regions of the Moon,
> And earth, half-deifi'd souls possess alone,
> Whom fiery wrath, in guiltless lives, has taught
> To brook the lower part of heaven, and brought
> Them to th'eternal sphears, which not they hold,
> That are with incense bury'd, tom'd in gold.
> There filled with true light, with wondring eyes
> The wandring planets, and fixt stars he sees.
> He sees our day involv'd in midst of night,
> And laughs at his torn trunks ridiculous plight.
> Then ore the Æmathian fields, his scatter'd fleet,
> And bloudy *Caesar's* troups he took his flight:
> And with revenge for these dire facts possest
> *Cato's* bold heart, and *Brutus* noble breast.
>
> (*LP* 209–10; 9.1–18)

But on earth "chance was doubtfull": the narrator soon turns to the grieving Cornelia, who throws her support wholly to Cato against Caesar and resolves to follow Pompey, "wheresoever / Th'art gone, through hell, if any hell there be, / Or empty chaos" (*LP* 212; 9.101–02). The episode of Pompey's lunar flight and his inspiration of Cato and Brutus – the only significant divine "machinery" in the *Pharsalia* – is transferred by Philips into the form of her entr'acte. A crucial difference, of course, is that in Lucan Cornelia does not know what Pompey knows. By turning Pompey's Stoic apotheosis into a song sung by Pompey himself to Cornelia, amid "*Cynthia's* borrow'd Beams," Philips rewards her political resolution and answers her metaphysical doubts with providential knowledge.

Armed with the knowledge of "future things," Cornelia makes a decision in act 4 that may seem impolitic on its face but which, given her providential perspective, is fully rational: she exposes the Egyptians' plot to kill Caesar. Cornélie does the same thing in *La Mort de Pompée*, and she and Cornelia both act on strict principle: Caesar's death has been "with too much Justice sought, / That it should now, be with a Treason bought" (4.4.29–30). In *Pompey*, however, Pompey's "sublimer Theams" have revealed to Cornelia that she is, in fact, in a much stronger position than Caesar. In act 5, scene 1, she exclaims:

> O formal Grief! how easie is that Tear
> That's shed for Foes whom we no longer fear!
> How soon revenge for others fills that brest
> Which to it, is, by its own danger prest?
> And when the Care we take to right the dead
> Secures our Life and does our glory spread.
> *Caesar* is generous 'tis true, but he

> By the King wrong'd, and from his Rival free,
> Might in an envious mind a doubt revive,
> What he would do were *Pompey* yet alive.
> His courage his own safety does provide,
> Which does the Beauty of his actions hide.
> Love is concern'd in't too, and he does fight
> In *Pompey's* Cause for *Cleopatra's* Right.
> So many Int'rests with my Husband's met,
> Might to his Virtue take away my debt.
> But as Great Hearts judge by themselves alone,
> I choose to guess his honour by my own.   (5.1.85–102)

Good Stoic that she is, Cornelia bestows upon Caesar two benefits: first, his life; and second, an analytical admiration of his "Virtue." And, because she is sure of her political and providential causes – more so, I think, than Corneille's Cornélie – her words here and elsewhere in act 5 amount to more than casuistry. True magnanimity comes to rest squarely on the shoulders of a worthy republican, and Cornelia is free to practice that virtue – for all that it is worth morally and politically, given a politics understood under a providential horizon – in relation to a Caesar whose ultimate character has been exposed by prophecy and who we know can have no place in the republican Elysium. Philips does not deny the "generous" Caesar his worldly glory. She simply insists that, *sub specie aeternitatis*, it does not matter.

Moreover, Cornelia's admiration of Caesarian "Virtue" does not mean that she has forgotten the "Duty" that drives her emotionally and politically. She addresses Caesar in scene 4:

> My Loss can never be repair'd by Fate,
> Nor is it possible t'exhaust my Hate.
> This Hate shall be my *Pompey* now, and I
> In his Revenge will live, and with it die.
> But as a Roman, though my Hate be such,
> I must confess, I thee esteem as much.
> Both these extreams justice can well allow:
> This does my Virtue, that my Duty show.
> My sense of Honour does the first command,
> Concern, the last, and they are both constrain'd.
> And as thy Virtue, whom none can betray,
> Where I should hate, makes me such value pay:
> My Duty so my Anger does create,
> And *Pompey's* Widdow makes *Cornelia* hate.
> But I from hence shall hasten, and know then,
> I'll raise against thee Gods, as well as Men.   (5.4.58–73)

Cornelia's Stoic "enjoyment" of her self is traumatic, involving a division of the self into "extreams" that violently contradict but do not cancel one another: "they are both constrain'd." The effect is reminiscent of Philips's poem on "Submission," in which the poet's resolve figures, as well, as irresolution:

> Thus I compose my thoughts grown insolent,
> As th'Irish Harper doth his Instrument;
> Which if once struck doth murmur and complain,
> But the next touch will silence all again.   (*CW* I,180–81)

And what, then, of "the next touch"? The complaining and silencing go on and on. Yet in *Pompey* this psychological problematic is not limited to Cornelia and is not, in any case, a liability to her. Indeed, such balancing of opposites becomes a norm in the latter scenes of the play, and her Stoic resolution puts in doubt the resolves of the politically and militarily successful characters to do this or that in the world. Caesar and Cleopatra must discuss Cleopatra's impending coronation in the ominous context of Cornelia's prophecy that Caesar's "offended Friends will at the Price / Of thy best Blood revenge their scorn'd Advice" (5.4.88–89); and Cleopatra herself is plagued by worries over wearing the crown inherited from Ptolemy, which, "As it obliges, Does afflict me too" (5.5.36). Caesar has the last word, but in terms of the broader history – from the *Pharsalia* through May's *Continuation* of the *Pharsalia* – Caesar's exhortation is heavy with dramatic irony. And, whereas in *La Mort de Pompée* the irony is directed at Cornélie – for we know that she and Caton will fail – in *Pompey* the future as disclosed in Pompey's song frowns on Caesar far more than it does on Cornelia.[35]

"KINGS ARE IN SOME SENSE CALLED GODS"

"Hate shall be my *Pompey* now," Cornelia says, and the severity of that dissident hatred figures from a strongly sympathetic angle the base ingratitude condemned over and over again by Stuart partisans throughout the seventeenth century. The Tory attack on ingratitude would sharpen its polemical edge during the course of the Exclusion Crisis of 1678–81, but the Senecan problem of ingratitude for benefits supposedly received was already a political issue in the early 1660s.[36] Caesar is too "generous" to accuse Cornelia of ingratitude, but the ready-made application for readers and audience members in 1663 was that such a woman as Cornelia could accept the magnanimous virtues of Charles's Declaration from Breda and the celebrated Act of Indemnity and Oblivion, the foundation of the Restoration "settlement," and still hate the giver himself.

Indeed, the issue of clemency had been at the forefront of English politics since the early 1640s, or ever since the King's divinely ordained prerogatives had been seriously questioned. The Rump had passed its own Act of Oblivion in 1652, but clemency, to put it bluntly, had always been a public relations tool for the Stuarts. Hyde knew that clemency was the only way that Charles I could maintain his divine stature and also avoid, first, open war and, later, utter defeat. Nevertheless, the rhetoric of clemency had little or no purchase in the 1640s because the members of the Commons did not as a whole feel that they were doing anything wrong in asserting their "ancient rights." Such clemency, they declared in a petition to the King in 1642, "could be no security to their fears and jealousies, for which his majesty seemed to propound it; because they arose not from any guilt of their own actions, but from the evil designs and attempts of others."[37] These feelings changed over time, as Hyde had trusted they would, and the passage of the Act of Indemnity and Oblivion under Charles II realized propositions that he had been advancing since the earliest challenges to Charles I.

Well before landing at Dover, Charles had made it clear that he did not intend to "Augment his Fame" by exacting revenge on his old Parliamentary and Cromwellian enemies in any thorough manner. In the Declaration from Breda of 4 April 1660, he offered a "free and general pardon . . . excepting only such persons as shall hereafter be excepted by Parliament"; and he stated that he was "desiring and ordaining that henceforth all notes of discord, separation and difference of parties be utterly abolished among all our subjects, whom we invite and conjure to a perfect union among themselves, under our protection."[38] The King's first problem was to convince Parliament that elimination of "discord, separation and difference of parties" was both possible and desirable. After months of withering conference debate on the indemnity bill in both Houses, he addressed the Lords on 27 July 1660 by restating the "Promise" of the Declaration and emphasizing the political expediency of a general pardon:

My Lords, if you do not joyn with me in extinguishing this Fear, which keeps the hearts of men awake, and apprehensive of Safety and Security; You keep Me from performing My Promise, which if I had not made, I am perswaded neither I nor You had been now here; I pray let us not deceive those who brought or permitted Us to come together. I knew well there were some men who could neither forgive themselves, or be forgiven by Us, and I thank you for your *Justice* towards those, the immediate murtherers of my Father, and I will deal truly with you, I never thought of excepting any other. I pray think well upon what I have offered, and the benefit you and I have received from that offer, and encourage and oblige all other persons, by not excluding them from the benefit of this Act. This Mercy and Indulgence is the best way to bring them to a true repentance, and to make them more severe to themselves, when they find We are not so to them. It will make them good Subjects to me, and good Friends and Neighbors to you; and We have then all Our end, and you shall find this the securest expedient to prevent future mischief: therefore I do earnestly Desire and Conjure you to depart from all particular Animosities and Revenge, or memory of past Provocations, and that you will pass this Act without other exceptions, then of those who were immediately guilty of that *Murder* of my Father. My Lords I have told you My opinion, and I hope you will be of the same.[39]

To be sure, the King's clemency was a gift that reflected very well upon its giver. As I have mentioned above, Seneca had established the moral and political excellence of clemency in *De Clementia*. There this virtue combines the severest Stoic wisdom with the prince's desire for absolute power; the prince's anger is to be checked, not by "feminine" pity, but by clemency, which for Seneca is an act of the intellect and will involving overwhelming and quite deserved self-regard. Fittingly following *De Ira* in the standard Latin and English editions of Justus Lipsius and Thomas Lodge, *De Clementia* is addressed to Nero, "to the end that in some sort I may serve thee for a mirrour, and shew thee to thy selfe, in such sort, as thou mayest receive a perfite contentment thereby" (*WS* 583; 1.1.1). In the "Argument" to book 1 of Lodge's translation, *A Discourse of Clemencie*, one is told of "how greatly it beseemeth Kings"; of how it "well becommeth them, because they are heads of the Commonweale, and we as the bodie and members"; and that by practicing clemency kings follow "the example of the gods, who spare us" (*WS* 582). In a remarkable passage arguing that the greatest revenge is clemency, Seneca provides a gloss on Caesar's desire to pardon the republicans and also lays out the cherished intellectual groundwork of what Hyde called "the excellent Example and Vertue of the King . . . this blessed Act of Oblivion":

A Servant, a Serpent, an Arrow have slaine a King. No man hath saved a King, except he that saved him were greater then himselfe. He therefore that hath attained the power over life and death, ought to use so great an authoritie bestowed upon him by the gods couragiously, especially towards those, who in his knowledge have sometime opposed themselves against his greatnesse:

having attained this dignitie, he is sufficiently revenged, and hath done that
which was requisite for an entire punishment. For he that should die, hath lost
his life, but whosoever from a high degree, hath beene prostitute at his enemies
feet . . . liveth to his greater glorie, that preserveth him: and addeth more to his
renowne by his life, then if he had sentenced him to death. For he is the
continuall spectacle of another mans vertue. (*WS* 599–600; 1.21.1–2)

It is not only Lodge's prose style that leads us to question in places which
"he" is which. For, at its most sublime, the psycho-political dynamic of
clemency merges the identities of victor and victim: as Hyde would
claim in September 1660, the King wanted "to finde all His subjects at
once in His arms, and himself in theirs";[40] or, as Caesar claims in
Pompey, "the worst Enemies I have met, / When they are conquer'd, I as
Brother Treat." But, of course, this is only a temporary confusion: the
glory goes finally to the prince, and it is an absolute glory. In Lipsius's
popular *Politicorum sive Civilis Doctrinae Libri Sex* clemency expresses the
pinnacle of honor and power: princes "purchase unto them selves
immortall glorie by this meanes; *For there is nothing that causeth men to
approach so neare unto God, as to give life, and safetie to men.*"[41]

But did the King's wonderful "Mercy and Indulgence" have any
reality for the nation beyond its brief, happy union with the expedient?
Having accepted his "Promise," the questions for Parliament became
whether his "perfect union" was politically workable and just what
being forever grateful to him entailed. The slow, circuitous progress of
the bill through the Lords and Commons in the spring and summer of
1660 – a story told in grim detail by David Masson in his monumental
omnibus, *The Life of John Milton* – did not bode well for the blessed "Act
of Free and General Pardon, Indemnity, and Oblivion" that did finally
become law.[42] A general pardon became, in fact, a patchwork of
unclement provisions against those political players active in the 1640s
and 1650s, "regicides" and non-"regicides" alike, who were to be
"absolutely excepted," "excepted with a saving clause," "excepted but
not capitally," "excepted but for incapacitation only," "excepted under
perpetual brand of incapacitation," and "incapacitated by description,
but not by name."[43] Even after the bill was finished and had received the
King's assent in late August, Hyde still felt it necessary in September
1660 to remind both Houses of their clement natures:

Give me leave to tell you, That as any name or names, or other words of
reproach are expressly against the letter, and punishable accordingly, so evil
and envious looks, murmuring and discontented hearts, are as directly against
the equity of this Statute, a direct breach of the Act of Indempnity, and ought to

be punished too; and I believe they may be so. You know Kings are in some sense called Gods, and so they may in some degree be able to look into mens hearts; and God hath given us a King who can look as far into mens hearts, as any Prince alive; and He hath great skill in Physiognomy too, you would wonder what Calculations He hath made from thence; and no doubt, if He be provoked by evil looks, to make a further enquiry into mens hearts, and findes those corrupted with the passions of Envy and Uncharitableness, He will never choose those hearts to trust and rely upon. He hath given us a noble and princely example, by opening and stretching His arms to all who are worthy to be His subjects, worthy to be thought English men, by extending His heart, with a pious and grateful joy, to finde all His subjects at once in His arms, and himself in theirs: and shall we fold our arms towards one another, and contract our hearts with Envy and Malice to each other, by any sharp memory of what hath been unneighbourly or unkindly done heretofore? What is this but to rebel against the Person of the King, against the excellent Example and Vertue of the King, against the known Law of the Land, this blessed Act of Oblivion?

My Lords and Gentlemen, The King is a Suiter to you, makes it His suite very heartily, That you will join with Him in restoring the whole Nation to its primitive temper and integrity, to its old good manners, its old good humor, and its old good nature . . . and that you will by your example, by the candor of your conversation, by your precepts, and by your practice, and by your Interest, teach your neighbors and your friends, how to pay a full obedience to this clause of the Statute, how to learn this excellent Art of Forgetfulness.[44]

Here the twenty-year background, replete with political and personal meanings for both Hyde and the King, combined with clemency's august intellectual heritage to produce one of the most remarkable rhetorical performances of Hyde's remarkable career. Nevertheless, even this exactingly retributive product of the Convention Parliament – and one which Seneca, Lipsius, and Hyde himself would have said was divinely inspired – came to be seen during the first six sessions of the Cavalier Parliament (1661–67) as a typical example of the foolish leniency of that earlier body, "an illegal makeshift, all whose acts required revision."[45] As Ronald Hutton has observed, the term "restoration settlement" is "a misnomer, for there were two settlements in these years, of different character and produced by different groups of men working in different circumstances."[46] Hyde himself wanted to maintain the Act of Indemnity and Oblivion as passed in 1660, but of course he and the King also wanted to crush any republican and nonconformist hopes that remained alive; clemency towards republicans and nonconformists did not mean countenancing them. A supplementary bill was quickly approved in the summer of 1661 that had the effect of widening the "exceptions" to the original Act and making them more severe. Several unfortunate men, though by law not actually "excepted capitally," were now "liable to be drawn through the streets on sledges, with ropes about their necks, to the gallows at Tyburn, and thence back to prison" – such cruelly theatrical clemency being a "continuall spectacle of another mans vertue" if ever there was one.[47]

Indeed, it was not long before the clement King's "noble and princely Example" was itself becoming something less than exemplary. The notorious execution of Sir Henry Vane in June 1662 was the direct result of a *retraction* of regal clemency. The King had agreed in September 1660 to a Parliamentary petition asking that, in the event Vane and John Lambert were capitally condemned at their trials, they would be spared execution through royal remission.[48] These men were not "regicides" and had enjoyed the respect of influential members of the Convention Parliament. The King had agreed to the spirit and letter of the petition – it had been suggested by Hyde as a solution to a dispute between the Lords and Commons – but by the summer of 1662 the King had changed his mind. It seems that Vane had defended himself rather too ably at his trial. Having heard of this eloquent defense, the King wrote to Hyde on 7 June 1662: "If he has given new occasion to be hanged, certainly he is too dangerous a man to let live, if we can honestly put him out of the way."[49] And so, after one more speech, the head of the man whom Milton called "young in years, but in sage counsel old," was cut off on Tower Hill on 14 June 1662.

In the end, although the Act of Indemnity and Oblivion "was an almost complete formal success in that there seems to have been only one prosecution under it (in Dorset in 1663) for berating somebody for his wartime record,"[50] it did little or nothing to inspire the feelings and virtues that Hyde and the King had invoked in its support. Nor was their government so clement as they liked to say, as may be gathered from the case of Vane. "On closer inspection," Hutton writes, the government's "position loses much of the disinterested generosity which filled the speeches of its members and appears to contrast so nobly with the attitude of the Commons."[51] Clemency went against some of the lamentable facts of political life and also against some vices that can appear quite virtuous in desperation and comfort alike. In simultaneously praising and retreating from the supposed healing powers of clemency, Hyde, the King, and Parliament were responding to and expressing attitudes and desires that the Restoration "settlement" did nothing to moderate or satisfy. Indeed, these attitudes and desires only grew more severe as the 1660s wore on. They are given energetically vicious expression by Sir Roger L'Estrange in *A Caveat to the Cavaliers* (1661) and *A Modest Plea both for the Caveat, and the Author of It* (1661). In the former tract, L'Estrange, who would soon be appointed Surveyer of the Imprimery and Printing Presses, attacks James Howell, a moderate royalist who had made the mistake of too happily pronouncing on the virtues of the Act of Indemnity and Oblivion – who had suggested, in a pleasant Senecan spirit, that "the noblest way of Revenge is to forget, and scorn injuries":

This is to enter further than becomes us into the Actions of our Soveraign. We do not blame the King's *Indulgence*, but rather adore that Divine Sweetnesse of his Nature; yet we detest those wretches that abuse it, and we affirm, that *Mis-placed Mercy was his Fathers Ruine*. To say that the *Snake kill'd the man that gave it Life, and warm'd it in his Bosome*, reflects upon the *Serpent*, not the *Charity*.

Nor by your Favour Sir, is the *Exercise* of *Mercy*, a Virtue, in all Cases. Suppose *Six* Persons ready to perish for want of Bread; *Three* of them, *Murtherers*, and my *Enemies*; the other *Three* my *Honest Friends*: I can relieve but *Half*, which *Three* shall I save? Or if I be uncertain how my stock will hold out, with which shall I begin? In this case, were not *Mercy* to the *Guilty*, *Cruelty* to the *Innocent*? *Love your Enemies*, is not *Hate your Friends: A will to save All*, is indeed a *Princely Virtue*, but he that makes the *Experiment*, shall most Infallibly *destroy the best*.

And, several pages further along, but in the same vein:

As to the *Act of Indempnity*: That saves them from the *Law*, but *in Foro Conscientia* 'tis no acquittal: It discharges the *Penalty*, but not the *Crime*, only an effectual *Repentance* can do that, which cannot be admitted without *Restitution*. 'Tis not an *Act of State*, that can dissolve a *Ty of Conscience*: that were to argue, as if a *Parliament* could forgive *Sins*.

At the last day, when Inquisition shall be made for *Bloud, Theft, Oppression, &c.* – We dare appeal to the Sworn Patrons of the Cause, *Smectymnuus* themselves: what will an *Act of Indempnity* avail, in Plea before the Great Tribunal?

So many *Parents* made *Childlesse* by *Thy Sword*; so many *Children Fatherlesse*; the Bloud of so many thousand *Loyal Subjects* spilt like water, *Common*, and *Noble*, and at last the *KINGS*: and all this in a Cause where every *Thought, Word, Action of Agreement* was a *Murther*. Why shouldest not thou be *Damn'd*?

Lord (saies he) MURTHERS *are Pardoned by the Act of INDEMPNITY*.[52]

Although most were grateful for the King's clement intentions, there were enough outspoken critics like L'Estrange, both in and out of Parliament, to hold up passage of the Act of Indemnity and Oblivion for several months; to turn it into something other than Hyde and the King had once hoped for; and, once it had passed in patchwork form, to conduct in the name of "gratitude" an unending if not finally successful campaign against the very ideas of clemency, oblivion, and mutual trust.

What L'Estrange and his impoverished royalist fellows hated most was the Miltonic "wise Man" from *Eikonoklastes* (1649), who with "constancie and solid firmness" could scorn even the glorious "Trophies of Charity" once offered by Charles I (*CPW* III, 601). What they feared most was that Charles II would be too clement to Smectymnuus and too ungenerous to them.

Clemency, then, for all its antiquity, was not simply a theory or a body of prescriptions. It named a troubled and troubling controversy, a crisis. Perhaps the best that can be said of Hyde and the King in regard to this crisis is that they occupied a rather moderate position within it. That, of course, is precisely the position they wanted to occupy; but, as politicians know, even the most moderate positions can be difficult to govern from. On one side were those like Vane, Milton, Marvell, and James Philips (I descend a hierarchy of Saints, from very high to very low) who had no love of punishment but who did not want to say that they wanted or needed clemency. On the other side were the much more audible voices of L'Estrange and all those who were deeply suspicious of royal clemency because they did not want to lose what they had just lately seemed to gain back, and who were determined not to let "*Mercy* to the *Guilty*" become "*Cruelty* to the *Innocent*" nor to let anyone – not even the King – forget that "*Love your Enemies*, is not *Hate your Friends*." From all sides clemency was praised to the skies, but its proper political use by the King was disputed and its true glory, in the eyes of God, was doubted.

"WE READ *CORNEILLE*, AND *ORINDA* TOO"

Returning now to *Pompey*, it should be clear enough that the stance taken by Cornelia in response to Caesar's clemency would have disturbed Hyde deeply had he thought to make the obvious application to contemporary political situations. *Here is a woman*, he might have thought, *who folds her arms in ingratitude when our noble Caesar extends his in pious and grateful joy.* It is also possible that the censorious L'Estrange may have approved the rationale for executing Pompey that Ptolemy gives the clement Caesar: "We fear'd your Mercy would your Right withstand: / For to that pitch your sense of Honour flies" (3.2.88–89). The dilemma that Philips captures so well is that, because Caesar acts in a proper Stoic manner in extending clemency to Cornelia, there is no way for her to accept it without either finding some means of returning the benefit or compromising the same Stoic "self" that he would have her "Enjoy." The only proper Stoic thing to do in Cornelia's situation is to return

Caesar's benefit, but the return she chooses – admiration for his apparent magnanimity – is linked, indissolubly, with the gift of her duty-bound *hatred*. Cornelia is quite close in spirit to the poor philosophical benefactors found in Seneca's *De Beneficiis*, who give to princes the timeless gifts of contempt and criticism. Seneca is passionate when he argues that beneficial exchange is a combat of virtue, where one may be bested but not conquered: "No man ... can be overcome in benefits, if he ... have a will to recompence, and if that which he cannot attaine in act, he equalleth in minde and will" (*WS* 94; 5.4.1). Minds and wills can be subversive, however, and criticism is usually the only thing that kings and tyrants do not already have enough of. Socrates, it is true, refused to receive benefits from Archelaus of Macedon, saying that he could never repay them. But Seneca is not impressed by this: "Might not *Socrates* then have requited *Archelaus*, if he had given him instructions how to governe his Kingdome? As little as you make of it, it had beene a great benefit in *Socrates*, and greater any wayes then *Archelaus* could have given him" (*WS* 97; 5.6.6).[53] Such "instructions" may have been good for King Archelaus, but any Stoic's hatred was a medicine too strong for King Charles II.

In the autumn of 1663, just a few months before she died of smallpox, Philips wrote a poem "To the Queen's Majesty, on her late Sickness and Recovery" from the same disease. In November she wrote to Cotterell, her trusted friend at court, of her new "verses":

I leave them therefore wholly to your mercy, of which you can give no greater an Instance, than by committing to the Flames a Paper, which, I fear, is past all Correction. And this I must injoin you to do, if any other Poem has been seen on the same Subject; for then I am sure this would appear with as much Disgrace, as covers my poor Translation of POMPEY, since the Lustre of the other obscur'd it. But if no other Person has been before-hand with me, and you resolve to expose me, be pleas'd to make me address my selfe not as I do, but as I ought to do to so great and sacred a Person. I know how difficult it is to speak of Princes as we ought; how much more difficult it is then for one born and bred in so rude and dark a Retreat as I have been, to accost them in such a manner as to deserve their Pardon? (*CW* II, 117–18)

Such deference is partly strategic and figures a deeply competitive impulse. But it is also clear that Philips is really worried here, and that her worries over the poem's reception at court are colored by the mixed response apparently given there to *Pompey*. Her reference to the "Pardon" of "Princes" suggests that she still has the central political issues of *Pompey* on her mind. As she had adapted it from Corneille, the language of Cornelia and Pompey was not the language of the court, and this could only have exacerbated her awareness of "how difficult it is to speak of Princes as we ought." After all, the product of her "rude and dark . . . Retreat" had been a Lucanic drama highlighting an eloquent character who hates a clement Caesar. For Philips, being a better translator than the suave "Persons of Honour" meant dealing seriously with the Lucanic and republican "History" at the heart of *La Mort de Pompée*. Perhaps all this, as L'Estrange had argued to Howell, was "to enter further than becomes us into the Actions of our Soveraign." To "speak of Princes" in this way was to do more than criticize a network of ancient *topoi*: Philips was exposing herself to the suspicions of those who were sure that the worst, most ungrateful intentions lurked behind the kind of Stoic integrity and resolution displayed by Cornelia.

Given the political context, what we know of the reception of *Pompey* at court is not surprising. In May 1663 Philips thanked Cotterell "for presenting POMPEY to his MAJESTY, and for the favourable Account you give me of his Royal Goodness for that Trifle" (*CW* II,90). The "Royal Goodness" did not last long: only a few months later Philips claimed that the "poor translation" had been put in "Disgrace" by the "Lustre of the other." The King may have considered the implications of Philips's final song, sung in duet "by two Egyptian Priests" at the close of act 5:

1

What cannot Glorious *Caesar* do?
How nobly does he fight and woo!
On Crowns how does he tread!
What mercie to the weak he shews,
How fierce is he to living Foes,
How pious to the dead?

2

Cornelia yet, would challenge Tears,
But that the sorrow which she wears,
So charming is, and brave.
That it exalts her Honour more,
Then if she all the Scepters bore
Her Generous Husband gave.

Chorus.

Then after all the Blood that's shed,
Let's right the living and the dead:
Temples to *Pompey* raise;
Set *Cleopatra* on the Throne;
Let *Caesar* keep the World h'has won;
And sing *Cornelia's* praise.   (5.5.71–88; italics reversed)

The song moves from questions about Caesar – whether they are serious or merely "rhetorical" is ambiguous, and depends on the way they are voiced – to confident statements about Cornelia. This was not the best way to praise the King and his relatives "in such a manner as to deserve their Pardon." For Philips asks that Cornelia be praised finally, not Caesar or Caesarism. If any pardon or benefit is to be given, it is not to *her*, but to *him*.

At this level of discourse, one at once thoroughly fictive and intensely political, personal motives tend to fall away as ephemera. A pardon may well have been coveted by her husband, but that possibility is beside the point when the relevant point of view is the role that she adopted when playing the Stoic. In the letter in which Philips first mentions her work on *Pompey* to Cotterell, she writes:

> I am indeed of your Opinion, and could never govern my Passions by the Lessons of the Stoicks, who at best rather tell us what we should be, than teach us how to be so; they show the Journey's end, but leave us to get thither as we can. I would be easy to my self in all the Vicissitudes of Fortune, and SENECA tells me I ought to be so, and that 'tis the only way to be happy; but I knew that as well as the Stoick. I would not depend on others for my Felicity; and EPICTETUS says, if I do not, nothing shall trouble me. I have a great Veneration for the Philosophers, and allow they give us many Instructions that I find applicable and true; but as far as I can see, the Art of Contentment is as little to be learn'd, tho' it be much boasted of, in the Works of the Heathens, as the Doctrine of forgiving our Enemies. 'Tis the School of Christianity that teaches both these excellent lessons. (*CW* II, 46)

Philips was willing to defend the reputation of her Christian piety with the usual commonplace attacks on Stoic "Heathens," but nobody bothers to turn the other cheek in *Pompey*. The ideas she espouses in the play and the letter are Stoic, urbane, and quite confident of an audience. One should not, after all, expect Philips to be any less "easy" about her husband's fortunes than her own. Nevertheless, the tendency to read Philips's work in narrow emotional contexts has become deeply ingrained. Even the so-called "long speeches" of *Pompey* have been cited recently as evidence of Philips's "own need to control her disordered emotions."[54] They are nothing of the sort, of course, unless all attempts at public discourse are to be taken as such. I have shown above that to criticize clemency in the 1660s was not a *private* thing to do. Clemency was not only a respected virtue in an age that respected virtues: it was a topic for debate with a broad range of positions argued *pro* and *con*. Philips's *Pompey* was a part of that larger argument, and was no doubt seen and read as staking out a position, however complex, casuistical, and perhaps unpopular, within it. The clemency of *Pompey* is not only the wonderful clemency of Hyde and Charles II; nor is it only the unwise, ungodly clemency of L'Estrange; nor is it only the foolish clemency contemned by Vane and Milton; nor is it only the convenient clemency coveted by lesser Vanes such as James Philips. The clemency of *Pompey* is, rather, the clemency of all these political men, combined as a dramatic whole, and criticized from the deeply Stoic and also deeply providential perspective of Cornelia, a woman who refuses to bow to her clement conqueror in this life and knows that the greatest clemency awaits in another.

Like most of the learned and natural Stoics of the seventeenth century, Philips was a cosmopolitan or had desires in that direction. Indeed, the "rude and dark . . . Retreat" in which she wrote *Pompey* and her many poems is a trope for writing itself: it names by paradox a way of branching out into the larger world of letters and learning, and there can be no doubt that in the 1650s and 1660s the literary world was also a political world. Of the "two Common-weales" that Seneca writes of in *De Otio* Philips could serve the "truely publique" one as well as any other writer, and we should not call this an aesthetic realm if by doing so we mean to oppose it to actual social and political circumstances. If her "lesser" commonwealth was Wales, the "greater" one was London or Dublin; if the possibilities for women in London and Dublin seemed too limited, then the worlds of ancient Rome and Egypt, brought to life with exemplary force on the stage, could serve her goals. The "truely publique" commonwealth is "greater" than the "lesser" local one, not because it is removed from reality, but because it is in fact, to the Stoic's literal mind, a larger reality. Seneca's *language* could sometimes present barriers to women readers – as when he says in the first sentence of *De Constantia Sapientis* that "there is as much difference betwixt the *Stoickes* and other Philosophers, as betweene Females and Males" – but his *doctrine* was often not only consolatory but empowering.[55] Serving the commonwealth of mankind, not merely obeying it, could be quite attractive to women intellectuals of the 1660s – intellectuals who were, of course, excluded from both Houses of Parliament and who could hardly expect rational commerce with members of the royal households. Like Paulina in *The Gallery of Heroick Women*, Cornelia shows "that Constancy belonged to her Sex no less than to [men]; and that Women might be Philosophers . . . without making Dilemmaes or Syllogismes."[56] The answer to the "Moral Question" that follows Paulina's story in that book must have seemed obvious to Philips and the many women and men who admired *Pompey* in the 1660s: "we must boldly say, and without fearing to do her injury, that [Stoic philosophy] hath no Sex. . . that she is come as well for Women as Men; and she being the last perfection of the Understanding, and the compleatment of Reason, all rational Souls are equally capable of her Discipline."[57] Philips was working on *Horace* (1641), Corneille's bleak deliberation on loyalties divided by family and state, when she died to the sorrow of Cowley, Orrery, and a host of other "friends" in the commonwealth of mankind and the republic of letters. One of these was the poet "Philo-Philippa" who, Philips thought, "pretends to be a Woman" and "writes very well":

> Woman Translate *Pompey*! which the fam'd
> *Corneille* with such art and labour fram'd!
> To whose close version the Wits club their sense,
> And a new Lay poetick SMEC springs thence!
> Yes, that bold work a Woman dares Translate,
> Not to provoke, nor yet to fear mens hate.
> . . .
> *Pompey*, who greater than himself's become,
> Now in your Poem, than before in *Rome*;
> And much more lasting in the Poets Pen,
> Great Princes live, than the proud Towers of Men.
> He thanks false *Egypt* for its Treachery,
> Since that his Ruine is so sung by thee;
> And so again would perish, if withall,
> *Orinda* would but celebrate his Fall.
> Thus pleasingly the Bee delights to die,
> Foreseeing, he in Amber Tomb shall lie.
> . . .
> This makes *Cornelia* for her *Pompey* vow,
> Her hand shall plant his Laurel on thy brow:
> So equal in their merits were both found,
> That the same Wreath Poets and Princes Crown'd:
> And what on that great Captains Brow was dead,
> She Joies to see re-flourish'd on thy head.
> In the French Rock *Cornelia* first did shine,
> But shin'd not like her self till she was thine:
> Poems, like Gems, translated from the place
> Where they first grew, receive another grace.
> Drest by thy hand, and polish'd by thy Pen,
> She glitters now a Star, but Jewel then:
> No flaw remains, no cloud, all now is light,
> Transparent as the day, bright parts more bright.
> . . .
> In your own fancy free, to his sence true,
> We read *Corneille*, and *Orinda* too.[58]

The final line, with its subtle homophony between *Corneille* and *Cornelia*, links the great Frenchman, the fearless Englishwoman, and the ancient Roman heroine in an honorable poetic trio worthy of the republic of letters. Cornelia is not the "real" Katherine Philips, of course, but that Stoic character does exemplify the most aggressive and productive aspects of Philips's authorial *persona*. If the Stoic pose was sometimes less one of bravery than withdrawal, it was most often one of bravery *in* withdrawal. This, at least, is the attitude of Philips in her "rude and dark ... Retreat," and we shall see such brave retreats at work again when we return in the following chapter to Marvell and consider his imitation of Jonson and his praise of Milton.

CHAPTER 4

Jonson, Marvell, Milton: the Stoicism of friendship and imitation

A wise man only is a friend: Friendship is only amongst the wise, for in them only is an unanimity as to things that concern life and community, so as our friends may make use of them as freely, as we our selves . . . But amongst the wicked, there is no friendship; for friendship being real and not feigned, it is impossible it should consist without faith and constancy. But, in the wicked, there is infidelity, and inconstancy, and hostility.

Thomas Stanley, *The History of Philosophy*, paraphrasing Diogenes Laertius, *Lives* 7.124.[1]

In this chapter I shall be dealing again with the writings of Andrew Marvell, but they in turn will lead us to John Milton and his sublime and iconoclastic epics. I suspect that some admirers of the "radical" Milton will bristle at the suggestion that his work should be associated in any positive way with Stoicism. The rhetoric of constancy, the idea of retirement to a Stoic garden, or a "rude and dark . . . Retreat" of the sort practiced by Katherine Philips, may seem to lead necessarily to the solitary, formalist Milton imagined by Louis Martz in *Poet of Exile* – to the view that *Paradise Regain'd* (1671), for instance, deals primarily with a "mind . . . exploring its own problems."[2] Such "exile" would be a dead-end indeed, but Martz's "exile" is not Milton's. I can only stress the paradoxical and political nature of virtually all claims to individual constancy, retirement, and silence in the face of political change and competition in the seventeenth century. Such claims are *instances* of change and competition. One intelligent reader of *Paradise Lost* and *Paradise Regain'd* who was willing to entertain the idea of a Stoic Milton was his friend Andrew Marvell, with whom he shared much "unanimity as to things that concern life and community." Marvell, of course, was deeply concerned in the political and religious controversies of the day and, as we saw in chapter 2, he was ready to deploy subtle Stoic arguments whenever he thought they were needed. That Marvell used such rhetoric in representing Milton in the 1670s is in any case one of the main contentions of this chapter, and it is from his perspective that I shall begin considering Milton's own complex revisions of the Stoic tradition.

MILTON'S ''RETIRED SILENCE''

Some may recall Marvell's defense of Milton in *The Second Part* of *The Rehearsal Transpros'd* against the attacks of Samuel Parker, once an associate of sorts, but by 1673 a champion of religious intolerance. Parker had written in his *Reproof* that *The Rehearsal Transpros'd* afforded ''as good Precedents for Rebellion and King-killing, as any we meet with in the writings of *J. M.*'';[3] and towards the end of *The Second Part* Marvell makes a point of rebutting this claim as yet another instance of Parker's malicious immoderation:

> You do three times at least in your *Reproof*, and in your *Transproser Rehears'd* well nigh half the book thorow, run upon an author *J. M.* which does not a little offend me . . . *J. M.* was, and is, a man of great Learning and Sharpness of wit as any man. It was his misfortune, living in a tumultuous time, to be toss'd on the wrong side, and he writ *Flagrante bello* certain dangerous Treatises. His Books of *Divorce* I know not whether you may have use of; but those upon which you take him at advantage were of no other nature then that which I mentioned to you, writ by your own father . . . At His Majesties happy Return, *J. M.* did partake, even as you your self did for all your huffing, of His Regal Clemency and has ever since expiated himself in a retired silence. It was after that, I well remember it, that being one day at his house, I there first met you. Since that I have been scarce four or five times in your Company, but, whether it were my foresight or my good fortune, I never contracted any friendship or confidence with you. But then it was, when you, as I told you, wander'd up and down *Moor-fields* Astrologizing upon the duration of His Majesties Government, that you frequented *J. M.* incessantly and haunted his house day by day.[4]

This defense may strike some modern readers as unnecessary or unserious, but it is important in our context and, I think, expressive of the political situations of both writers at the time. Milton is represented as a perfect example of Stoic constancy and a man who could appreciate the equally Stoic virtue of "Regal Clemency." This may seem rather too moderate coming from a friend, but it does provide grounds for an effective attack on their common enemy. The "faith and constancy" that for the Stoics mark those capable of friendship have, of course, always been lacking in Marvell's Parker; in him there is only "infidelity, and inconstancy, and hostility." Indeed, Marvell is able to turn the language of Stoicism and its "retired silence" to political advantage. Marvell's running allusion to the Duke of Buckingham's burlesque, *The Rehearsal* (1672), is braced here by the moral world of Jonsonian satire. Parker is both "Mr. Bayes" and a modern-day Sir Politic Would-Be, someone more taken with *verba* than *res*, a man like the vain "Stirrer" of Jonson's Cary-Morison ode who can do nothing but "die late" (*BJ* VIII, 243). Milton, however, has always accepted "misfortune" and the consequences of being "toss'd on the wrong side." Having like Marvell made *"Destiny* [his] *Choice,"* Milton was uncompromised in the company of the inconstant Parker in the early 1660s, and is untouched by his attacks now.

Milton is a silent Stoic in Marvell's prose defense, but by 1673 this "retired silence" had produced *Paradise Lost, Paradise Regain'd*, and *Samson Agonistes* (1671). The fact that Milton needs to be *defended* at all suggests that there is a rhetoric to such silence and, quite likely, a politics to it as well. Within the controversial context shared by Marvell, Milton, and Parker, such retirement is always a function, not of actual withdrawal – *"Death* to the *Muses*, and a real *literal quitting* of this *World,"*5 as Cowley had imagined it in 1656 – but of controversy itself. The "retired silence" of Marvell's Milton has a secure place in a politically charged tradition of Stoic resistance that seventeenth-century readers understood much better than we, one that reaches back to the censored eloquence of Tacitus's republican martyrs for inspiration. "Punitis ingeniis gliscit auctoritas," writes Tacitus of the republican historian Cremutius Cordus in *Annals* 4.35 – a thought nicely translated by Ben Jonson in *Sejanus his Fall* (1605): "the punishment / Of wit, doth make th'authoritie [of wit] increase" (*BJ* IV, 408; 3.475–76).6 Of course, Marvell's language of clemency and retirement also recalls Philips's *Pompey* in which Caesar's offer of clemency and his beneficent invitation to "Enjoy your self" poses severe ethical and political challenges to the Stoic. Stoic discourse joins victor with vanquished in an ethical bond which is also a vexing political competition to see who can bestow the superior clemency. "Benefits oblige," observes Hobbes in *Leviathan* (1651), "and obligation is thraldome; which is to one's equall, hatefull."7 In Marvell's defense of Milton, however, "Regal Clemency" is less an ethical *problem* than a political *fiction* with the purpose of driving an ideological wedge between the King and official and unofficial spokesmen such as Parker. Clemency was a king's politic alternative to outright punishment and, as we have seen in the writings of Lipsius and Clarendon, its godlike aura could also appeal to a king's vanity. But honor and authority could still be gained in the study if not in the forum, and the traditional Stoic critique of the tyrant's generosity as worthless translated powerfully for censured republicans and nonconformists like Milton in the wake of civil war and the still disputed "settlement." Thus, although the "retired silence" that Marvell claims for Milton is allowed and indeed enforced by "Regal Clemency," it could also be a direct challenge to the King's rule.

"TO MY CHOSEN FRIEND"

Marvell's Stoic and Stoically republican attitudes toward Milton ran much deeper than the rhetoric of this prose defense. Indeed, "On *Paradise Lost*," his famous poem of "misdoubting" prefixed to the 1674 edition of Milton's epic, has a clear model in an earlier commendatory poem in the English Stoic tradition: Ben Jonson's "*To My Chosen Friend, The Learned Translator of Lucan, Thomas May*, Esquire." The translation referred to in Jonson's title is Thomas May's very popular *Lucan's Pharsalia*, a work that, though obscure to twentieth-century eyes, caught the attention of Jonson and held the attention of the critically and politically savvy Marvell. "To My Chosen Friend" welcomed readers to every edition of *Lucan's Pharsalia*, and it is reasonable to think that Marvell knew the commendation as well as he knew the epic.[8] In their larger outlines, Jonson's poem on May and *Lucan's Pharsalia* and Marvell's longer poem on Milton and *Paradise Lost* share the unusual rhetorical procedure of severe doubt followed by enthusiastic approbation of form and content. In praising Milton and his "vast Design" (line 2), Marvell adopts the critical language used by Jonson in praising the heroic coherence of Lucan's "whole frame" (line 20). And, in praising Milton as a poet who "above humane flight dost soar aloft" (line 37), Marvell follows Jonson's commendation of May's success as a translator in having faithfully "interpreted" the gods Phoebus and Hermes (line 19). Verbal, formal, and philosophical similarities link these poems as poems and, as I hope to show in the latter pages of this chapter, these links were likely to function as political commentary in 1674. John Aubrey noted that May's "translation of Lucan's excellent poeme made him in love with the republique, which tang stuck by him."[9] The same "tang" pervades both "To My Chosen Friend" and "On *Paradise Lost*." *Lucan's Pharsalia* brought the wars and ideas of Caesar, Pompey, and Cato home to English readers during years when they could relate directly to the experience of civil war. To praise Milton in a Jonsonian manner was, in this outstanding case, to praise him for having written a Lucanic poem.

Perhaps the most striking thing about "On *Paradise Lost*" is its skeptical rigor, Marvell's willingness to revise the generic conventions of commendatory verse by repeatedly straining praise through a sieve of doubt. The poem, writes Joseph Wittreich, was "calculated to portray Marvell as a poet different in kind from Milton, with an integrity of his own, and an honour. What has seemed to many readers a self-effacing poem is, at least covertly, a self-justifying one."[10] But, whatever they have thought of his motives, critics have usually assumed that Marvell had models – that the poem did not spring unbidden from his forehead. Reasonably enough, the most popular place to look for models has been *Paradise Lost* itself. "The first passage of the poem," thought Colie, "is written in a formal Miltonic syntax."[11] This may be true, but if Marvell adopts a Miltonic style in "On *Paradise Lost*," the result is Milton blended with a heavy dose of Jonson. Here is Jonson's "To My Chosen Friend," which I quote from the 1650 edition of *Lucan's Pharsalia*:

> WHen, *Rome*, I read thee in thy mighty pair,
> And see both climbing up the slippery stair
> Of Fortunes wheel by *Lucan* driv'n about,
> And the world in it, I begin to doubt,
> At every line some pin thereof should slack
> At least, if not the general Engine crack.
> But when again I view the parts so peiz'd,
> And those in number so, and measure rais'd,
> As neither *Pompey's* popularity,
> *Caesar's* ambition, *Cato's* liberty,
> Calm *Brutus* tenor start; but all along
> Keep due proportion in the ample song,
> It makes me ravish'd with just wonder, cry
> What Muse, or rather God of harmony
> Taught *Lucan* these true moodes! replies my sence
> What gods but those of arts, and eloquence?
> *Phoebus*, and *Hermes*? They whose tongue, or pen
> Are still th'interpreters twixt gods, and men!
> But who hath them interpreted, and brought
> *Lucans* whole frame unto us, and so wrought,
> As not the smallest joynt, or gentlest word
> In the great masse, or machine there is stirr'd?
> The self same *Genius*! so the work will say.
> The *Sun* translated, or the Son of *May*.   (*LP* A7)

Certainly, "To My Chosen Friend" is a much less ambitious poem than "On *Paradise Lost*." Marvell can, of course, stand on his own. Nevertheless, if the allusive structure that I see is not chimerical, I am sure that it is not a coincidence – not simply a matter of generic tradition working itself out without respect to particular exemplary texts. If Marvell imitates Jonson's poem he does so by practicing an imitative poetic close to Jonson's own, one in which "the poet's materials are not inert and suppressed 'sources,' merely a part of the genesis of the poem, but allusions meant to be recognized – signs in the finished work that its originality, organization, and continuing life depend on suggestive links to the great writers of antiquity."[12] Sir Roger L'Estrange was no friend to Milton or Marvell, but he characterized the Stoic ethic of literary imitation quite well in his *Seneca's Morals by Way of Abstract*: "He that puts a Good *Hint* into my *Head*, puts a good *Word* in my *Mouth* . . . The *Text* is beholden to him that *Reads* upon't, for *Emproving* it; and the *Latter* had never *thought* of the *Subject* perhaps, if the *Former* had not *Bolted* it."[13] Writers are by nature beholden to one another in bonds of obligation and competition, sometimes to their frustration; but the honest ones, says the Stoic, are willing to make their debts their themes. This describes Jonson's approach to the classics, but much the same may be said of Marvell's approach to Jonson.

The basic link between the poems is the similarity of their rhetorical occasions, occasions that are, in a sense, their subjects as well. Jonson begins with, "WHen, *Rome*, I read thee in thy mighty pair," and builds arrestingly to, "I begin to doubt, / At every line"; and that doubt is followed two lines later with a reconsideration beginning, "But . . ." Marvell follows the outlines of Jonson's skeptical sequence in the first eleven lines of "On *Paradise Lost*":

> When I beheld the Poet blind, yet bold,
> In slender Book his vast Design unfold,
> *Messiah* Crown'd, *Gods* Reconcil'd Decree,
> Rebelling *Angels*, the Forbidden Tree,
> Heav'n, Hell, Earth, Chaos, All; the Argument
> Held me a while misdoubting his Intent,
> . . .
> Yet as I read, soon growing less severe . . .   (lines 1–6, 11)

In both poems, we move from beholding and reading, to doubting and misdoubting, and then to a significant "But" and a profound "Yet." The occasion that Marvell represents – the temporal process of doubting and discrimination when reading another's texts, a process that seems so characteristic of Marvell – is also a recurrent concern for Jonson. Indeed, metaphor describing this process is one of Jonson's favorite poetic tropes, and a thoroughly Stoic habit of "defensive self-affirmation" runs throughout his prose *Discoveries* as well.[14] Jonson's habit has a rhetorical model and philosophical grounding in Seneca's *Epistulae Morales*, in which Epicurus's sayings are treated as "gifts" (*mercedula*) that must nevertheless be handled with great care. Properly used, they are salutary to the novice Stoic; improperly used, they are dangerous.[15] But how does this critical process work in "To My Chosen Friend" – and what was there for Marvell to notice most when he wrote of Milton?

Perhaps the first thing to notice about "To My Chosen Friend" is that the "misdoubt" posed and then answered in regard to form and decorum is associated – as such doubt so often is in Jonson's texts – with serious ethical and political misgivings. It is remarkable that the title and first line indicate different addressees, the former being discarded for the latter throughout most of the poem. For, when Jonson begins "to doubt, / At every line," he is addressing, not Thomas May, but Rome "WHen . . . I read thee." Literally speaking to Roman political history, not a "Chosen Friend," Jonson addresses a state overwhelmed by civil war and the ambitions of "thy mighty pair," Caesar and Pompey, to climb "the slippery stair / Of Fortunes wheel." This historical subject becomes interchangeable with Lucan's poem as a formal construct, although Jonson's "strong lines" – Lucanic in the use of the *comma* to shape rhythm and sense – make it difficult to say exactly how this happens.[16] "Some pin thereof" and "the general Engine" which may "crack" seem to refer to "Fortunes wheel," "the world in it," and finally to the poetic "world" of the *Pharsalia* itself. The situation is dramatic. Jonson had used similar language in *Catiline his Conspiracy* (1611); Catiline wishes, with perverse Senecan egotism, "That I could reach the axell, where the pinnes are, / Which bolt this frame; that I might pull 'hem out, / And pluck all into *chaos*, with my selfe" (*BJ* V, 474; 3.175–77). Jonson's ideal reader fears that Lucan's formal, ethical, and political construction is in danger of a similar "slack" and "crack"; and perhaps that reader also fears the "slippery stair" of the reading process itself. Jonson may be suggesting that, when one reads this unusual poem about violent civil war, one's critical skills are in danger of failing, that one may be overwhelmed by the narrative, and that one may draw unwise political conclusions from the text.

Finally, however, there is a very characteristic Jonsonian turn: "But when again I view the parts so peiz'd, / And those in number so, and measure rais'd / . . . It makes me ravish'd with just wonder, cry. . . !" In the course of this long exclamation, Jonson argues that the ethical and political claims of Pompey, Caesar, Cato, and Brutus "all along / Keep due proportion in the ample song"; and he suggests that the poet, having studied with a "God of harmony," has attained heroic status himself in holding the difficult, centrifugal subject together. Pompey, Caesar, Cato, and Brutus – along with their "popularity," "ambition," "liberty," and "tenor" – remain uncompromised in their resolute differences. The task has not been easy. With "parts so peiz'd," Jonson suggests that the various "parts" of the poem have been balanced as one balances weights on a scale, and also hints, recalling "the *Muses* anvile" of his poem on Shakespeare, that they have been shaped by terrific force as if hammered in a forge.[17] It has been a balancing act at once delicate and fierce, a task fit for a poetic Hercules or Cato. It is significant that Jonson, who had written commendatory poems for the 1609 edition of Sir Clement Edmondes's *Observations upon Caesars Commentaries*, does not choose one hero over the others, "so peiz'd" (*BJ* VIII, 71–72). Indeed, he suggests that to do so would be to disregard Lucan's true formal achievement in the *Pharsalia*, the "due proportion" which his handling of its various heroes and themes does in fact "Keep."[18]

Returning now to the first few lines of "On *Paradise Lost*" – to Marvell's description of the vast subject of Milton's poem – one can see that he has been reading Jonson all along. Milton writes of "*Messiah* Crown'd, *Gods* Reconcil'd Decree, / Rebelling *Angels*, the Forbidden Tree, / Heav'n, Hell, Earth, Chaos, All. . . " (lines 3–5). Although Marvell's lengthy sentence with its enjambed lines and breathless participles has been taken by some critics to be a close imitation of Milton's style in *Paradise Lost*, it is just as close, and perhaps closer, to the "climbing" and "driv'n" verse used by Jonson when describing the *Pharsalia*. Messiah, God, angels – beings linked by *asyndeton* as Jonsonian as it is Miltonic – take the place of Jonson's four Lucanic characters; while "Heav'n, Hell, Earth, Chaos, All" are thrust together, or apart, as violently as are the elements of Lucan's "world."

As I have suggested above, the second sentence of "To My Chosen Friend" concludes with an exclamation that raises the question of divine inspiration: "What Muse, or rather God of harmony / Taught *Lucan* these true moodes!" For Jonson, of course, this is a rhetorical, not a theological, question. It is a fitting topic of praise, and answering it takes the form of more rhetorical questions: "replies my sence / What gods but those of arts, and eloquence? / *Phoebus*, and *Hermes*?" And Jonson says that Thomas May, in turn, artfully and eloquently interprets *them*. But Marvell takes these rhetorical questions and doubts and turns them into other questions:

> the Argument
> Held me a while misdoubting his Intent,
> That he would ruine (for I saw him strong)
> The sacred Truths to Fable and old Song,
> (So *Sampson* groap'd the Temples Posts in spight)
> The World o'rewhelming to revenge his Sight.
>
> Yet as I read, soon growing less severe,
> I lik'd his Project, the success did fear;
> Through that wide Field how he his way should find
> O'er which lame Faith leads Understanding blind;
> Lest he perplext the things he would explain,
> And what was easie he should render vain.
>
> Or if a Work so infinite he spann'd,
> Jealous I was that some less skilful hand
> (Such as disquiet alwayes what is well,
> And by ill imitating would excell)
> Might hence presume the whole Creations day
> To change in Scenes, and show it in a Play.   (lines 5–22)

The last verse paragraph would seem to allude both to Dryden's Miltonic "opera," *The State of Innocence* (apparently composed for the marriage of the Duke of York and Mary of Modena in 1673 but not published until 1677) and to the disquieting confusions to which Sir William Davenant had subjected epic and dramatic theory in the "Preface" to *Gondibert* (1650). Davenant thought that he had, "by that regular species" of drama, "though narratively and not in Dialogue . . . drawn the body of an Heroick Poem"; for he "did not onely observe the Symmetry" of English drama in *Gondibert*, "proportioning five Books to five *Acts* and *Canto's* to *Scenes* . . . but all the *shadowings, happy strokes, secret graces*, and even the *drapery*."[19] When theory becomes a mere pretext for rhetorical conceit a culture of "ill imitating" is the sure result, one from which Marvell and Milton were both happily excluded. But given that Milton himself deals with "The sacred Truths" in *Paradise Lost*, the question is whether a careful, critical reader can be sure that Milton has been a faithful interpreter, as it were, "twixt gods, and men." The problem was all the more serious now that Jonson's "God of harmony" had been supplanted by a God whose ways, Milton thought, needed to be *justified*. Marvell has initially described his subject in Jonson's terms, and he seems to have found hints for his answer, not in theological tracts, but in Jonson's poem as well. Marvell's answer to his own "misdoubt" concerning the theological politics of *Paradise Lost* recalls "To My Chosen Friend" in two stages centering first on formal decorum and, second, on translation and prophecy. First, there is the praise of Milton's mastery of form:

> Pardon me, *mighty Poet*, nor despise
> My causeless, yet not impious, surmise.
> But I am now convinc'd, and none will dare
> Within thy Labours to pretend a Share.
> Thou hast not miss'd one thought that could be fit,
> And all that was improper dost omit:
> So that no room is here for Writers left,
> But to detect their Ignorance or Theft.   (lines 23–30)

This recalls Jonson's claim that May has brought "*Lucans* whole frame unto us, and so wrought, / As not the smallest joynt, or gentlest word / In the great masse, or machine there is stirr'd." Similarly, Marvell's final couplet – "Thy verse created like thy *Theme* sublime, / In Number, Weight, and Measure, needs not *Rhime*" (lines 53–54) – echoes Jonson when he views "again . . . the parts so peiz'd, / And those in number so, and measure rais'd." Jonson and Marvell share a common source for these lines in the Book of Wisdom – "thou hast ordered all things in measure, and number, and weight" (11:20) – but I suspect that Marvell's use of this verse followed from a sense that Jonson had used it well in "To My Chosen Friend."

Mastery of decorum can be so crucial only when subject matter is thought to be profound, and indeed both poems tell of writers confronted by mysterious originals. Although Jonson is writing about a translation and *Paradise Lost* is obviously *not* a translation, Marvell does seem to have thought of its "Project" as in some respects being the task of a translator. This appears to lie behind his "misdoubting" as it is elaborated in the second verse paragraph, where Marvell says that he "did fear" Milton's "success," "Lest he perplext the things he would explain, / And what was easie he should render vain." Both May and Milton are praised for daring to "render" divine "things," and for doing so successfully. Much as Jonson elevates May's translation of Lucan's "great masse" to a matter of communication with the "gods . . . of arts, and eloquence," so Marvell in his fifth and sixth verse paragraphs shifts the perspective that he takes on Milton's "Project" from the arena of those writers who "by ill imitating would excell" to the realm of the gods – or rather God – and prophecy:

> That Majesty which through thy Work doth Reign
> Draws the Devout, deterring the Profane.
> And things divine thou treatst of in such state
> As them preserves, and Thee inviolate.
> At once delight and horrour on us seize,
> Thou singst with so much gravity and ease;
> And above humane flight dost soar aloft,
> With Plume so strong, so equal, and so soft.
> The *Bird* nam'd from that *Paradise* you sing
> So never Flags, but alwaies keeps on Wing.   (lines 31–40)

But how, he asks, is such writing possible?

> Where couldst thou Words of such a compass find?
> Whence furnish such a vast expense of Mind?
> Just Heav'n Thee, like *Tiresias*, to requite,
> Rewards with *Prophesie* thy loss of Sight.   (lines 41–44)

Jonson's answer to his analogous doubt in "To My Chosen Friend" – "But who hath them [Phoebus and Hermes] interpreted . . . ?" – had been provided by a pun on the names of Thomas *May* and Hermes, the son of *Maia*: "The selfe same *Genius*! so the work will say. / The *Sun* translated, or the Son of *May*." Marvell could not follow Jonson's witty example completely and Stoically *identify* the sage-like Milton with God, but he does suggest that his old friend has special privileges of access. There had been many who claimed that God rewarded Milton for his controversial efforts in the 1640s and 1650s with humiliating blindness and nothing more. A typical attack was made by Sir Roger L'Estrange in *No Blinde Guides* (1660) when he questioned whether Milton really expected "to *see* Christ, Reigning upon Earth, even with *those very eyes* you *Lost* (as 'tis reported) *with staring too long, and too sawcily upon the Portraiture of his Vicegerent, to breake the* Image, as your Impudence Phrases it" referring to *Eikonoklastes*.[20] Of course, Marvell's answer also recalls Milton's own reference in *Paradise Lost* to Homer, Thamyris, Teiresias, and Phineus, those "Prophets old" who, though blind to lesser things, could see greater ones; they are for Milton "equall'd with me in Fate" though superior in "renown" (3.33–36). But it is especially interesting that Marvell singles out for comparison Teiresias, the sage who tells the hard truths of fate to Oedipus and Creon. If, as Jonson has it, kings and

tyrants fall hardest down "the slippery stair / Of Fortunes wheel,"
Milton is, like Lucan's Cato, *deo plenus*, "full of *Jove*, / Whom in his secret
breast he carryed ever" (*LP* 225; 9.564)

"A JUST AND NOBLE *CAUSE*"

The point of this reading is not simply that Marvell imitates Jonson in
"On *Paradise Lost*." That would not be so remarkable. What must be
recognized is that Marvell takes one special route among many other
possibilities within the capacious Jonsonian tradition, a route that Jonson himself laid down, line by line, in quiet protest against the vices of
arbitrary rule. For while "To My Chosen Friend" is not itself a poem of
protest, it may be allied with those poems, written in honor of the texts
of admired and trusted contemporaries, that engage in substantial
ethical and political criticism. Unlike many of Jonson's less serious
commendatory poems, it eschews witty satire at the expense of the
object of praise. It rivals in sincerity the much longer poems to Sir
Henry Savile on his translation of Tacitus (1591) and to Sir John Selden
on his *Titles of Honour* (1614) (*BJ* VIII, 61–62, 158–61). This is the
historicist and political Jonson, the grave author of *Sejanus his Fall* and
Catiline his Conspiracy, a man more than once accused of sedition.[21]

Indeed, "To My Chosen Friend" is perfectly at home in a politically
charged, oppositional context. It follows naturally after a dedication to
William Cavendish, second Earl of Devonshire, in which May writes
of Rome at "that unhappy height, in which she could neither retaine
her freedom without great troubles nor fall into a *Monarchy* but most
heavy and distastful" (*LP* A3v–A4). Of course, Jonson would have
known Lucan's tragic personal history as well: his early literary fame
and remarkable public distinctions; his part in Calpurnius Piso's failed
conspiracy against Nero; his suicide at the age of twenty-five. In suicide Lucan took what was thought to be the best of a limited range of
options open to senatorial dissidents during the principate. "The Roman could do no more than turn in upon himself," writes Frederick
Ahl, "following the example of Cato, transforming the act of self-
destruction into a symbolic defiance of temporal authority."[22] Such
symbolism was not likely lost on Jonson who, as witnessed in *Sejanus his
Fall* and elsewhere, was quite willing to regard suicide, not as a matter
of defeat or self-hatred, but as a final act of self-control that can secure
lasting honor.[23] The point was emphasized by May in lines, facing the
1627 title page, that compare Lucan to Vergil: "twas an act more

great, and high to moove / A Princes envy, then a Princes love." And, in "The Life of Marcus Annaeus Lucanus," May relates the story of the dying Lucan who recites verses from the *Pharsalia* on a wounded soldier while his own hands and feet grow cold – thus turning poetry into death and death into poetry (*LP* A6–A6v). Similarly, the Lucan of "To My Chosen Friend" continues living in the history of his text and translator. Jonson uses a conventional topic of praise, of course, but in this case literary tradition is at odds with the tradition of hereditary monarchy.

Long after Jonson's death – and May's death in 1650 – *Lucan's Pharsalia* was still enjoying such praise. Lucan's blood flows freely above Caesar, Pompey, and their battling armies on the title page of *Lucan's Pharsalia* in 1627, 1631, and 1635 (see fig. 4). A bust of "MARCUS ANNAEUS LUCANUS," set in a scene perhaps representing his burial "at Rome in his own most fair and sumptoous gardens" (*LP* A6v), is the subject of the frontispiece in 1650. His thirsty ghost haunts the frontispiece of the 1650 edition of May's *Continuation of Lucan's Historicall Poem till the Death of Julius Caesar*. In the accompanying "Mind of the Picture Or, Frontispiece," the Muse fills a cup with sacrificial blood, gives it to "her dear Poets Ghost," and makes this "command":

> Thou, once the Glorie of th'Aonian Wood,
> But now their sorrow, *Lucan*, drink this Bloud.
> No other Nectar *Phoebus* gives thee now;
> Nor can the Fates a second life bestow;
> A second voice by this charm'd cup they may,
> To give some progress to that stately Lay
> Thou left'st unfinish'd. End it not until
> The Senates swords the life of *Caesar* spill;
> That he, whose conquests gave dire *Nero* Reign,
> May as a sacrifice to thee be slain.
> The Ghost receiv'd the cup in his pale hand,
> Drunk, and fulfill'd *Calliopes* command.[24]

Lucan's spirit speaks through May, a "second voice." In the poet's opinion, at least, the *Continuation* brings to the *Pharsalia* a formal, historical, and political coherence that it had not possessed before. It is symptomatic of the emphasis placed on political history in the Lucanic tradition that royalists may so often be seen attacking the *Pharsalia* on generic grounds. In his famous "Preface," for instance, Davenant argues that Lucan's "enterprize rather beseem'd an Historian, then a Poet: for wise Poets think it more worthy to seek out truth in the

Figure 4   *Lucan's Pharsalia*, trans. May (London, 1627).

Passions, then to record the truth of Actions."[25] Indeed, May's translation of Lucan was a favorite of those republicans who dominated literary and political discourse from the execution of Charles I in 1649 to the dissolution of the Long Parliament in 1653 – men with whom one may associate Marvell and identify both May and Milton.[26] Their favorable opinion was no doubt encouraged by May's deft combination of historical objectivity and party bias in *The History of the Parliament of England* (1647), an important source for Milton when he wrote *Eikonoklastes*.[27] Marchamont Nedham, editor of *Mercurius Politicus*, quotes twenty-eight lines from *Lucan's Pharsalia* in November 1651 to show that "It was the glory of *Pompey* . . . that both in Peace and War he approved himself the grand Patron of *Publick Liberty*," and that "it is not fortune, but a just and noble *Cause*, that makes men truely great, even after the greatest miseries and misfortunes." Pompey's "Character," Nedham writes, has been "translated to the life by the best of Poets, *Thomas May* our *English Lucan*, more excellent than the *Roman*."[28] In January 1652 Nedham links luxury and tyranny as cause and effect, and quotes a "copy of old *Catos* countenance, as it was drawn by *Lucan*" – thirteen lines from *Lucan's Pharsalia* – as a corrective; after Caesar's rise to power, "onely *Cato* remained as a monument of that Temperance, Vertue, and Freedom, which Flourished under the Government of the people."[29] But even the most stridently republican discourse is never far from knowledge of the poet's dramatic suicide. Lucan's political failure was one part of his political strength, for it encouraged elegiac response in poetry and prose, and an iconography appropriate to what may be termed the republican sublime.[30]

Praise of Lucan was circumspect and of May virtually impossible after the Restoration. The exhumation of May's body from Westminster Abbey was ordered in 1661 – a lurid "part," as Norbrook says, "of a ritual expulsion of republicanism from the nation's political culture."[31] But Lucan's image, if properly packaged, could still be used to praise honest, retired poets over their hated Caesars. Consider the scene conjured by Sir George Mackenzie in *A Moral Essay, Preferring Solitude to Publick Employment* (1665):

Compare *Julius Cesar* . . . with *Lucan*, who wrote the story of his wars, and ye will find *Lucan* the much happier: Consider *Cesar*, macerat oft with hunger, stiffned with unrewarded toil, jealous of his own souldiers, and apprehensive of the Senat, tortured with the uncertain events of the war, and terrified by the having kill'd his Son in law *Pompey*, after he was sure of the victory. And then return your reflections upon *Lucan*, sitting in the bosome of a shaddowie grove, flanckt with a christal stream, and there creating those noble lines, which have since carried his fame as far as *Cesars* actions . . . But to conclude the folly of *Fame*, consider even this generous *Lucan*, falling under the sword of *Nero*; because that cruel Prince was ashamed to see himself so far out-done in wit by one of his own Subjects: and from this learn, that *Fame* is suspicious to its dependers, when it bestows its favours, and unjust, when it denyes them.[32]

Mackenzie lived to the right of May, Milton, and Marvell, but even such Stoic commonplaces as these may have had something of a political "tang" amid the Caesarian pretenses of the Restoration court. The preference for Lucan over Julius and Nero Caesar seems almost subversive when compared with the monarchist *vita activa* imagined by John Evelyn in his reply to Mackenzie, *Publick Employment and an Active Life Prefer'd to Solitude* (1667):

> Behold *here* a *Sovereign* sitting in his august Assembly of *Parliament* enacting wholesome *Laws*: next him my *Lord Chancellor* and the rest of the reverend *Judges* and *Magistrates* dispensing them for the *good* of the *People*: Figure to your self a *Secretary* of *State*, making his *dispatches* and receiving *intelligence*; a *Statesman* countermining some pernicious *Plot* against the *Common-wealth*: Here a *General* bravely *Embattailing* his *Forces* and vanquishing an *Enemy* . . . In a word, behold him in the neerest resemblance to his *Almighty* maker, always in *action*, and always doing *good*.[33]

In his dismissive account of the *Moral Essay*, Vickers asks: "How many have heard of Lucan?"[34] Fewer today than in the seventeenth century, it would seem. The numerous reprintings of *Lucan's Pharsalia* and of May's *Continuation* indicate that many readers had not only heard of Lucan but had actually read his "noble lines" – with admiration or outrage, but seldom indifference.

"The punishment / Of wit," as Tacitus and Jonson put it, "doth make th'authoritie [of wit] increase." Thomas Hobbes, developing a comment from Quintilian that Jonson had apparently chosen to ignore, argued in his essay "Concerning the Vertues of an Heroique Poem" (1677) that the virtue of impartiality is lacking in Lucan, who "shews himself openly in the *Pompeyan* Faction, inveighing against *Caesar* throughout his Poem, like *Cicero* against *Cataline* or *Marc Antony*; and is therefore justly reckon'd by *Quintilian* as a Rhetorician rather than a Poet. And a great part of the delight of his Readers proceedeth from the pleasure which too many men take to hear Great persons censured."[35] In fact Quintilian remarks simply that Lucan's sententiousness means that he is better imitated by orators than poets, a proviso that amounts to praise in a study of oratory (*Inst. Orat.* 10.1.90). Davenant attacks

Lucan for his historicism and Hobbes attacks him for his supposedly insolent rhetoric; but the question whether Lucan wrote history or oratory was less important to most seventeenth-century readers than whether he also wrote poetry, and answering *that* question was nearly always a political exercise.[36] He is a poet, and a fine one indeed, in Jonson's "To My Chosen Friend," in republican discourse and iconography of the 1650s, and also in less contentious works like Mackenzie's *Moral Essay*. In "On *Paradise Lost*" Marvell extends these imitative continuities to include Milton, yet another poetic "voice" and writer of "noble lines" in the long Lucanic tradition. The temporal and tonal disjunctions among Marvell's models (Lucan, Jonson, May, Milton) and the immediate controversial context were not causes to reject those models or criticize them as being inadequate to the situation. "To My Chosen Friend" gave him a point of departure for responding to attacks on Milton by suggesting that Milton's political situation could be placed within a subtly unified intertextual history running from Lucan through Jonson and May to Milton himself. This move was by no means a retreat from those attacks: it was rather a political strategy itself. "No room is here for Writers left," one might have said at the time, knowing that many of the writers in question were pamphleteers like Samuel Parker.

Although this intertextual history is heavy with feelings of political discontent, it is also, as in much of Jonson's work, a coming-to-terms with discontent. Marvell was quite sure of what he was doing, and he took care not to play his cards too openly. Jonson's poem serves as an implicit principle of order that, much like the Stoic conception of order itself, "pushes from behind, so to say, and does not lead from in front"; it serves as a "*whole* Frame," not just a frame, that organizes and inspires Marvell's various themes and gives the poem its special perspective on contemporary events and characters.[37] Whether or not we recognize this perspective as being specifically Jonsonian or Stoic, without it "On *Paradise Lost*" would be much less interesting as a poem than as a document in the history of poetic taste. As it stands, however, the various topical matters take on added significance for their relation to Jonson's rigorous Stoic ethos and its republican posterity. For instance, when Marvell praises "That Majesty which through thy Work doth Reign," he is asserting in literary terms the Stoic preference for rule of the passions over rule of the state, and is also, as Christopher Hill argues, having "a good joke" with his republican friend.[38] Indeed, he may also have recalled that the same Stoic preference is expressed by the Son in book 2 of *Paradise Regain'd*. Marvell's self-conscious criticism of rhyme and his apparent attack on Dryden, "the *Town-Bays*," also have their place in the Stoic *ars vivendi*:

> Well mightst thou scorn thy Readers to allure
> With tinkling Rhime, of thy own Sense secure;
> While the *Town-Bays* writes all the while and spells,
> And like a Pack-Horse tires without his Bells.
> Their Fancies like our bushy Points appear,
> The Poets tag them; we for fashion wear.   (lines 45–50)

The identification here, so characteristic of Seneca and Jonson, of linguistic purity with moral integrity directs the reader's attention to the note on "The Verse" of *Paradise Lost*, where Milton claims to have recovered "ancient liberty" for the English epic.[39]

Marvell's use of "To My Chosen Friend" is a matter, then, not so much of borrowings patched together, as an allusive intertext meant to communicate to knowing readers a political and critical style. Although the Stoic often claims to be most secure among others when using a private language – as when Milton is of his "own Sense secure" – it is quite likely that Marvell expected that at least some of his readers would see the closeness of his poem to Jonson's poem and, by profound extension, the closeness of Milton's poem to Lucan's. Surely Marvell noticed that the *Pharsalia* shares with the 1667 edition of *Paradise Lost*, the version that he would have had at hand while writing his poem, the distinction of being a ten-book epic. Moreover, both poems end in similarly remarkable ways: Lucan's abruptly, in the midst of a sentence, and Milton's quietly, in the midst of the lives of its hero and heroine. "By insisting upon the open-endedness of history," writes David Quint, Lucanic epics of loss and failure assert "that the setback may only be temporary, that continuing resistance may turn the tables on the victorious enemy. *Paradise Lost* most fully belongs to the tradition of Lucan in the resistance to closure that makes its ending into a new beginning for Adam and Eve, in their carrying on the memory of Eden as a 'paradise within thee happier far' (12.587)."[40] In fact, Michael speaks of much more than happy memories in book 12. With the wisdom that Adam can express already (lines 553–73), with "Deeds to . . . knowledge answerable," and with the proper virtues, the "paradise within" is said to be a far happier one than Eden – perhaps happier even than Eden had been before the loss to Satan in book 9. If in the *Pharsalia* the open-ended, often circuitous course of history – the "slippery stair / Of Fortunes wheel" – allows for the possibility of something better *because* it is open-ended and circuitous, in *Paradise Lost* we are told that "wand'ring steps, and slow" (12.648) will eventually lead to another, better paradise. They walk into the unknown world "solitary," but Adam knows that, in the most important sense, they are not going to be "solitary" at all. Their lives in this greater if also more frightening world will bring them, as Michael tells Adam in book 11, into the presence of their creator:

> *Adam*, thou know'st Heav'n his, and all the Earth,
> Not this Rock only; his Omnipresence fills
> Land, Sea, and Air, and every kind that lives,
> Fomented by his virtual power and warm'd. (11.335–38)

God is everywhere. In their solitary wandering they will join with a God who is for them a greater God than the one they had known before. A very similar idea is expressed at a critical moment in *Pharsalia* 9 when Cato and his republican soldiers are wandering in the Saharan wilderness dying of hunger and thirst, cut off from Rome and, it seems, their gods. But in fact "The great Creator" is with them still, Cato tells his men:

> Nor did he chuse these barren sands to shew
> (Hiding it here) his truth but to a few.
> Is there a seat of gold, save earth, and sea,
> Air, heaven, and virtue? Why for gods should we
> Seek further? What ere moves, what ere is seen
> Is *Jove*. (*LP* 226; 9.576–80)

"Milton imitated these impressive lines" in *Paradise Lost*, remarks Charles Martindale, "but hardly improved on them."[41] Indeed, the differences here between Lucan's Stoic physics and Milton's religion may not seem crucially important to all readers: for Milton, God "fills / Land, Sea, and Air, and every kind that lives," while for Lucan "What ere moves, what ere is seen / Is *Jove*." Seneca makes much the same point in his *Quaestiones Naturales*: "What is God? All that thou seest, & and all that thou seest not" (*WS* 761; 1.pr.12). Pantheism, we may gather, can be inspiring in desperate circumstances.

Returning to Jonson, we may conclude that, in spite of his services to James I and Charles I, he could be readily interpreted in what Annabel Patterson has termed the "vocabulary" of the Good Old Cause.[42] The sticking point here, of course, is "Tom May's Death," a fascinating poem of uncertain date and uncertain authorship in which Jonson's ghost condemns May as, among other things, a "Most servil' wit, and Mercenary Pen."[43] The argument of this chapter may confound those who feel that "Tom May's Death" is "in many ways a quintessential Marvellian poem," that it *"ought* to be Marvell's," and that May was merely "a time-serving follower of fate and fortune, betrayer of his friends and of the king who had extensively patronized him."[44] Although such critics may not be guilty of what Norbrook calls the "revisionist view" of English history, which "assumes that monarchism was natural to Renaissance poets, that the republicanism of the mid-century was a fleeting aberration to be explained largely in terms of personal grievances,"[45] surely they have not done justice to the *positive* presences of May's Lucan in "Tom May's Death." Here, after sixty–two lines of abuse, the poet pauses to consider his own ideals:

> When the Sword glitters ore the Judges head,
> And fear has the Coward Churchmen silenced,
> Then is the Poets time, 'tis then he drawes,
> And single fights forsaken Vertues cause.
> He, when the wheel of Empire, wirleth back,
> And though the World's disjointed Axel crack,
> Sings still of ancient Rights and better Times,
> Seeks wretched good, arraigns successful Crimes.
> But thou base man first prostituted hast
> Our spotless knowledge and the studies chast.
> Apostatizing from our Arts and us,
> To turn the Chronicler to *Spartacus.*   (lines 63–74)

Thus the conservative satirist makes his stand, apparently, in the realm of pure poetry, opposed to republican history (*The History of the Parliament of England*) and republican historical epic (*Lucan's Pharsalia*). Remarkably enough, however, these lines fuse allusions, not only to Jonson's "To My Chosen Friend," but also to book 2 of *Lucan's Pharsalia* where Cato praises Stoic virtue practiced actively in the republican cause:

> We confesse,
> *Brutus,* that civil war's great wickednesse:
> But where the Fates will lead, vertue shall go
> Securely on; to make me guilty now
> Shall be the gods own crime; who would endure
> To see the world dissolve, himselfe secure?
> Who could look on, when heaven should fall, earth fail,
> And the confus'd world perish, and not wail?
> . . .
> I will not leave thee, Rome, till I embrace
> Thy hearse, and liberty, thy dying face,
> And fleeting Ghost with honour do attend. (*LP* 31; 2.286–303)

It is choice irony, and one wholly characteristic of seventeenth-century satire, that Jonson's ghost should be made to attack a man whom Jonson had praised in life. Public, Jonsonian virtues are used to castigate what are, for the most part, private vices. But perhaps it is something other than irony that allows Jonson's ghost to espouse a public ideal drawn from May's most famous work. If "Tom May's Death" was written by Marvell, it was a Marvell who had already begun to accept, perhaps more than he realized, the tradition that he was to defend in "On *Paradise Lost*."

Indeed, the political stakes of Marvell's association of Lucan, Jonson, May, and Milton in 1674 may have been set by Marvell himself more than twenty years earlier. But situations, as Marvell knew, are critical. Civil war was no longer the problem: a reactionary political climate that could not suffer the existence of an elderly poet was the problem. Marvell's manner of engaging with the texts of his culture was always open and dynamic, and Marvellians will always be at work gathering the evidence. In regard to *Lucan's Pharsalia* and "To My Chosen Friend," his critical engagement may be said to run from "Tom May's Death," through the ambivalent "Horatian Ode," to "On *Paradise Lost*," in which Jonson's May comes to serve as a positive model for Marvell's Milton. Thus, those who admire both Jonson and Marvell may now say happily that if Marvell looked to Jonson's legacy for authoritarian prescriptions in the early 1650s, he could see something much more expansive and liberating in it when he set about to praise Milton in 1674. And, whatever Marvell had once thought of May as a person, he evidently concluded in the 1670s that certain political themes and literary examples from the Stoic tradition – a tradition that May had done much to popularize – were worth preserving. They were worth preserving, at the very least, for the sake of preserving Milton against reactionary attacks.

Marvell's defense of Milton in *The Second Part* of *The Rehearsal Transpros'd* and the intertextual poetic tradition that he constructs in "On *Paradise Lost*" are very much of a piece. Temporally, of course, they are close and impose an artful period on Milton's career. Moreover, both interpretations of Milton and his work celebrate aspects of ethical and formal balance that Marvell apparently had come to associate with Stoic wisdom, and these things must have held profound poetic and political significance for him in the 1670s. In this case, I am sure that we can learn a great deal from Andrew Marvell, a poet who, as Colie thought, wrote a *Poetry of Criticism*. For, if Marvell's deft imitation of

Jonson's "To My Chosen Friend" sheds new light on Marvell himself in the 1670s, it should also be taken as an invitation to consider more closely Milton's own engagements with Stoic tradition. Of course, neither Marvell's idea of Milton's "retired silence" nor his allusions to Jonson's "To My Chosen Friend" make Milton a Stoic. But when we consider Milton's texts and the controversial exigencies that he faced as a writer, we shall find that Marvell was essentially correct to place him in the tradition of Lucan and the Stoics. Aubrey says that a republican "tang stuck by" Thomas May, and we should not be surprised to find that Jonson, Marvell, Milton, and their most sympathetic readers were "by *Lucan* driv'n about" as well.

CHAPTER 5

John Milton: the Stoicism of history and providence

> To seek to extinguish anger utterly is but a bravery of the Stoics.
> We have better oracles: *Be angry, but sin not: let not the sun go down on
> your anger.* Francis Bacon, "Of Anger."[1]

In *Paradise Regain'd* "one man's firm obedience" is "fully tried / Through
all temptation" and, in the process, that man raises "*Eden* . . . in the waste
Wilderness" (1.4–5, 7). If we agree with Christopher Hill in *Milton and the
English Revolution* that this is also a story of "the triumph of reason over
passion," we must recognize that no such "triumph" can ever be quite
what it seems within the Stoic tradition of "retired silence" invoked by
Marvell when he wrote of Milton and his epic poetry in the 1670s.[2] We
have seen in various contexts that the "bravery" which for Bacon and
others marked the Stoic effort "to extinguish anger utterly" could be
"bravery" in several multi-layered senses: prideful show, steadfast courage, and a sophisticated effort to manipulate anger in the politically
meaningful attitudes of retirement and constancy. Certainly, the man
"call'd the Son of God" (1.136) is capable of real, human anger. "Get
thee behind me," he orders Satan in book 4, and the "Evil one" can only
reply "with fear abasht" (4.193–95). The Son recalls that he has considered violence as a possibility (1.215–20), and God the Father refers to
the coming trial in the desert as an "exercise" in which the Son – we may
recall "the rudiments of . . . Souldiership" outlined in *Of Education* –
"shall first lay down the rudiments / Of his great warfare" (1.156–58).
This "great warfare" will be one in which the Son regains "by Conquest
what the first man lost / By fallacy surpris'd" (1.154–55). For now it is
Satan's turn to be "surpris'd" – to be "smitten with amazement" and to
fall (4.562) – because he has not thought that a man's "constant persever-
ance" (1.148) alone could be so daunting or that the mere effort to "try"
this man's "constancy" (2.225–26) could be so explosive. Indeed, there is

much of the "bravery of the Stoics" in the Son's dealings with Satan and a strong sense throughout that, no matter how "unalter'd" (1.493) he seems by Satan's baiting, the righteous, angry militarism which he displays in book 6 of *Paradise Lost* is still in play in the wilderness-garden of *Paradise Regain'd* under a different name – *constancy*.³

The question of how the Son of God should "Publish his Godlike office now mature" (1.188) and yet remain constantly indifferent to the tempting things that Satan offers him is answered when he declares himself the "living Oracle" (1.460) and predicts the coming of an "inward Oracle" (1.463) within each person that will lead eventually to the violent destruction of "All Monarchies" (4.149) in the world. Quite against the spirit of Paul's advice in Ephesians 4:26 – the "better oracles" heard by Bacon – the sun goes down and will rise again on the climacteric violence promised by the "living Oracle." Thus, the Son's taming of violent passion by cool reason – as well as his rejection of "policy, and projects" (3.391) and even such philosophical doctrines as that of the "*Stoic* severe" (4.280) in favor of Gospel revelation and an "inward Oracle" – together promise the most prodigious violence and far-reaching knowledge imaginable in Milton's world. These things are deeply paradoxical, of course, and in this final chapter I shall argue that their meanings are to be most fully understood in the light of Stoic tradition.

"FULL OF *JOVE*"

When first we meet the Son of God we are told that he has been having "such thoughts / . . . of things past and to come" that "well might recommend / Such Solitude before choicest Society" (1.299–302). Although he can say at this point only that he has been led "Into this Wilderness" by "some strong motion" for a reason which "perhaps I need not know" (1.290–92), it turns out that he has gone into the "pathless Desert, dusk with horrid shades" (1.296) for one of the basic reasons that the wise man goes to his garden in the Stoic tradition: to engage in intense rhetorical activity concerned with the greater world and his proper roles in the world. We have seen in Lipsius and Marvell that Stoic gardens are not places of ease, and certainly the Son is not figuring on an easy retirement. To make a garden out of a desert – to raise "*Eden* . . . in the waste Wilderness" – requires *work*. Nor is *Paradise Regain'd*, for all its attention to the Son's "thoughts," a *psychomachia* of either the Son's or the poet's soul.⁴ The action of *Paradise Regain'd* does not take place in "choicest Society," but it is always represented to us as plain to the sight, effective, and – to borrow Satan's useful distinction – "Real," not "Allegoric" (4.390). The Son's thoughts "recommend" solitude precisely because they are *dangerous* thoughts and have the potential for public ramifications – "rescu[ing] *Israel* from the *Roman* yoke" and "subdu[ing] and quell[ing] o'er all the earth / Brute violence and proud Tyrannic pow'r" (1.217–19), among others. By choosing "Solitude before choicest Society," Milton's Son of God joins in league with such figures of moral and political resistance as the Lucan of Mackenzie's *Moral Essay* whose "noble lines . . . have since carried his fame as far as *Cesars* actions" and "Poor *Socrates*" – the Son himself mentions him as a model in book 3 – who "For truth's sake suffering death unjust, lives now / Equal in fame to proudest Conquerors" (3.96–99).

Neither Socrates nor the Jesus of the Gospels were Stoics, of course, but the "situation," of the Son in *Paradise Regain'd*, writes Malcolm Kelsall, "at once recalls the [Stoic] tradition, and the problem" that faced idealistic first-century Romans when "the cause of the republic, of liberty and of virtue, was guttering out."[5] The Son's withdrawal to a "Desert wild" (1.193) and then "his Mother's house" (4.639) are valid Stoic responses that preserve the possibility of virtuous action in the greater commonwealth of mankind; nor do they shrink from the fact that "silence implies *dissent*, and dissent threatens the order of the state."[6] To represent Jesus in such terms was, indeed, to represent him *historically* – to imagine how his "mind would have worked under Tiberius, how any intelligent, justly ambitious, and actively inclined philosophical man would have seen the world under tyrannical government."[7] It should be stressed, however, that while Milton's historical knowledge was immense, he was not a positivist historian interested in recovering the past for its own sake alone. "The historical setting of *Paradise Regained* – Israel under the rule of the Emperor Tiberius – would have had particular force in the Romanized England of the 1660s and 1670s," observes Laura Lunger Knoppers in a book dealing with Milton's reactions to the triumphal style of Restoration culture.[8] Both his friends and his foes were likely to sense a republican "tang" in the choice of Tacitus as his main authority on Tiberian Rome, in the Son's high estimation of "*Quintius, Fabricius, Curius, Regulus*" (2.446), and in the comparison of the Son to Seneca's admired Hercules (4.565).[9] And finally, when they sought to understand the political meaning of a Stoic Jesus who thinks dangerous "thoughts / . . . of things past and to come,"

I suspect that they were guided by the hero of the same epic that Marvell found exemplary when praising *Paradise Lost* – the Cato of Lucan's *Pharsalia*.

The vast deserts of the *Pharsalia* and *Paradise Regain'd* present Cato and the Son of God with the problem of escaping the failures of the past and somehow finding or making a better future for free men and women. It is fitting, given the apocalyptic fervor of seventeenth-century England and the first-century Empire, that in both Lucan and Milton this *political* problem is represented as a *prophetic* crisis in which present-day action is taken to depend upon competing descriptions of, and attitudes toward, the future. Prophecy may seem to have little to do with the dry rationalism which supposedly characterizes Stoicism, but it must be stressed that prophetic discourse is an especially complicated and loaded issue in Stoic contexts. "*Philosophers* were divided about the Subject of *Oracles*" in the ancient world, wrote the skeptical Fontenelle in his *Histoire des Oracles* (1687); "the *Platonists* and *Stoicks* were for them, but the *Cynics*, *Peripateticks* and *Epicureans* declared highly against them."[10] Indeed, most Stoics strongly *defended* popular belief in prophecy and oracles, and they faced much abuse from Skeptics and Epicureans, ancient and modern, for doing so. "With the possible exception of Panaetius," Edelstein writes, "all Stoic philosophers defended the belief in the science of omens that reveal to man the divine interest in his fate." Given their belief in the necessity of all actions, it seemed theoretically possible to them that "the future could be known at least by a mind able to follow all lines of causation; and if it is true that this cosmos is held together by sympathy and all its members form a unity or common body," it is "probable and even most likely that God's benevolence will share with the human being what is so important for him to have, insight into the future."[11] We shall see that when Cato spurns the oracle at the temple of Jupiter Ammon in *Pharsalia* 9 he is not rejecting superstition, irrationality, or even untruth but professing instead his own personal participation in the divine. He is asserting that he is himself as good as an oracle. Something very similar happens in *Paradise Regain'd* as Milton "revises and redeploys the prophecies of Daniel and Revelation integral to millenarianism" and "provides a model by which the saints can internalize their warfare" – a warfare, I shall argue, inspired not only by Scripture but by Cato's courageous Stoic generalship.[12] In both Lucan and Milton the self becomes the subject of prophetic discourse, and in both cases political integrity is achieved by revising, purifying, and internalizing that discourse.

Like Jesus, who was once "enforc't to fly" his homeland from Herod "who sought his life, and missing fill'd / With infant blood the streets of *Bethlehem*" (2.75–78), Cato in *Pharsalia* 9 is a political refugee with harrowing violence in his past and future. In the past lies the bloody failure at Pharsalia; in the future lie deaths rendered by Lucan in gruesome detail and, though Lucan did not live to write it, Cato's own painful, protracted suicide after the battle of Thapsus (see fig. 5). "In his hands," writes Martindale, "the desert march becomes a test of virtue, a Stoic obstacle race . . . Cato, the Stoic sage, guides his men through a series of trials (storms by sea and land, thirst, heat and deadly snakes) in which they prove themselves the true possessors of spiritual freedom."[13] The approach to the temple of Jupiter Ammon is through the Saharan desert, a vast waste, unwholesome to humans, in which "No paths, no difference now of ways are known," and in which one is "guided by the star alone" (*LP* 223; 9.494–95). He and his "Patrician" soldiers march in the "scorching day"; they flow "with sweat, / Their mouths with thirst . . . parch'd," before at last they find a stream. Cato is "with much adoe" offered a helmet filled with water, but he, "stirr'd with wrath [strikes] the helmet down" (*LP* 224; 9.498–510). Finally, they come "to Libya's onely temple plac'd / In Garamantis rude." This temple belongs to Jupiter Ammon, a "poor" and thus a "pure" god:

> *Jupiter Ammon* is adored there,
> Not arm'd with thunder like our *Jupiter*,
> But crooked horns. To whom the Libyans build
> No sumptuous Fane, no orient jewels fill'd
> The house with lustre. Though the Indians,
> The Æthiopes, and rich Arabians
> *Jupiter Ammons* name do all adore,
> And no god else, yet still that god is poor.
> No wealth corrupts his Fane, a god of th'old
> Pureness, his temple guards from Roman gold.
> That place of all the Countrey onely green
> Shews a gods presence.   (9.512–23)

Libya's latitude means that the temple is especially favorable for astrological interpretation: the "signs oblickly rise not, but direct" (*LP* 225; 9.533). With plentiful water, green grass, shade, and clear "signs," the temple of Jupiter Ammon is a promising place for Cato's republicans to rest and take stock of their cause and learn about its doubtful future.[14] "The Eastern people standing at the door" of the temple step aside for the great Cato, and his soldiers "plie" him to "be taught" by the

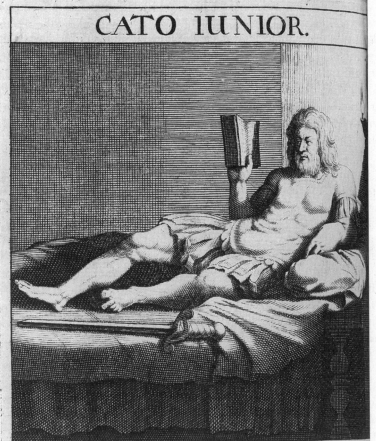

Figure 5   *Plutarch's Lives* (London, 1683–86).

"far-famed deitie" the truth about "future fates" (9.544–48). One of these, a former Caesarian named Labienus, is particularly anxious that Cato consult the oracle:

> Chance, and the fortune of our war (quoth he)
> Lend us the mouth of that great deitie,
> And his sure counsels: we may now implore
> His powerful guidance through this war, and ore
> The dangerous Syrtes. For to whom should I
> Believe the gods would trulier certifie
> Their secret will, than *Catos* holy breast,
> Whose life to heavenly laws was still addrest,
> And follow'd god? Behold we now have here
> A freedom given to talk with *Jupiter*,
> *Cato*, enquire of wicked *Caesars* fate,
> And know what shall be Romes ensuing state,
> Whether this civil war be made in vain,
> Or shall our laws, and liberties maintain,
> Let *Ammons* sacred voice thy breath inspire.
> Thou lover of strict virtue, now desire
> To know what virtue is; seek from above
> Approvement of the truth.   (9.550–63)

But Cato rejects such "Approvement" utterly and attacks Labienus with a long series of questions and paradoxes that summarizes the full range of his Stoic virtue and make plain his fighting spirit:

> He full of *Jove*,
> Whom in his secret breast he carried ever,
> These temple-worthie speeches did deliver:
> What, *Labienus*, should I seek to know?
> If I had rather die in arms, then bow
> Unto a Lord? If life be nought at all?
> No difference betwixt long life and small?
> If any force can hurt men virtuous?
> If fortune lose, when virtue doth oppose,
> Her threats; if good desires be happiness,
> And virtue grow not greater by success?
> Thus much we know, nor deeper can the skill
> Of *Ammon* teach. The gods are with us still;
> And, though their oracles should silent be,
> Nought can we do without the gods decree;
> Nor need he voices; what was fit to know
> The great Creator at our births did show.
> Nor did he chuse these barren sands to shew

(Hiding it here) his truth but to a few.
Is there a seat of gold, save earth, and sea,
Air, heaven, and virtue? Why for gods should we
Seek further? What ere moves, what ere is seen
Is *Jove*. For oracles let doubtful men
Fearful of future chances troubled be:
Sure death, not oracles ascertain me.
The coward and the valiant man must fall;
This is enough for *Jove* to speak to all:
Then marching thence, the temple's faith he saves,
And to the temple untry'd *Ammon* leaves. (*LP* 226; 9.564–86)

The future, as Labienus should know by now, holds no particular importance for Cato beyond its aspect as a continual moral and political trial (some of these lines, it will be recalled, have been quoted above in connection with *Paradise Lost* and the presence of God even in the dangerous, unknown wilderness that faces Adam and Eve beyond Eden). It is not for nothing that Lucan writes so many lines on the geography, poverty, and purity of the temple; they are essential to the episode because they make Cato's rejection of prophetic aid seem all the more heroically "pure." Indeed, the knowledge that Cato rejects here is not a faulted knowledge at all. His reasons for spurning "the skill / Of *Ammon*" are bound up with the Stoics' reasons for believing in the science of oracles in the first place. He already knows "what virtue is" because he is himself "full of *Jove*." As a Stoic sage he is *deo plenus* and shares freely in the truth of "The great Creator" that he feels in and all around him. He possesses, as Edelstein puts it above, "a mind able to follow all lines of causation." Cato speaks *for* Jupiter Ammon – he "temple-worthy speeches did deliver" – in the very act of turning *from* the temple because he is himself a "better oracle."

The problem, of course, is that he expresses himself in paradoxes that may seem to put in question the purpose of having a future. But that is Cato's point: he wants to focus himself and his men on their *immediate* purpose. The "paradoxes of the Stoa," Edelstein writes, "are often quoted in order to prove that . . . Stoic moralism was indifferent to the content of moral action; but nothing could be farther from the truth, for [they] were meant to show that man must always take responsibility himself, that the choice is his, that he can never find an excuse in external circumstances, and that even in the last extremity of moral action he and his reason must be the sole point of reference."[15] For Epictetus in *Enchiridion* 32, the reality of oracles entails that one should always listen to the "greater Oracle":

When you go to a Foreteller of things to come, no doubt, but you are ignorant of what is to happen. For it is, to be inform'd by him, that you consult him. But, to know whether that which shall happen will be good or bad, you have no need of the Foreteller, because you know it already, if you are a Philosopher. For if it be not something dependent on your self, . . . you may confidently affirm, that it is neither good nor bad. When therefore you go to consult the Fortune-teller, be not prepossess'd with either Desire or Aversion; otherwise you will never approach him without trembling. Hold it for a Maxime, that every Event is indifferent, that it can never give any obstruction to what you had purposed to do, and, whatever it may be, that it is always in your power to apply it to a good use . . . So that when the question is concerning the defence of your Country, or of your Friend, there is no necessity of going to the South-sayer; inasmuch as if the South-sayer tell you, that the entrails of the Victime presage ill success, it is an infallible sign, either that you will dye, or that you will be crippled, or that you will be banish'd, which might haply divert you from the design you were engaged in. In the mean time Reason advises, that you should relieve your Friend and Country, even with the hazard of your Life. Make your applications then to a greater Oracle.[16]

The "greater Oracle" for Epictetus and Lucan is always reason, or God, who tells the Stoic to perform his social and political "offices" whenever possible – and sometimes even when *not* possible. Cato's decision to continue doing what he is doing – marching on in the desert without listening to the oracle, confident in his own oracular knowledge that he "had rather die in arms, then bow / Unto a Lord" – unites Stoic obstinacy and political action, Stoic fatalism and a strong sense of personal and communal freedom together in a way that, while not hopeful in a Christian sense, is not without religious qualities. Indeed, Cato can seem strikingly Christlike at times. In book 2 he rejects the inactivity advised by Brutus and embraces instead an active, fearless *virtus* that would "redeem the people":

> Would the gods
> Of heaven, and Erebus would now strike dead
> For all our crimes this one condemned head.
> Devoted *Decius* by his foes could fall:
> Me let both Roman hosts assault, and all
> Rhines barbarous troups; let me i'th' midst receive
> All darts, all wounds, that this sad war can give.
> Let me redeem the people: Let my Fate
> What ere Romes manners merit, expiate.
> Why should the easily conquer'd people die,
> That can endure a Lord? Strike onely me,
> Me with all the swords, and Piles, that all in vain
> Our wronged laws, and liberties maintain:
> This throat shall peace to Italie obtain. (*LP* 31–32; 2.306–18)

For most of the *Pharsalia* it seems that this redemptive office must be Cato's alone. The other candidates waver between passionate extremes of inactivity and activity. Brutus, for instance, who had been dangerously close in his thinking to Appius Claudius, whose republicanism is extinguished after he consults the Delphic oracle in book 5, has now been made rather "too far / . . . in love with civil war" (*LP* 32; 2.325) by Cato's stirring speech.[17] But Cato's knowledge of the basic truths given by "The great Creator at our births" leads him to insist finally that virtue, however opposed it is to fortune and even fate, must be a *common* cause. Soon after his eulogy on Pompey in book 9, he reclaims a group of deserters with these words:

> Fought you, young men, with *Caesars* armies hopes
> (No more true Roman, but Pompeyan troups)
> To gain a Lord? since for no Lord you fight,
> But live to do your selves, not tyrants right,
> Since your spent blouds can no mans rule procure,
> But your own safetie, you'll not now endure
> The wars; to live in bondage you desire,
> And for your slavish necks a yoak require.
> Your danger's worthie now, the cause is good;
> *Pompey* perhaps might have abus'd your bloud
> And will you now, when libertie's so nigh,
> To aid of Rome your swords, and throats denie?
>
> (*LP* 217; 9.256–65)

Cato offers the redemptive office, which he had claimed for himself alone in book 2, to *all* his soldiers in this speech. Indeed, with Pompey dead the men may now fight for themselves, not a "tyrants right." In the desert of their defeat Cato tells his men that the great alternative between Pompey and Caesar had not constituted a real choice at all. Even when there is absolutely no hope of success – even when the "greater Oracle" makes this quite clear – the Stoic will continue to fight, not so much because the Stoic is a republican, but because the Stoic is fighting for himself and recognizes that this fight links him with all other virtuous persons.

ORACLES "CEAST," "LIVING," AND "INWARD"

Just as Lucan is concerned with oracles, prophecies, and their true value to the virtuous and wise throughout the *Pharsalia*, so Milton leads us from the first lines of *Paradise Regain'd*, as Barbara Lewalski observes, "to regard the temptation episode in the double perspective of the past and future, as indeed the turning point between past and future."[18] From Satan's first greeting to the Son in book 1 to the allusion to Oedipus and the Sphinx during Satan's fall in book 4, prophetic discourse guides the action and arguments of the brief epic. And, insofar as Satan strives to interpret the intentions of the "living Oracle," prophetic discourse may be said to constitute the *form* of their encounter and to function as the general rhetorical medium or arch-temptation through which each of the temptations proper – to food, riches, power, knowledge – emerge. Milton, writes Dick Taylor, Jr., "was inimical to vulgar and hysterical sign reading, [but] he believed that God revealed his mind and will to man at the proper times" and that "man must distinguish by his reason the true from the false."[19] On the one hand, Milton treats "with great prominence the various true prophecies and revelations concerning the Messiah," especially "the prophecy concerning Christ's accession to the throne of David"; on the other hand, "Satan himself is shown to be aware of the prophecies" and "uses them in his temptation of Christ."[20] It is thus not simply a matter of rejecting prophetic discourse as Satanic, because oracles, prophecies, and portents, much like books in *Areopagitica*, are occasions for the exercise of an individual's virtue.

The prominence given to prophetic discourse is all the more remarkable since prophecy is not an important feature in the accounts given by Luke and Matthew. Jesus prefaces his statements with "it is written" in the Book of Luke; but this writing refers to given law, not the future. Luke's devil ventures on prediction once: "For it is written, He shall give his angels charge over thee, to keep thee: And in *their* hands they shall bear thee up" (4:10–11); but his words, quoted almost verbatim by Milton (4.556–59), do not prepare us for the prophetic obsessions of Satan who, when he first meets the Son of God, remarks that he "seem'st the man whom late / Our new baptizing Prophet" has "honor'd" (1.327–29). Nor, perhaps, are we prepared when the Son, responding to Satan's suggestion that he could best fulfill expectations by turning "hard stones" to bread (1.343), invokes the prophet Moses who "nor eat nor drank" and the prophet Elijah who "forty days . . . without food / Wander'd this barren waste" (1.351–54). "The same I now," the Son concludes, and so it seems reasonable to Satan, as he tries to ingratiate himself with this remarkably terse prophet, to note that he, too, has been involved in various prophetic adventures over the years. Indeed, he once "undertook [God's] office" in destroying King Ahab (I Kings 22:19–23) by "glibb[ing]" "the tongues / Of all his flattering

Prophets" (1.374–76). Satan "dwell[s] / Copartner" with men and women, and he has always been happy to give them his "aid" and "advice" by means of "presages and signs, / And answers, oracles, portents and dreams, / Whereby they may direct their future life" (1.393–96). The Son responds "sternly" to this and at great length before making a prophecy about *prophecy*:

> all Oracles
> By thee are giv'n, and what confest more true
> Among the Nations? That hath been thy craft,
> By mixing somewhat true to vent more lies.
> . . .
> But this thy glory shall be soon retrench'd;
> No more shalt thou by oracling abuse
> The Gentiles; henceforth Oracles are ceast,
> And thou no more with Pomp and Sacrifice
> Shalt be inquir'd at *Delphos* or elsewhere,
> At least in vain, for they shall find thee mute.
> God hath now sent his living Oracle
> Into the World to teach his final will,
> And sends his Spirit of Truth henceforth to dwell
> In pious Hearts, an inward Oracle
> To all truth requisite for men to know.   (1.430–64)

God's Word silences Satan's oracles. They are as "dumb" as the oracles of the ode "On the Morning of Christ's Nativity" (line 173). But we are not done with oracles quite yet. The rhetorically sophisticated Son of God is still happy to use the word if not the thing itself. In the very act of silencing these oracles he announces the arrival of two new and, as Bacon would say, "better oracles": God's "living Oracle" (himself) and "an inward Oracle" that will "dwell / In pious Hearts" of men.

This was at once an old metaphor and something rather different, I think, than a metaphor.[21] The term "Oracle" is introduced and re-iterated so carefully in these lines that it becomes every bit as *historical* and *realistic* as any other narrative device that Milton uses for "lik'ning," as Raphael says of his history of the War in Heaven in *Paradise Lost*, "spiritual to corporal forms" (5.573).[22] To call the Holy Spirit an "inward Oracle" was to conceive it by seventeenth-century standards in historical terms, to place it in a narrative running from the priests of Delphos to England's Fifth Monarchists and "the English people's racking concern over the interpretation of prodigies" which had been "rising to a high pitch" during the years he was writing his poem.[23] The "living Oracle" and "inward Oracle" are not, of course, the stuff of Thomas Bromhall's *History of Apparitions, Oracles, Prophecies, and Predictions* (1658) in ancient and modern times, but they do participate in its *mundus significans* and respond to the expectations of such books' readers. Oracles, whether "ceast" or not, were *real* for most seventeenth-century readers, and Bromhall confidently asserts that reality against "scoffers" of "all Ages": the "*Sadduces . . .* and the *Epicures,* and the greatest part of the *Peripateticks,* and all sorts of *Atheists* whatsoever" do Satan's work when they try, against experience and common sense, to divorce spiritual from bodily realities.[24] To Plutarch's objection to the presence of devils in Chrysippus's Stoic world – "that in this universall body of the World, so well ordained and framed, [God] should grant so great an inconvenience, (to wit) that there should be Devils afflicting and tormenting men" – the Puritan comes to the Stoic's defense by replying that "God hath placed, and left here below in this World, Devils and wicked Spirits, to be as tormenters and executioners to wicked men: that so his Justice might shine the more glorious, to the comfort of the godly, and of his Elect, that live in the love and fear of him."[25] Similarly, the author of the seditious *Mirabilis Annus, Or the Year of Prodigies and Wonders* (1661) does "not dare to be positive in a particular application of all, or any portents mentioned in the following History," but he is sure of "a few of those *general* things which commonly prove the *issues and events* of such *prodigious apparitions.*" These include the propositions that "They usually fore-signifie some remarkable *changes* and *revolutions,*" that "They do bode very much misery and calamity to the *prophane* and *wicked* part of the World," and that "They do usually Prognosticate very much good to the *Sober* and *Religious* part of the World."[26]

Although the messianic hopes of the Fifth Monarchists and other radicals are deferred in *Paradise Regain'd,*[27] Milton does not dispute the prophetic as a category of true knowledge. Indeed, he revivifies and historicizes prophetic discourse by placing what had been its most plainly historical manifestation – oracles – quite literally *inside* his readers' "pious Hearts." The doctrinal equivalent to the "Spirit of Truth" and "inward Oracle" in the *Christian Doctrine* is, of course, the Holy Spirit, and the "truth requisite for men to know" is the Gospel, "THE NEW DISPENSATION OF THE COVENANT OF GRACE . . . MUCH MORE EXCELLENT AND PERFECT THAN THE LAW." Here, too, he traces a history running from favored prophets to innumerable individuals with the means of prophecy held within them: "FIRST ANNOUNCED, OBSCURELY, BY MOSES AND THE PROPHETS, AND THEN WITH

ABSOLUTE CLARITY BY CHRIST HIMSELF AND HIS APOSTLES AND
THE EVANGELISTS," the Gospel "HAS BEEN WRITTEN IN THE
HEARTS OF BELIEVERS THROUGH THE HOLY SPIRIT, AND WILL
LAST UNTIL THE END OF THE WORLD. IT CONTAINS A PROMISE
OF ETERNAL LIFE TO ALL MEN OF ALL NATIONS WHO BELIEVE IN
THE REVEALED CHRIST, AND A THREAT OF ETERNAL DEATH TO
UNBELIEVERS" (*CPW* VI, 521). This is clear doctrine – more clear,
perhaps, than the "inward Oracle" announced in Milton's poem – but
there is, I think, an imagistic, irreducibly numinous core to the doctrine
itself. In his development of "WRITTEN IN THE HEARTS," Milton
quotes several Scriptural passages that place prophetic powers physical-
ly in mouths, hearts, and minds before concluding that "all true believers either prophesy or have within them the Holy Spirit, which is as
good as having the gift of prophecy and dreams and visions" (*CPW* VI,
523–24). Such imagery lies at the *heart* of Milton's understanding of
Christian liberty. Although it "is not a less perfect life that is required
from Christians but, in fact, a more perfect life than was required of
those who were under the law," the potentially innumerable prophets
who follow their own "inward Oracles" cannot be said to *follow* in the
usual sense of that word. Christ "leads them as willing followers" (*CPW*
VI, 535) but "willing followers," as Stanley Fish observes, "are those
who are in a sense following themselves."[28] The natural consequence of
this gradual democratization of prophetic power is political freedom:
"CHRISTIAN LIBERTY MEANS THAT CHRIST OUR LIBERATOR
FREES US FROM THE SLAVERY OF SIN AND THUS FROM THE RULE
OF THE LAW AND OF MEN, AS IF WE WERE EMANCIPATED SLAVES"
(*CPW* VI, 537). To possess an "inward Oracle" is, as Cato demonstrates
in *Pharsalia* 9, to have no need of oracles, prophets, or any other forms of
information oral or written. Moreover, it is to be free from the "bond-
age" and "yoak" of tyranny (Lucan) and "THE RULE OF THE LAW
AND OF MEN" (Milton).

To Satan, apparently, the Son's identification of himself as the "living
Oracle" sounds something like pride, and he soon changes tack and
casts the Son in the role of a prophet or oracle and himself as that
oracle's fawning auditor. Truth is hard to act on but "pleasing to
th'ear," he says; "What wonder then if I delight to hear / Her dictates
from thy mouth?" (1.478–82). On his return in book 2, ready now to
"try" the Son's "constancy" with "manl[y] objects" (2.225–26), Satan
reminds the Son that he is hungry although the "Prophet bold / Native
of *Thebez* wand'ring here was fed" (2.312–13) and tempts him with "A

Table richly spread, in regal mode" (2.340). Food is only the beginning of what becomes an attempt to "try" the "living Oracle" with the sort of "sumptuous" accouterments, "orient jewels," and "Roman gold" that characterize untruthful oracular temples in the *Pharsalia*. But when Satan claims that "Fortune is in my hand" (2.429) and offers riches and the kingly power that they can buy, the Son responds with this sage advice:

> Extol not Riches then, the toil of Fools,
> The wise man's cumbrance if not snare, more apt
> To slacken Virtue and abate her edge,
> Than prompt her do aught may merit praise.
> What if with like aversion I reject
> Riches and Realms; yet not for that a Crown,
> Golden in show, is but a wreath of thorns,
> Brings dangers, troubles, cares, and sleepless nights
> To him who wears the Regal Diadem,
> When on his shoulders each man's burden lies:
> For therein stands the office of a King,
> His Honor, Virtue, Merit and chief Praise,
> That for the Public all this weight he bears.
> Yet he who reigns within himself, and rules
> Passions, Desires, and Fears, is more a King;
> Which every wise and virtuous man attains:
> And who attains not, ill aspires to rule
> Cities of men, or headstrong Multitudes,
> Subject himself to Anarchy within,
> Or lawless passions in him, which he serves.   (2.453-72)

The Son is as "poor" and "pure" as Jupiter Ammon and as contemptuous of wealth and tyrants as Cato. This statement has usually been passed over as something of a commonplace, but in fact it is a strong, politically pointed version of the Stoic paradox that "*A wise man only is a King*: For Monarchy is a principality subordinate to none, which only consists in the wise."[29] The anti-monarchical tenor of such Stoic abstractions in Restoration culture can be grasped through contrast with the attitude of the conscientiously obedient Christ of Gilbert Sheldon's *Monarchy Triumphing over Traiterous Republicans* (1661): "Christ was born under an *Emperor*, not during the time of the *Roman Commonwealth*," writes this self-described "lover of Loyalty"; he appeared when "the Temple of *Janus* shut, which never fell out during the time of the *Republican Constitution* of *Rome*"; and although "he first made it appear, that *Peter* and he, (being *children* and not *strangers*) were free from the *payment of Tribute*, yet payed it, and wrought a miracle to that end."[30]

Indeed, the Son's contempt for kings and their "headstrong Multitudes" recalls "the constancie and solid firmness of any wise Man" who in *Eikonoklastes* is said to contemn the "Prayers" of Charles I in *Eikon Basilike* and the "inconstant, irrational, and Image-doting rabble" (*CPW* III, 601) that believes them.

Satan stands for a moment "mute confounded what to say, / What to reply" to the Son's rigorous Stoic indifference. He is himself, after all, a "great Dictator" (1.113) always "inly rackt" by emotions of various kinds (3.203). But then, still remembering that the Son is the "living Oracle," he thinks to make this response:

> I see thou know'st what is of use to know,
> What best to say canst say, to do canst do;
> Thy actions to thy words accord, thy words
> To thy large heart give utterance due, thy heart
> Contains of good, wise, just, the perfect shape.
> Should Kings and Nations from thy mouth consult,
> Thy Counsel would be as the Oracle
> *Urim* and *Thummim* those oraculous gems
> On *Aaron's* breast, or tongue of Seers old
> Infallible; or wert thou sought to deeds
> That might require th'array of war, thy skill
> Of conduct would be such, that all the world
> Could not sustain thy Prowess, or subsist
> In battle, though against thy few in arms.   (3.7–20)

He begins by praising the Son's discourse in Stoic terms reminiscent of Seneca and Jonson, equates human wisdom with oracular power in a Stoic manner, and then subtly turns all of these things toward militarism. When he again addresses the Son as a prophet later in book 3 he does so by comparison to Judas Maccabaeus, who "Retir'd unto the Desert, but with arms" (3.166). By warring with Rome the Son would "best fullfil, best verify / The Prophets old, who sung thy endless reign" (3.177–78). The Son, who holds a typological relationship to all true prophets of the past, is, much like Cato at the hands of Labienus, being asked to "verify" himself – to say what he already knows and to be what he already is – and this is quite vexing to him: "But what concerns it thee when I begin / My everlasting Kingdom? Why art thou/Solicitous?" (3.198–200). The Parthian temptation follows, and Satan places it, too, in relation to prophetic discourse. Unless the Son "Endeavor, as . . . *David* did," he will never obtain his "Kingdom though foretold / By Prophet"; for "prediction still / In all things, and all men, supposes means" (3.351–55). Satan's attempt here to convince the Son to use the Parthians to regain *"David's* royal seat" (3.373) recalls Pompey's proposal in *Pharsalia* 8 "To use the Parthian arms to overthrow / That land, and mix their ruin with our woe" (*LP* 191; 8.323–25).[31] Like the Roman senators, however, the Son rejects a military alliance with the Parthians, and indeed all "prediction" involving "policy, and projects deep / Of enemies, of aids, battles and leagues" (3.391–92). He rejects Satan's strategic projections just as Cato rejects Labienus's efforts to interest him in "wicked *Caesars* fate," and "what shall be Romes ensuing state." He is also "unmov'd" (4.109) by the suggestion that he conquer Rome's "wide domain" (4.81):

> What wise and valiant man would seek to free
> These thus degenerate, by themselves enslav'd,
> Or could of inward slaves make outward free?
> Know therefore when my season comes to sit
> On *David's* Throne, it shall be like a tree
> Spreading and overshadowing all the Earth,
> Or as a stone that shall to pieces dash
> All Monarchies besides throughout the world,
> And of my Kingdom there shall be no end:
> Means there shall be to this, but what the means,
> Is not for thee to know, nor me to tell.   (4.143–53)

His dismissal of Rome's "inward slaves" recalls at once Tacitus on the general servitude of the Empire (*Annals* 1.7) and, in a crucial contrast, his own prophecy of the "inward Oracle" in book 1.[32] The "means" of his kingdom's "spreading and overshadowing" – the "means" of the dashing "to pieces" of "All Monarchies besides throughout the world" – is "not for [Satan] to know, nor me to tell" because, on the one hand, Satan does not possess an "inward Oracle" and, on the other hand, because "pious Hearts" do not *need* to be *told* – not even by the Son of God. They *will* the law of God and so make the law their own just as they may be said to make the future their own.

Indeed, the "inward Oracle" of *Paradise Regain'd* is the possession of "pious Hearts" like those presumably possessed by the "Children of that Kingdom" in *Eikonoklastes* – "Children" whom Milton invented to bring about the "ancient Prophesies" of Daniel 2:44: "Kings of this world have both ever hated, and instinctively fear'd the Church of God," either because its members' "doctrine seems to favour two things to them so dreadful, Liberty and Equality, or because they are Children of that Kingdom, which as ancient Prophesies have foretold, shall in the end break to peeces and dissolve all thir great power and Dominion" (*CPW* III, 509). In *Areopagitica* political liberation and individual prophetic power are knit together as "branches" that grow like those of the Son's "spreading and overshadowing" tree before – lo! a wonder – metamorphosing into military units:

For now the time seems come, wherein *Moses* the great Prophet may sit in heav'n rejoycing to see that memorable and glorious wish of his fulfill'd, when not only our sev'nty Elders, but all the Lords people are become Prophets. No marvell then though some men, and some good men too perhaps, but young in goodnesse, as *Joshua* then was, envy them. They fret, and out of their own weaknes are in agony, lest these divisions and subdivisions will undo us. The adversarie again applauds, and waits the hour, when they have brancht themselves out, saith he, small anough into parties and partitions, then will be our time. Fool! he sees not the firm root, out of which we all grow, though into branches: nor will beware untill he see our small divided maniples cutting through at every angle of his ill united and unweildy brigade. (*CPW* II, 555–56)

Prophetic discourse invites the interpretation of figures, the conversion of figures into literal statements. But in Milton this is often a process without a clear end. Figures are followed by more figures: "Prophets" become "branches" which in turn become "maniples cutting through" an "unweildy brigade." And so, paradoxically, these things come to seem not apposite figures but apposite facts, with the "means" of their realization as facts at once unclear and unimportant to believers.

To the unbeliever, of course, they are likely to become wholly meaningless, and it is natural enough for Satan at this point to try to reclaim knowledge and its conventional categories as his own by tempting the Son with "sage Philosophy" (4.272). The "living Oracle" is indifferent to the knowledge Satan recommends, and thus he "sagely" replies:

> Think not but that I know these things; or think
> I know them not; not therefore am I short
> Of knowing what I ought: he who receives
> Light from above, from the fountain of light,
> No other doctrine needs, though granted true. (4.286–90)

The Son's rejection of philosophy is complete. Socrates professed only "that he nothing knew"; Plato "to fabling fell"; the Skeptics "doubted all things"; and Epicurus placed felicity in "corporal pleasure . . . and careless ease" (4.293–99). As for Satan's "*Stoic* severe" (4.280), he places felicity

in Philosophic pride,
By him call'd virtue; and his virtuous man,
Wise, perfect in himself, and all possessing
Equal to God, oft shames not to prefer,
As fearing God nor man, contemning all
Wealth, pleasure, pain or torment, death and life,
Which when he lists, he leaves, or boasts he can,
For all his tedious talk is but vain boast,
Or subtle shifts conviction to evade.
. . .
Much of the Soul they talk, but all awry,
And in themselves seek virtue, and to themselves
All glory arrogate, to God give none,
Rather accuse him under usual names,
Fortune and Fate, as one regardless quite
Of mortal things.   (4.300–18)

The Son is quite serious here – he has no need to misrepresent himself to Satan – but his lengthy rejection of Stoicism is itself the necessary terminal point of Milton's logic of Stoic indifference. For it is "not simply that the doctrine of things indifferent is to be found everywhere in *Paradise Regained*," as Fish observes, "but that *Paradise Regained* is a working out of the doctrine."[33] The "working out" of Stoicism requires in this case that Stoicism itself be rejected as doctrine.

On the one hand, Milton had good political reasons to repudiate the "soft" Stoicism of such popular texts as *Eikon Basilike* and Mackenzie's *Religio Stoici* (first published 1663). Like Milton, if with infinitely less precision, Mackenzie imagines Jesus in his first-century intellectual context: "if men had . . . listened (as the *Stoicks* Book of Discipline injoyned) to their own private consciences, and had by retiredness abstracted themselves from the reach of temptations, it had facilitated much their conversion: for if the young Lawyer, who came to consult Christ how to draw up his Securitie of Heaven . . . had believed their Oracle, which decry'd riches as the unnecessary baggage of man's life . . . he had never refused our Saviour's yoke."[34] But a Stoic Jesus entails for this moralist what was always unacceptable to Milton: a conforming Christian, one willing to keep his opinions to himself if the state does not punish his body. "As every private Christian should be tolerated by his fellow-subjects to worship God inwardly according to his conscience: so all should conspire in that exterior Uniformity of Worship, which the Laws of his Country enjoy" – or so we are told in "THE STOICK'S Friendly ADDRESSE To the PHANATICKS Of all Sects and Sorts," prefixed to *Religio Stoici*.[35] And yet, on the other hand, Milton also had good political reasons – as I hope to have shown in these five chapters – to rely on a more grave Stoicism for its powerful critique of kings and tyrants, the vices characteristic of courts, and the inconstancy of "head-strong Multitudes." Situations always matter – they make indifferent things more or less valuable for the Stoic – and in *Comus, Eikonoklastes*, and *Defensio Secunda* Stoic rhetoric had been valuable to Milton. Stoicism is crucial to him in the "pathless Desert" of the Restoration as well, but now the doctrine must be attacked in favor of a goal which Zeno would have admired: an unfolding of a politically powerful inwardness, "Spreading and overshadowing all the Earth." The Son of God, a man who Stoically esteems the man "who reigns within himself, and rules / Passions, Desires, and Fears," has it both ways in book 4. That is surely within his power. We may recall that Cato, too, demonstrates his knowledge by spurning knowledge – a knowledge perhaps identical to his own. The Son deals with Satan's "*Stoic* severe" exactly as Cato deals with Labienus. They are both "living Oracle[s]" and reject knowledge for the very same reason. Whatever wisdom – whatever "doctrine . . . though granted true" – that can be found in an oracle or a book can sooner be found in oneself: as the Son says, the "inward Oracle" gives "all truth requisite for men to know"; and, as Cato says, "What was fit to know / The great Creator at our births did show."

It is fitting that one of the Son's most positive uses of Stoic rhetoric comes in the wake of his rejection of the "*Stoic* severe":

> many books
> Wise men have said are wearisome; who reads
> Incessantly, and to his reading brings not
> A spirit and judgment equal or superior
> (And what he brings, what needs he elsewhere seek)
> Uncertain and unsettl'd still remains,
> Deep verst in books and shallow in himself,
> Crude or intoxicate, collecting toys,
> And trifles for choice matters, worth a sponge;
> As Children gathering pebbles on the shore.   (4.321–30)

Milton did not make this opinion up; nor, I think, was it dictated by a rush of religious enthusiasm. It is true that King Solomon said that "of making many books *there is* no end; and much study *is* a weariness of the flesh" (Ecclesiastes 12:12). But, as Milton himself suggests, other "wise men" have said very much the same thing. Indeed, it is a commonplace of Stoic educational theory, and the Son's phrasing as he searches after just the right metaphor is especially close to Seneca's manner in *Epistulae Morales* 2. "Beware lest this desire to reade many Authors, and all sorts of bookes, containe not giddiness and inconstancie of mind," Seneca writes, beginning a barrage of apposite metaphors: "Those that passe their life in travel take up many Innes, but entertaine few friendships"; "That meate never nourisheth the bodie, which is no sooner taken in, but is delivered out"; "The tree prospereth not that is transported from one place to another"; "The stomacke is distempered, that longeth after divers sorts of meates." All in all – and this is Seneca, not King Solomon – "The multitude of bookes distracteth and distempereth the under-standing" (*WS* 164; 2.2–4). This passage and others like it in the *Epistulae Morales* run through Lipsius, Bacon, Jonson, and all subsequent profes-sors of the Senecan style in the seventeenth century. The Son of God rejects Stoicism in *Paradise Regain'd*, but he does so on Stoic grounds.

Having found the "living Oracle" so inscrutable, Satan resorts finally to astrology:

> Now contrary, if I read aught in Heaven,
> Or Heav'n write aught of Fate, by what the Stars
> Voluminous, or single characters
> In their conjunction met, give me to spell,
> Sorrows, and labors, opposition, hate,
> Attends thee, scorns, reproaches, injuries,
> Violence and stripes, and lastly cruel death.   (4.382–88)

His syntax and vision are both horribly vexed. Satan cannot understand the meaning, "Real or Allegoric," of the Son's "Kingdom," nor its temporal nature: "no date prefixt / Directs me in the Starry Rubric set" (4.389–93). After the stormy night, Satan makes sure to "read" it as a portent of ill: such storms "oft fore-signify and threaten ill: / This tem-pest at this Desert most was bent" (4.464–65). But the Son is not "worse than wet" and the "terrors" of the storm mean nothing to him: "what they can do as signs / Betok'ning or ill-boding I contemn" (4.489–90). His contempt for Satan's interpretation of the "Tempest" leaves the latter "swol'n with rage" (4.499). The whole episode recalls their dispute over oracles "ceast" and "inward" in book 1, as well as the contest earlier in book 4 between their predictions of what the Son's kingdom will be like. Indeed, Satan uses the storm in the same way he has always used prophetic discourse: as an encouragement to the Son to take "*David's* Throne" (4.471) immediately – and with *his* aid. When Satan finally falls, he falls both like Antaeus at the hands of Hercules and like the Sphinx, "that *Theban* Monster that propos'd / Her riddle" (4.572–73). He falls like the Sphinx because the Son of God, writes Northrop Frye, "has solved the riddle of human life, putting all the words which are properly attributes of God into their rightful context."[36] He has also replaced Satan's riddles, prophets, and oracles with a better, "inward Oracle": the place of this oracle is, in Oedipus's famous word, *man*.

It will be helpful here to review and compare the meaning of oracles and prophetic discourse in Milton and the Stoic tradition. The Stoic takes oracles very seriously, believing them philosophically valid in the face of considerable derision from other schools. He takes them so seriously that he sometimes likens them, as Lucan does in the *Pharsalia*, to the *sapiens*. But then, having conflated oracular knowledge with the "greater Oracle" of reason, the Stoic restricts the scope of that knowledge to a few basic, unchanging truths. We have seen that Milton takes prophetic discourse seriously as well, believing it valid even at a time when enthusistic prognosticators were giving it a bad name. Indeed, he speaks of Jesus as the "living Oracle" and of the Holy Spirit as the "inward Oracle," places this latter "Oracle" in each believer, and makes such imagery all but inseparable from the idea of Christian liberty. But then, having democratized prophecy Milton severely restricts prophetic knowledge to one unchanging "promise of eternal life" to believers and "eternal death to unbelievers." We may seem to reach a similar impasse in both Milton and the Stoics, but in practice the restriction of prophetic knowledge to basic unchanging things – Stoic paradoxes and offices on the one hand, Christian promises on the other – can lead to the empowering confidence that one's hopes will be fulfilled. Thus, while there is no need for Milton to believe that prophecy will be realized in a year, or two, or ten for him to believe in its truth, there is also no reason for him to argue in *Paradise Regain'd* that "true knowledge requires escape from the motions of temporal experience," that "the Christian soul must escape from the confusing 'now' of temporal sequence," or that prophecy is "the way out of time."[37] If Milton drew anything from the Stoics it was that although there is in fact *no* way out of time for us, we can control the significance of future events as well as we can control the significance of past ones, and that by knowing the truths we were born with we will know the truths of the future.

Those who wanted to follow the example of Jesus in 1671 were faced with several options. Some no doubt still admired the Caesarian Jesus of *Monarchy Triumphing over Traiterous Republicans*. Some probably admired the conforming Jesus of Mackenzie's *Religio Stoici*. Others may have heard in the Son's careful responses to Satan the wisdom of Epictetus as rendered the year before by John Davies in *The Life, and Philosophy, of Epictetus* (1670): "Keep silence, as much as you can. Never speak any thing but what is absolutely necessary, and to do that, spend as few words as you can . . . But above all things, be careful, in your Conversation, to avoid both Praise and Dispraise, and making Comparisons between any." They may also have admired the fact that during Satan's several temptations, the Son follows perfectly Epictetus's advice to "take only so much as necessity requires, and the Mind stands in need of, in order to its well-being, and reject whatever contributes to Luxury and Delicacy."[38] Still other readers may have looked to *Paradise Regain'd* for the triumphant King Jesus of the Fifth Monarchy. If so they were disappointed. Milton, as Knoppers says, "does not attempt to raise an army or even the national consciousness."[39]

Yet their hopes may not have been wholly dashed. For *Paradise Regain'd*, as Knoppers also points out, does "not end with a repudiation of force; rather, force is overcome or superseded by the Son's full internalization of the divine will."[40] Fully internalizing the divine will is easy enough for the Son of God to do, of course, but my goal has been to undertstand how the feat was most likely to have been understood by those familiar with the republican "tang" that had been tasted by Jonson, May, Marvell, Philips, Milton, and many others during the seventeenth century. By tracing the internalization of revolutionary purpose in *Paradise Regain'd* through the imagery of the "inward Oracle," we have seen that Milton constructs the Son's encounter with Satan as an encounter with the limiting horizons of prophetic discourse, and that this narrative opens on a problematic of knowledge and self-determination whose origins may be traced productively in the Stoic tradition.

Cato's spurning of the oracle in *Pharsalia* 9 is bound up with his larger political exemplarity: his unshakable purpose to "receive / All darts, all wounds" in order to "redeem the people," his need to share that inner purpose with others, and to show them that by fighting for themselves – by living "to do your selves, not tyrants right" – they are in fact fighting for all virtuous men and women. Cato spurns the oracle not because knowledge of the future is impossible but because he already knows the truth of the future that pertains to him as a human being and citizen of the world. He knows, among other things, that he would "rather die in arms, then bow / Unto a Lord"; that there is "No difference betwixt long life and small"; that no "force can hurt men virtuous"; that "virtue

grow[s] not greater by success"; and that "The gods are with us still."
He is even willing, when necessary, to advance communal political
ideals in a thoroughly fatalistic spirit: "will you now, when libertie's so
nigh, / To aid of Rome your swords, and throats denie?" The answer
given by his soldiers is a tacit negative followed by more marching. At
this point they know as well as Cato does that the liberty of the Roman
republic is out of their reach and that any future liberty will be purchased by their blood. "History shows that even fatalism was not always
a hindrance to energetic, practical action," writes George Plekhanov in
a passage that makes Stoicism and dialectical materialism seem morally
interchangeable; "in certain epochs it was a *psychologically necessary basis
for such action* . . . Those who think that as soon as we are convinced of the
inevitability of a certain series of events we lose all psychological possibility to help on, or counteract these events, are very much mistaken."[41]
Cato and his men are fatalists, certainly, but they are not dead to the
choices that fate brings upon them. In *Paradise Regain'd* the Son faces
"Sorrows, and labors, opposition, hate, / . . . Violence and stripes, and
lastly cruel death" as he sounds the voice – and the meaningful silence –
of the "inward Oracle" amid a world of tyrannous control. Indeed, the
"inward Oracle" is most at home in a world of tyranny and violence. It
revels in the knowledge that the true Kingdom will someday be like "a
stone that shall to pieces dash / All Monarchies." This is the language of
Daniel and the Fifth Monarchists, but it is also in the spirit of Cato,
Lucan's great philosophical "General," poised against tyranny and "All
darts, all wounds."

"ONE'S *PATRIA*"

Six years after the King's return and five years before the publication of
Paradise Regain'd, Milton received a letter from Peter Heimbach, an
acquaintance from the 1650s who had since become councillor to the
Elector of Brandenburg. Addressed as "A Man above Praise," Milton
wrote back quickly and at some length. "It is no wonder," he writes, if
"among so many deaths of my countrymen, and in a year so poisonous
and plague-ridden . . . you believed that I too (as you write) had been
borne away" (*CPW* VIII, 3). 1666 was a plague year, of course, but as
Milton thanks God for having "prepared a safe place for me in the
country" there is a hint that the plague – along with the Dutch war and
the London fire – had been carried along by the royalist "epidemic"
predicted in *The Readie and Easie Way to Establish a Free Commonwealth*

(1660). Having thanked Heimbach for "admiring" in him "the marriage of so many various virtues" and noted that "virtues grow and flourish most in straitened and difficult circumstances," he observes that "One of those Virtues has not so pleasantly repaid to me the charity of hospitality": "the one you call *Policy* (and which I would prefer you call *Patriotism* [*quam enim Politicam tu vocas, ego Pietatem in Patriam dictam abs te mallem*]), after having allured me by her lovely name, has almost *ex-patriated* me, as it were" (*CPW* VIII, 4).[42] Milton is playing with Heimbach's rhetoric, turning the terms first one way, then another, and trying to find ones adequate to his own situation. When he corrects *politica* to *pietas in patria* he does so not, I think, to correct the lesser Latinist's diction but to put his own political rhetoric to the test. Indeed, he characterizes what is for him the supreme civic virtue with the qualities of *fortuna*. By loving his country constantly he has, by some trick of Lady Fortune, been betrayed by her inconstancy. And yet, after all this, he concludes that "One's *Patria* is wherever it is well with him [*Patria est, ubicumque est bene*]" (*CPW* VIII, 4).

It is worth pausing on this sentence from a letter which, according to E. M. W. Tillyard, catches "the mood of *Paradise Regain'd*, with which Milton was [then] occupied."[43] Milton was thinking of Cicero's *Tusculan Disputations* 5.37 – "Itaque ad omnem rationem Teucri vox accomodari potest, 'Patria est, ubicumque est bene'" – yet in his bemused manner he is more akin to Langius in *De Constantia* when that sometimes sarcastic sage criticizes *pietas in patria* as being wholly inappropriate to the life of constancy. "You cannot endure, you say, the Publick Calamity" (*DC* 22) he says to Lipsius, who would rather "*change Land for Land*" and "fly any wither" rather than see his native country despoiled. "Do you speak thus in *earnest*," asks Langius, "or do you *personate*, and *counterfeit it?*" (*DC* 22). "'Tis for my Country, *Langius*, Onely for *Her sake*, that I thus grieve," says the pious Lipsius. Langius can only shake his head:

We men, I confesse, complain oftentimes of the *Publick Evills*, nor is there any Grief more Common, and *appearing* . . . in our *Foreheads*: But if you examine it nearer, you shall find a dissent betwixt the *Tongue* and the *Heart*. Those are *proud* words; *The affliction of my Country pierces Mee*! not *true* ones; borne with the *lips only*, not deeper within the *breast*. That which is reported of *Polus*, the famous *Athenian Actor*, who, being to present upon the stage a Part, wherein he was to expresse much passion, brought privately in, the *Urne*, and bones of his *dead Sonne*, and by that meanes fill'd the Theater with *true sorrow*; The same may be said of most of you. You do but *Act* this *Tragedy*, and appearing under the *vizard* of your *Country*, you lament your *Own miseries*, with true and warmer teares. (*DC* 22–23)

Pietas is "a high, and Eminent *Vertue*," Langius admits, but it is "properly nothing else, than the *Lawful, due Honour, and love which wee bear towards God, and our Parents*" (*DC* 30). Langius then establishes – in a passage that puts in question Oestreich's thesis that Lipsius was a flag-waver for the absolutist state – the proper attitude toward one's country: "This" – speaking of the *place* where they happen to live – "is not our *Country*; But, one certain *State*, as I said, and (as it were) *common ship*, under *one Law*, or under *one King*: which if of Right you will have to be loved, and defended by its people, I will *confesse* it: If you will have Death under gone in its Quarrell, I will *permit* it: But I will never permit you to *grieve*, and *lament* for it" (*DC* 34). *Fateor, agnoscere, permittere*: Langius lets the degrees and kinds of concession and indifference come gradually, one by one.[44] He is willing to do these things – and nothing more – because, while his Stoicism makes him willing to fight and die for the virtue of his country, it also makes him a cosmopolitan unwilling to commit himself finally to this or that national identity. "No! The *whole World* is thy *Country*," he had exclaimed earlier: "A Great and large Mind does not *withdraw*, and *retire* itself within those narrow Bounds, which *Opinion* sets him; but his Thoughts spread, and advance *beyond* them, as he looks upon the *whole Universe*, as his *Own*" (*DC* 25).

The "mood" of the letter to Heimbach is Stoic indifference, but this need not be taken to signal a turn from the political involvements that mark so much of Milton's career. Indeed, we have found that the indifference of *Paradise Regain'd* expresses a broadening and even intensi-fication of those involvements. The place of Milton's liberty after the Restoration – his true *patria* – was the widening universe of his readers; and if we are unwilling to allow this statement to be anything more than an aesthetic commonplace I fear we shall never be able to feel the pulse of liberty as Milton and his contemporaries felt it. *Punitis ingeniis gliscit auctoritas*: forced into "retired silence," Milton turned his punishment into authority. Similarly, it is to privacy, to retirement, that the Son returns in the final lines of *Paradise Regain'd*: "hee unobserv'd / Home to his Mother's house private return'd" (4.638–39). But we know that privacy is less an alternative to violence than a further challenge to the realization of the "inward Oracle." Like Cato's inner *deus*, the "inward Oracle" is not limited to an inner life; nor, of course, will the Son of God be limited to his mother's house. He is not done yet, nor does Milton tell Heimbach that one's *patria* is wherever one *lives*. He says, rather, that one's *patria* is wherever one lives *well*.

Notes

INTRODUCTION

1 Quentin Skinner, *The Foundations of Modern Political Thought*, 2 vols. (Cambridge: Cambridge University Press, 1978), II, 279.
2 Ibid., II, 282.
3 Guillaume Du Vair, *A Buckler against Adversity: Or a Treatise of Constancie*, trans. Andrew Court (London, 1622), 120.
4 Markku Peltonen, *Classical Humanism and Republicanism in English Political Thought, 1570–1640* (Cambridge: Cambridge University Press, 1995), 136.
5 Andrew Milner, *John Milton and the English Revolution: A Study in the Sociology of Literature* (Totowa, NJ: Barnes and Noble, 1981), 147.
6 David Norbrook, "The Monarchy of Wit and the Republic of Letters: Donne's Politics," in *Soliciting Interpretation: Literary Theory and Seventeenth-Century English Poetry* (Chicago: University of Chicago Press, 1990), 7–8.
7 Maurizio Viroli, *From Politics to Reason of State: The Acquisition and Transformation of the Language of Politics, 1250–1600* (Cambridge: Cambridge University Press, 1992), 1.
8 Such rhetorical and situational complexities are not considered by Gilles D. Monsarrat in his fine thematic survey, *Light from the Porch: Stoicism and English Renaissance Literature* (Paris: Didier-Érudition, 1984).
9 Gordon Braden, *Renaissance Tragedy and the Senecan Tradition: Anger's Privilege* (New Haven: Yale University Press, 1985). My debts to Braden will be clear to anyone familiar with his argument that in Stoicism "the classical drive for self-esteem is not . . . suppressed but only redirected toward a more secure and elite kind of self-esteem" (18).
10 Ibid., 21, 24.
11 Sir William Cornwallis, *Essayes*, ed. Don Cameron Allen (Baltimore: Johns Hopkins University Press, 1946), 5.
12 *The Workes of Lucius Anneus Seneca*, trans. Thomas Lodge, 2nd edn. (London, 1620), 639; hereafter cited in text and notes as *WS*, followed by section numbers from the Loeb Classical Library editions.
13 See Ludwig Edelstein, *The Meaning of Stoicism* (Cambridge, Mass. : Harvard University Press, 1966), 19–44.
14 Ibid., 79.

15 Maren-Sofie Røstvig, *The Happy Man: Studies in the Metamorphoses of a Classical Ideal, 1600–1700*, 2nd edn. (Oslo: University of Oslo Press, 1962); Earl Miner, *The Cavalier Mode from Jonson to Cotton* (Princeton: Princeton University Press, 1971); Raymond A. Anselment, *Loyalist Resolve: Patient Fortitude in the English Civil War* (Newark: University of Delaware Press, 1988).

16 Thomas Stanley, *The History of Philosophy in Eight Parts* (London, 1656), VIII, 86, paraphrasing Diogenes Laertius, *Lives* 7.108.

I   CONFLICT AND CONSTANCY IN SEVENTEENTH-CENTURY ENGLAND

1 *The Poetical Works of Sir John Denham*, ed. Theodore Howard Banks, Jr. (New Haven: Yale University Press, 1928), 288–89.

2 Ibid., 289.

3 Braden, *Renaissance Tragedy*, 30, 26.

4 D. H. Pennington, *Europe in the Seventeenth Century*, 2nd edn. (London: Longman, 1989), 279.

5 George N. Clark, *War and Society in the Seventeenth Century* (Cambridge: Cambridge University Press, 1958), 24–25. For profound arguments that war has *never* been the extension of policy by other means, see John Keegan, *A History of Warfare* (New York: Random House, 1994), esp. 3–60.

6 Pennington, *Seventeenth Century*, 341.

7 Clark, *War and Society*, 9–10.

8 Ibid., 22.

9 Ibid., 9.

10 Pennington, *Seventeenth Century*, 281.

11 Robert Thomas Fallon, *Captain or Colonel: The Soldier in Milton's Life and Art* (Columbia: University of Missouri Press, 1984), 128.

12 *The Complete Prose Works of John Milton*, ed. Don M. Wolfe et al., 8 vols. (New Haven: Yale University Press, 1953–82), II, 561; hereafter cited in text and notes as *CPW*.

13 David Loewenstein, *Milton and the Drama of History: Historical Vision, Iconoclasm, and the Literary Imagination* (Cambridge: Cambridge University Press, 1990), 44.

14 Michael Lieb, *Milton and the Culture of Violence* (Ithaca: Cornell University Press, 1994), 263. For contrasting interpretations of Milton's response to war, see Michael Lieb, *Poetics of the Holy: A Reading of "Paradise Lost"* (Chapel Hill: University of North Carolina Press, 1981), 246–312; James Holly Hanford, "Milton and the Art of War," *Studies in Philology* 18 (1921): 232–66; Stella P. Revard, *The War in Heaven: "Paradise Lost" and the Tradition of Satan's Rebellion* (Ithaca: Cornell University Press, 1980); James A. Freeman, *Milton and the Martial Muse: "Paradise Lost" and European Traditions of War* (Princeton: Princeton University Press, 1980); and Fallon, *Captain or Colonel*.

15 J. R. Hale, *War and Society in Renaissance Europe, 1450–1620* (Leicester: Leicester University Press, 1985), 39.

16 Robert Burton, *The Anatomy of Melancholy*, ed. Floyd Bell and Paul Jordan-Smith (New York: Tudor Publishing, 1941), 47.

17 Justus Lipsius, *Two Bookes of Contancie*, trans. Sir John Stradling (1594), ed. Rudolph Kirk with notes by Clayton Morris Hall (New Brunswick: Rutgers University Press, 1939), 83; hereafter cited in text and notes as *TBC*.

18 See John Guy, ed., *The Reign of Elizabeth I: Court and Culture in the Last Decade* (Cambridge: Cambridge University Press, 1995), 1–19.

19 Graham Parry, "A Troubled Arcadia," in *Literature and the English Civil War*, ed. Thomas Healy and Jonathan Sawday (Cambridge: Cambridge University Press, 1990), 46.

20 Mervyn James, *English Politics and the Concept of Honour, 1485–1642* (Oxford: Past and Present Society, 1978).

21 Pennington, *Seventeenth Century*, 261. Cf. Brian Manning: "The nobility looked to the crown to provide the honours, employments, and economic resources, on which depended their social pre-eminence: but there were not enough to go round. As one aristocratic faction moved into favour its disappointed rivals tended to drift into opposition" ("The Nobles, the People, and the Constitution," *Past and Present* 9 [1956]: 55).

22 See Braden, *Renaissance Tragedy*, x, 11–12.

23 That those moorings did unravel was not remarkable in the European context. "A large part of the history of seventeenth-century Europe is made up of violent resistance to authority. Rebellion at every level of society was as much a part of life as were famine, plague, and war" (Pennington, *Seventeenth Century*, 259). Here and throughout I am indebted to James, *Concept of Honour*, esp. 72–91; but whereas he sees providentialism and its "image of the Christian warrior and the Holy war . . . as an alternative to the remodelled heroic image which the man of honour drew from Aristotle and the Stoics," I see these two images as combined and complementary in several important Jacobean and Caroline texts. For instance, Fulke Greville's *Life of Sir Philip Sidney*, which James discusses at 83–84, is itself an excellent example of the combination of Stoic and providentialist thought in a writer who found himself increasingly at odds with the Stuarts.

24 James, *Concept of Honour*, 66.

25 Gerhard Oestreich, *Neostoicism and the Early Modern State*, ed. Brigitta Oestreich and H. G. Koenigsberger, trans. David McLintock (Cambridge: Cambridge University Press, 1982), 30; my emphasis.

26 Samuel Daniel, *Poems and A Defence of Rhyme*, ed. Arthur Colby Sprague (Cambridge, Mass. : Harvard University Press, 1930), 112. In Joseph Hall's *Mundus Alter et Idem* (1605) the traveller comes to "a plaine where there were certaine old coines digged up whilest I was there." One has a Janus head and the other "was round, having on one side one in a gowne, seeming to bee of middle age, leaning his right hand upon the head of a little prettie dogge, and holding in the left hand, a booke; and on the other side was a *Chamaeleon* enameled in all her altering colours, and over her, these wordes, *Const. Lips*" (John Healey, trans., *The Discovery of a New World* (1609), ed. Huntington Brown [Cambridge, Mass. : Harvard University Press, 1937], 85–86).

27 See Clark, *War and Society*, 130–49. A compact example of such thinking is George Wither's emblem on "PAX EX BELLO" in *A Collection of Emblemes, Ancient and Moderne, The Second Booke* (London, 1634), 90.

28 This paragraph is indebted to Braden, *Renaissance Tragedy*, 5–27. See also Joseph-François Maisonobe, "Caton Gladiateur dans le *De Providentia*, II, 8: Étude sur les Combats de Gladiateurs dans l'Oeuvre de Sénèque," *AFL-Nice* 35 (1979): 235–57. On the figure of the gladiator in Roman culture at large, see Carlin A. Barton, "The Scandal of the Arena," *Representations* 27 (1989): 1–36.

29 *The Five Days Debate at Cicero's House in Tusculum* (London, 1683), 136.

30 Plutarch, *The Lives of the Noble Grecians and Romans*, trans. Sir Thomas North (London, 1657), 638.

31 See Henry W. Sams, "Anti-Stoicism in Seventeenth- and Early Eighteenth-Century England," *Studies in Philology* 41 (1944): 65–78; and Monsarrat, *Light from the Porch*, 81–108.

32 *The Booke of Marcus Tullius Cicero Entitled Paradoxa Stoicorum*, trans. Thomas Newton (London, 1569), A3.

33 Ibid., A2v.

34 Ibid., A3v.

35 Ibid., A4v, B2, B4v, C1v, C5v, D4.

36 John Bramhall, *Castigations of Mr. Hobbes* (London, 1658), 158.

37 Robert Johnson, *Essayes* (London, 1638), B2.

38 *The Basilikon Doron of King James VI*, ed. James Craigie (Edinburgh: William Blackwood & Sons, 1944), 156–57. The bracketed words appear only in the 1599 text.

39 Roger Ascham, *The Scholemaster*, ed. John E. B. Mayer (London: G. Bell & Sons, 1934), 180–81; I have modernized the spelling.

40 Wesley Trimpi, *Ben Jonson's Poems: A Study of the Plain Style* (Stanford: Stanford University Press, 1962), 33.

41 Ibid., 42. Cf. Kenneth J. E. Graham on Sir Thomas Wyatt's "plainness": "It rejects the goal of communal knowing as too dependent on the good faith of others . . . It proposes instead a self determined to uphold its convictions by claiming and enacting a privilege that, on the one hand, protects the self's purity by withdrawing its judgment and standards from questioning and, on the other, attacks the enemies of those convictions" (*The Performance of Conviction: Plainness and Rhetoric in the Early English Renaissance* [Ithaca: Cornell University Press, 1994], 38).

42 Cicero, *De Oratore Book III, De Fato, Paradoxa Stoicorum, De Partitione Oratoria*, trans. H. Rackham (Cambridge, Mass. : Harvard University Press, 1942), 49.

43 Ibid., 53–55. Trimpi notes that, for Cicero, "discussion was dangerous . . . to the established order . . . when one was not simply arguing about how a thing should be said but about what should be said" (*Ben Jonson's Poems*, 248n).

44 Seneca was more comfortable writing letters than making speeches. "I would not stampe upon the ground, nor cast my hands abroad, nor lift up

my voice. I would leave that to Orators, and content my selfe to have made thee understand my conceit without inriching my speech" (*WS* 305–06; *Ep. Mor.* 75. 1–5).

45 Fulke Greville, *The Works in Prose and Verse Complete*, ed. Alexander B. Grosart, 4 vols. (1870; New York: AMS Press, 1966), II, 71–72.

46 Here Braden builds an alliance where there was at best, I think, an uneasy truce: "The Stoic critique of monarchic power, like its critique of honor, is only the first movement in a process of internalization . . . Imperium remains the common value, the desideratum of both sage and emperor" (*Renaissance Tragedy*, 21). A common language can make for allies but it can also make for enemies who know each others' motives all too well.

47 The Lipsian bibliography is large and growing. I have found the following studies to be especially useful: Jason Lewis Saunders, *Justus Lipsius: The Philosophy of Renaissance Stoicism* (New York: The Liberal Arts Press, 1955); Anthony Grafton, "Portrait of Justus Lipsius," *The American Scholar* 56 (1987): 382–90; Mark Morford, *Stoics and Neostoics: Rubens and the Circle of Lipsius* (Princeton: Princeton University Press, 1991); and Justus Lipsius, *Principles of Letter-Writing*, ed. and trans. R. V. Young and M. Thomas Hester (Carbondale: Southern Illinois University Press, 1996), xiii–lvii.

48 John Earle, *Micro-Cosmographie* (1628), ed. E. Arber (London, 1868), 32. On the "hopping" qualities of Lipsian style, see George Williamson, *The Senecan Amble: Prose Form from Bacon to Collier* (Chicago: University of Chicago Press, 1952), 121–49.

49 Sir William Cornwallis, *Essayes of Certaine Paradoxes* (London, 1616), B1–E3.

50 Lipsius, *Principles of Letter-Writing*, 35–41.

51 Morris W. Croll, "Juste Lipse et le Mouvement Anticicéronien à la Fin du XVIe et au Début du XVIIe Siècle" in *Style, Rhetoric, and Rhythm*, ed. J. Max Patrick et al. (Princeton: Princeton University Press, 1966), 26.

52 Trimpi, *Ben Jonson's Poems*, 33.

53 Lipsius, *Principles of Letter-Writing*, 41.

54 Degory Wheare, *The Method and Order of Reading both Civil and Ecclesiastical Histories*, trans. Edmund Bohun (London, 1685), 105–06; italics reversed.

55 Oestreich, *Neostoicism*, 29.

56 Cf. Jonathan Sawday: "To say . . . of identity that it is challenged under the conditions of civil war might seem axiomatic. Yet, the psychological model suggests that it is not so much what happens outside the subject which precipitates breakdown . . . so much as it is the very processes of retreat into an internal world in an endeavor to preserve a unified sense of selfhood which brings about the crisis" (" 'Mysteriously Divided': Civil War, Madness and the Divided Self," in *Literature and the English Civil War*, ed. Thomas Healy and Jonathan Sawday [Cambridge: Cambridge University Press, 1990], 131).

57 Lipsius's "violent" works – lavishly printed "cum figuris" in most editions – include *De Militia Romana, Libri Quinque* (1595); *Poliorceticon sive de Machinis, Tormentis, Telis, Libri Quinque* (1596); *De Ampitheatro Liber* (1584); *Saturnalium*

Sermonum Libri Duo, qui de Gladiatoribus (1585); and *De Cruce Libri Tres, ad Sacram Profanamque Historiam Utiles* (1592).

58 Oestreich, *Neostoicism*, 30. See also Michael Roberts, *The Military Revolution, 1550–1660* (Belfast: Queens University Press, 1956), 7.

59 Oestreich, *Neostoicism*, 14. Peter Burke observes in a review of this book that Oestreich "writes as if theory always preceded and shaped practice" and that he does not give sufficient attention to eclecticism and "stoic radicalism" in the Neostoic movement (*English Historical Review* 100 [1985]: 404).

60 J. H. M. Salmon, "Stoicism and Roman Example: Seneca and Tacitus in Jacobean England," *Journal of the History of Ideas* 50 (1989): 224.

61 Braden, *Renaissance Tragedy*, 24–25.

62 Sir William Cornwallis, *Discourses upon Seneca the Tragedian* (London, 1601), H1.

63 On the politics of things indifferent see Victoria Kahn, *Machiavellian Rhetoric: From the Counter-Reformation to Milton* (Princeton: Princeton University Press, 1994), esp. 135–48, 171–84.

64 Justus Lipsius, *War and Peace Reconciled; Or, a Discourse of Constancy in Inconstant Times*, trans. Nathaniel Wanley (London, 1672). The engraving on the title page of this book appears to have been copied from the title page of Thomas Hobbes's *Philosophical Rudiments Concerning Government and Civil Society* (London, 1651). Curiously enough, the oval portrait at bottom center pictures not Lipsius but Hobbes.

65 Jonathan Goldberg, *James I and the Politics of Literature: Jonson, Shakespeare, Donne, and Their Contemporaries* (Stanford: Stanford University Press, 1989), 33–34.

66 Ben Jonson, *King James's Entertainment in Passing to His Coronation*, in *Ben Jonson*, ed. C. H. Herford and Percy and Evelyn Simpson, 11 vols. (Oxford: Clarendon Press, 1925–52), VII, 97; hereafter cited in text and notes as *BJ*.

67 Goldberg, *James I*, 43.

68 See Raymond A. Anselment, "Clarendon and the Caroline Myth of Peace," *Journal of British Studies* 23 (1984): 37–54; and idem, *Loyalist Resolve*, 21–45.

69 See Peltonen, *Classical Humanism*, 289–96. On the Neostoic heritage of Puritan "spiritual warfare," see Michael Walzer, *The Revolution of the Saints: A Study in the Origins of Radical Politics* (Cambridge, Mass. : Harvard University Press, 1965), 286–88.

70 Greville, *Works*, II, 113–14.

71 Quoted in J. P. Kenyon, *The Civil Wars of England* (New York: Knopf, 1988), 11.

72 Quoted in D. J. Gordon, "Roles and Mysteries," in *The Renaissance Imagination*, ed. Stephen Orgel (Berkeley: University of California Press, 1975), 16.

73 Plutarch, *The Philosophie, Commonlie Called the Morals*, trans. Philemon Holland (London, 1603), 1055–56.

2 ANDREW MARVELL: THE STOICISM OF NATURE, WAR, AND WORK

1 Stanley, *History of Philosophy*, VIII, 116.
2 See Derek Hirst and Stephen Zwicker, "High Summer at Nun Appleton, 1651: Andrew Marvell and Lord Fairfax's Occasions," *The Historical Journal* 36 (1993): 247–69.
3 Ibid., 250.
4 R[ichard] G[oodridge], trans., *A Discourse of Constancy: In Two Books* (London, 1654), 2; hereafter cited in text and notes as *DC*.
5 John M. Wallace, *Destiny His Choice: The Loyalism of Andrew Marvell* (Cambridge: Cambridge University Press, 1968), 248.
6 Christopher Duffy, *Siege Warfare: The Fortress in the Early Modern World, 1494–1660* (London: Routledge & Kegan Paul), 250.
7 Ibid., 258.
8 See ibid., 58–105.
9 For Marvell's poems I follow *The Poems and Letters of Andrew Marvell*, ed. H. M. Margoliouth, rev. Pierre Legouis and E. E. Duncan-Jones, 3rd edn., 2 vols. (Oxford: Clarendon Press, 1971).
10 Donald M. Friedman, *Marvell's Pastoral Art* (Berkeley: University of California Press, 1970), 208. I am indebted to Friedman's fine reading of this poem on 200–09.
11 *Lucan's Pharsalia: Or the Civil-Wars of Rome, between Pompey the Great, and Julius Caesar*, trans. Thomas May, 4th edn. (London, 1650), 5; *Pharsalia* 1. 129–45. Hereafter cited in text and notes as *LP*, followed by book and line numbers from the Loeb Classical Library edition.
12 Don Cameron Allen, *Image and Meaning: Metaphoric Traditions in Renaissance Poetry*, 2nd edn. (Baltimore: The Johns Hopkins University Press, 1968), 217–18.
13 Wallace, *Destiny His Choice*, esp. 252–57.
14 Michael Wilding, *Dragons Teeth: Literature in the English Revolution* (Oxford: Oxford University Press, 1987), 163.
15 George de F. Lord, "From Contemplation to Action: Marvell's Poetical Career," *Philological Quarterly* 46 (1967): 214.
16 Diego Saavedra de Fajardo, *The Royal Politician, Represented in One Hundred Emblems*, trans. Sir James Astry (London, 1700), 36. I am indebted to James Turner for mentioning Saavedra's "widely-propagated" book in *The Politics of Landscape: Rural Scenery and Society in English Poetry, 1630–1660* (Oxford: Basil Blackwell, 1979), 70. For a closer investigation of the poem's military imagery, see Turner's fascinating essay on "Marvell's Warlike Studies," *Essays in Criticism* 28 (1978): 288–301.
17 Rosalie L. Colie, *"My Ecchoing Song": Andrew Marvell's Poetry of Criticism* (Princeton: Princeton University Press, 1970), 240; Turner, "Marvell's Warlike Studies," 292; Hirst and Zwicker, "High Summer at Nun Appleton," 254.
18 Lawrence W. Hymen, "Politics and Poetry in Andrew Marvell," *Publications of the Modern Language Association of America* 73 (1958): 477–78.

19 Lord, "Contemplation to Action," 213, 215.

20 Indeed, Milton may well have wished that the constancy of another Cromwell had expressed itself in battle at the end of the decade. "The greatest disappointment of his mature life, after the failure of his eyesight," writes Fallon, "was the Restoration, and the King returned precisely because no war was fought" (*Captain or Colonel*, 129).

21 See Wilding, *Dragons Teeth*, 169–71; and John Wilson, *Fairfax* (London: John Murray, 1985), 174–83.

22 Allan Pritchard, "Marvell's 'The Garden': A Restoration Poem?" *Studies in English Literature* 23 (1983): 371.

23 See Nigel Smith, *Literature and Revolution in England, 1640–1660* (New Haven: Yale University Press, 1994), esp. 1–19.

24 See Colie, *Ecchoing Song*, 141–77.

25 T. Katharine Thomason, "The Stoic Ground of Marvell's 'Garden,'" *Texas Studies in Language and Literature* 24 (1982): 222–41.

26 Brian Vickers, "Leisure and Idleness in the Renaissance: The Ambivalence of *Otium*," *Renaissance Studies* 4 (1990): 3.

27 Morford, *Stoics and Neostoics*, 66.

28 Colie, *Ecchoing Song*, 166.

29 "Ut pictores longa intentione hebetatos oculos ad specula quaeda & virores colligu[n]t: sic nos hic animu[m] desusum, aut aberrante[m]" (Justus Lipsius, *De Constantia Libri Duo* [London, 1586], 45). For other parallels, see Marvell, *Poems and Letters*, I, 268–69.

30 Colie, *Ecchoing Song*, 176.

31 Leon Battista Alberti, *On Painting*, trans. John R. Spencer (New Haven: Yale University Press, 1966), 51.

32 See Marvell, *Poems and Letters*, I, 268–69; Colie, *Ecchoing Song*, 163–65; Turner, *Politics of Landscape*, 36–48; Thomason, "Stoic Ground," 230, and the studies that she cites on 240.

33 See Edelstein, *Meaning of Stoicism*, 66–69.

34 For Milton's poems I follow *Complete Poems and Major Prose*, ed. Merritt Y. Hughes (Indianapolis: Bobbs-Merrill, 1957).

35 Thomason, "Stoic Ground," 232.

36 Ibid., 235.

37 Colie, *Ecchoing Song*, 176.

38 G. W. Pigman III, "Versions of Imitation in the Renaissance," *Renaissance Quarterly* 33 (1980): 4.

39 On bees, soldiery, and war, see Freeman, *Milton and the Martial Muse*, 191–99.

40 Cf. Thomas M. Greene: "We do not, perhaps cannot, know exactly how nectar becomes honey; analogously the assimilation of our reading is a process not to be codified, although the will is called upon to ensure the thoroughness of absorption" (*The Light in Troy: Imitation and Discovery in Renaissance Poetry* [New Haven: Yale University Press, 1982], 74).

41 Edelstein, *Meaning of Stoicism*, 38.

42 Friedman, *Marvell's Pastoral Art*, 226.

43 Edelstein, *Meaning of Stoicism*, 24. See also Thomason, "Stoic Ground," 231–32.
44 Edelstein, *Meaning of Stoicism*, 25.
45 Cf. Colie: "The plant-mixture of the garden reflects the world-mixture of experience, this mixture presented and offered in terms of the poet's craft, in *genera mixta*. Once the reflection is understood, the fusion of retirement and emergence makes sense, although it plays havoc with the tradition in which the poem seems to begin, apparently assuming an irrevocable opposition between active and contemplative life" (*Ecchoing Song*, 171).
46 Pritchard, "Marvell's 'The Garden,'" 385.
47 Ibid., 382.
48 J. G. A. Pocock, *The Machiavellian Moment: Florentine Political Thought and the Atlantic Republican Tradition* (Princeton: Princeton University Press, 1975), 406–07.
49 Ibid., 409.
50 Andrew Marvell, *The Rehearsal Transpros'd* (London, 1672), 119, 134.
51 Ibid., 119, 121.
52 Juvenal, *Mores Hominum: The Manners of Men, Described in Sixteen Satyrs*, trans. Robert Stapylton (London, 1660), 166.
53 Marvell, *The Rehearsal Transpros'd*, 122–23.
54 Ibid., 170.

3 KATHERINE PHILIPS: THE STOICISM OF HATRED AND FORGIVENESS

1 Elaine Hobby, *Virtue of Necessity: English Women's Writing, 1649–88* (Ann Arbor: University of Michigan Press, 1989), 131.
2 Abraham Cowley, "On *Orinda's* Poems," in *The Collected Works of Katherine Philips*, ed. Patrick Thomas, G. Greer, and R. Little, 3 vols. (Essex: Stump Cross, 1990–93), III, 192; hereafter cited in text and notes as *CW*.
3 Achsah Guibbory, "Sexual Politics / Political Sex: Seventeenth-Century Love Poetry," in *Renaissance Discourses of Desire*, ed. Claude J. Summers and Ted-Larry Pebworth (Columbia: University of Missouri Press, 1993), 207.
4 See Harriette Andreadis, "The Sapphic-Platonics of Katherine Philips, 1632–1664," *Signs* 15 (1989): 34–60.
5 Catherine Cole Mambretti, "Orinda on the Restoration Stage," *Comparative Literature* 37 (1985): 233–51.
6 Stephen Greenblatt, *Renaissance Self-Fashioning: From More to Shakespeare* (Chicago: University of Chicago Press, 1980), 115.
7 John Dryden, *Essay of Dramatick Poesie* (1668), in *Of Dramatic Poesy and Other Critical Essays*, ed. George Watson, 2 vols. (London: Dent, 1962), II, 60. John A. Winterbottom has observed that Dryden himself turned to "the philosophy of the Stoics" in his tragedies because it "brought counsels of restraint to the powerful and of resignation to the victims of power" ("Stoicism in Dryden's Tragedies," *Journal of English and Germanic Philology* 61 [1962]:883).

8 Philip Webster Souers, *The Matchless Orinda* (Cambridge, Mass. : Harvard University Press, 1931), 170.

9 Mambretti, "Orinda," 239. On James Philips's suspension from Parliament in 1661 and expulsion in 1662, see *CW* II, 157–62.

10 Mambretti, "Orinda," 243.

11 Ibid., 244.

12 See ibid., 246–47; and Dorothea Frances Canfield, *Corneille and Racine in England* (New York: Columbia University Press, 1904), 51–69.

13 *His Majesties Most Gracious Speech, Together with the Lord Chancellors, to the Two Houses of Parliament; On Thursday the 13 of September, 1660* (London, 1660), 11.

14 Jacqueline Pearson, *The Prostituted Muse: Images of Women and Women Dramatists, 1642–1737* (New York: Harvester Press, 1988), 122.

15 Nicholas Jose, *Ideas of the Restoration in English Literature, 1660–71* (London: Macmillan, 1984), 131.

16 Ibid. Christopher J. Wheatley also seems to stray from the plot when he states that the "theme of loyalty to the restored power of Caesar was apropos to the difficulties engendered by the [Irish] Act of Settlement, which was seen as too favorable to Catholics at the expense of Cromwell's adventurers" ("'Our Fetter'd Muse': The Reception of Katherine Philips's *Pompey,*" *Restoration and Eighteenth-Century Theatre Research* 7 [1992]: 21).

17 See John M. Wallace, "Dryden and History: A Problem in Allegorical Reading," *English Literary History* 36 (1969): 265–90; John M. Wallace, "'Examples are Best Precepts': Readers and Meanings in Seventeenth-Century Poetry," *Critical Inquiry* 1 (1974): 273–90; and Alan Roper, "Drawing Parallels and Making Applications in Restoration Literature," in *Politics as Reflected in Literature*, ed. Maximillian E. Novak (Los Angeles: University of California Press, 1989), 31–65.

18 Dryden, *Critical Essays*, II, 8.

19 See Pierre Corneille, *Œuvres Complètes*, ed. Georges Couton, 3 vols. (Paris: Gallimard, 1980), I, 1074–78. "Pour le style," Corneille writes, "la gloire n'en est pas toute à moy. J'ai traduit de Lucain tout ce que j'y ai trouvé de propre à mon Sujet, et comme je n'ai point fait de scrupule d'enrichir notre Langue du pillage que j'ai pu faire chez lui, j'ai tâché pour le reste à entrer si bien dans sa manière de former ses pensées et d'expliquer, que ce qu'il m'a fallu y joindre du mien sentît son Génie, et ne fût pas indigne d'être pris pour un larcin que je lui eusse fait" (I, 1077).

20 On Lucan, see Frederick M. Ahl, *Lucan: An Introduction* (Ithaca: Cornell University Press, 1976); W. R. Johnson, *Momentary Monsters: Lucan and His Heroes* (Ithaca: Cornell University Press, 1987); David Quint, *Epic and Empire: Politics and Generic Form from Virgil to Milton* (Princeton: Princeton University Press, 1993), 131–57; David Norbrook, "Lucan, Thomas May, and the Creation of a Republican Literary Culture," in *Culture and Politics in Early Stuart England*, ed. Kevin Sharpe and Peter Lake (Stanford: Stanford University Press, 1993), 45–66; and Smith, *Literature and Revolution*, 204–07.

21 Katherine Philips, *Letters from Orinda to Poliarchus* (London, 1729), quoted in

Souers, *Matchless Orinda*, 198–99. Cf. the autograph version, preferred by Thomas over the 1729 text, in *CW* II, 113–14. For Cleopatra's offensive lines, see Edmund Waller, et al., *Pompey the Great* (London, 1664), 38.

22 Corneille, *Œuvres Complètes*, I, 1714.

23 In the "EPILOGUE to the King at Saint *James's*" the "Royal Sir" is figured as Pompey; France is found to have been a wiser Egypt, one that readily welcomed him during his "long Retreat," and the "Story" as a whole describes a "Change of Scene" (Waller, et al., *Pompey the Great*, H4v). The masque-like *Pompey the Great* transcends strict allegory, however; Pompey as Charles did not necessarily entail Caesar as Cromwell. In the "EPILOGUE to the Dutchess at Saint *James's*" Pompey is an example of *Pompey the Great* itself, seeking "the Haven which he first design'd, / This Royal Audience"; Caesar is the "pattern" of the Duchess's warlike husband, James, "Whose matchless Conduct might our Lions lead, / As far as e're the *Roman* Eagle spread" (Il).

24 Ahl, *Lucan*, 56.

25 David Clarke, *Pierre Corneille: Poetics and Political Drama under Louis XIII* (Cambridge: Cambridge University Press, 1992), 252.

26 John Webster, *The Tragedy of the Dutchesse of Malfy* (London, 1623), K1.

27 Pierre Le Moyne, *The Gallery of Heroick Women*, trans. John Paulet, Marquis of Winchester (London, 1652), 67.

28 Ibid., 69.

29 Marc Fumaroli, "L'Héroïsme Cornélien et l'Éthique de la Magnanimité," in *Héros et Orateurs: Rhétorique et Dramaturgie Cornéliennes* (Geneva: Droz, 1990), 333.

30 Ibid., 343.

31 Serge Doubrovsky, *Corneille et la Dialectique du Héros* (Paris: Gallimard, 1963), 281.

32 Fumaroli, "L'Héroïsme Cornélien," 344.

33 Clarke, *Pierre Corneille*, 252.

34 Waller, et al., *Pompey the Great*, H2v.

35 Cf. H. T. Barnwell, ed., *Pompée* (Oxford: Oxford University Press, 1971): "Cornélie may threaten César with continuing war and ultimate defeat, but (though of course she does not realize it herself – and that is the irony) all her references to the future are to defeat for the Pompeians. This means that the audience, knowing the facts, cannot share Cornélie's hopes" (65). The irony is exactly reversed in *Pompey*.

36 See the following essays by John M. Wallace: "John Dryden's Plays and the Conception of a Heroic Society," in *Culture and Politics from Puritanism to the Enlightenment*, ed. Perez Zagorin (Berkeley: University of California Press, 1980), 113–34; "*Timon of Athens* and the Three Graces: Shakespeare's Senecan Study," *Modern Philology* 83 (1986): 349–63; and "Otway's *Caius Marius* and the Exclusion Crisis," *Modern Philology* 85 (1988): 363–72.

37 Quoted in Edward Hyde, Earl of Clarendon, *The History of the Rebellion and Civil Wars in England*, ed. W. Dunn Macray, 6 vols. (Oxford: Clarendon Press, 1888), II, 9.

38 Samuel Rawson Gardiner, ed., *The Constitutional Documents of the Puritan Revolution, 1625–1660*, 2nd edn. (Oxford: Clarendon Press, 1899), 465–66.

39 *His Majesties Gracious Speech to the House of Peers, the 27 of July, 1660, Concerning the Speedy Passing of the Bill of Indempnity & Oblivion* (London, 1660), 4–5.

40 *His Majesties Most Gracious Speech, Together with the Lord Chancellors*, 11–12.

41 Justus Lipsius, *Sixe Bookes of Politickes or Civil Doctrine*, trans. William Jones (London, 1594), 31.

42 David Masson, *The Life of John Milton: Narrated in Connexion with the Political, Ecclesiastical, and Literary History of His Time*, 7 vols. (1880; Gloucester, Mass. : Peter Smith, 1965), VI, 25–56. See also Ronald Hutton, *The Restoration: A Political and Religious History of England and Wales, 1658–1667* (Oxford: Clarendon Press, 1985), 132–83.

43 Masson, *Life of John Milton*, VI, 54–55.

44 *His Majesties Most Gracious Speech, Together with the Lord Chancellors*, 11–12.

45 Masson, *Life of John Milton*, VI, 222.

46 Hutton, *Restoration*, 125.

47 Masson, *Life of John Milton*, VI, 223–24.

48 Ibid., VI, 50–51, 230–31; see also Hutton, *Restoration*, 162–63.

49 Quoted in Masson, *Life of John Milton*, VI, 231.

50 Hutton, *Restoration*, 135.

51 Ibid., 163; see also 164–66, *passim*.

52 Sir Roger L'Estrange, *A Caveat to the Cavaliers* (London, 1661), 7–8, 27.

53 In fact, Lodge softens the Senecan *veto* of monarchy: "Socrates parem gratiam Archelao referre non posset, si illum regnare vetuisset?"

54 Andreadis, "Sapphic-Platonics," 48.

55 On women and Stoicism in an earlier context, see Mary Ellen Lamb, *Gender and Authorship in the Sidney Circle* (Madison: University of Wisconsin Press, 1990), 115–41.

56 Le Moyne, *Gallery of Heroick Women*, 68.

57 Ibid., 73.

58 Philo-Philippa, "To the Excellent *Orinda*," in *CW* III, 197–98, 201–02, 203; italics reversed. For Philips's comments on this poet, see *CW* II, 78.

4 JONSON, MARVELL, MILTON: THE STOICISM OF FRIENDSHIP AND IMITATION

1 Stanley, *History of Philosophy*, VIII, 99.

2 Louis L. Martz, *Poet of Exile: A Study of Milton's Poetry* (New Haven: Yale University Press, 1980), 261.

3 Samuel Parker, *A Reproof to the Rehearsal Transpros'd* (London, 1673), 212.

4 Andrew Marvell, *The Rehearsall Transpros'd: The Second Part* (London, 1673), 378–79.

5 Abraham Cowley, *Poems* (London, 1656), A3v.

6 See Annabel Patterson, *Censorship and Interpretation: The Conditions of Writing and Reading in Early Modern England* (Madison: University of Wisconsin Press,

1984), 60–61; and Blair Worden, "Ben Jonson among the Historians," in *Culture and Politics in Early Stuart England*, ed. Kevin Sharpe and Peter Lake (Stanford: Stanford University Press, 1993), 78–79.

7 Thomas Hobbes, *Leviathan*, ed. C. B. Macpherson (Harmondsworth: Penguin Books, 1968), 162–63.

8 Marvell's knowledge of Lucan and *Lucan's Pharsalia* has been discussed by numerous critics in connection with the "Horatian Ode"; see Legouis's commentary in *Poems and Letters*, I, 294–303. His knowledge of "To My Chosen Friend" has been asserted by Gerard Reedy, S. J., " 'An Horatian Ode' and 'Tom May's Death,' " *Studies in English Literature* 20 (1980): 137–51; Annabel Patterson, " 'Roman-cast Similitude': Ben Jonson and the English Use of Roman History," in *Rome in the Renaissance: The City and the Myth*, ed. P. A. Ramsey (Binghamton, NY: MRTS, 1982), 381–94; and Robert Wiltenburg, "Translating All That's Made: Poetry and History in 'Tom May's Death,' " *Studies in English Literature* 31 (1991): 117–30, in essays concerned in part with echoes of Jonson that they find in "Tom May's Death." There were editions or reprintings of *Lucan's Pharsalia* in 1626 (the first three books only), 1627, 1631, 1635, 1650, and 1659. There were editions or reprintings of May's *Continuation of Lucan's Historicall Poem till the Death of Julius Caesar* in 1630, 1633, 1650, 1657, and 1659; his Latin version was published in Amsterdam in 1640, in London in 1646, and was included in editions of Lucan in the seventeenth and eighteenth centuries. On *Lucan's Pharsalia*, see Norbrook, "Lucan, Thomas May," 57–60; and Smith, *Literature and Revolution*, 204–07.

9 John Aubrey, *Brief Lives*, ed. Andrew Clark, 2 vols. (Oxford: Clarendon Press, 1898), II, 56.

10 Joseph Anthony Wittreich, Jr., "Perplexing the Explanation: Marvell's 'On Mr. Milton's *Paradise Lost*,' " in *Approaches to Marvell: The York Tercentenary Lectures*, ed. C. A. Patrides (London: Routledge, 1978), 301.

11 Colie, *Ecchoing Song*, 7. Wittreich argues that "Marvell simulates the syntax and sweep of the Miltonic period and, simultaneously, makes his own poem an analogue to a Miltonic structure" ("Perplexing the Explanation," 287).

12 Richard S. Peterson, *Imitation and Praise in the Poems of Ben Jonson* (New Haven: Yale University Press, 1981), 3. See also Greene, *Light in Troy*, 264–93.

13 Sir Roger L'Estrange, "An After-Thought," *Seneca's Morals by Way of Abstract*, 4th edn. (London, 1688), 12.

14 I take the phrase from R. R. Bolgar, *The Classical Heritage and its Beneficiaries: From the Carolingian Age to the End of the Renaissance* (Cambridge: Cambridge University Press, 1954), 385.

15 Seneca's comment on his many quotations of Epicurus – "soleo enim et in aliena castra transire, non tamquam transfuga, sed tamquam explorator" (*Ep. Mor.* 2. 5) – inspired Jonson's motto, *Tanquam Explorator*. See *BJ* I, 261.

16 See Trimpi, *Ben Jonson's Poems*, 124–26.

17 See *OED*, s. v. "peise," v., 1–3, and 5, "To drive, bear down, etc. by impact of a heavy body, or (generally) by force; to force." Cf. "To . . . Mr. William

Shakespeare": "Who casts to write a living line, must sweat, / (Such as thine are) and strike the second heat / Upon the *Muses* anvile: turne the same, / (And himselfe with it) that he thinkes to frame" (*BJ* VIII, 392).

18 Jonson refers to "that excellent Lucan" and "the divine Lucan" in his marginal commentary to *The Masque of Queenes* (*BJ* VII, 284, 292), although Drummond of Hawthornden recalls him saying once in private "that Lucan taken in parts was Good divided, read alltogidder merited not the name of a Poet" (*BJ* I, 134).

19 Sir William Davenant, *Works* (London, 1673), 7. On Marvell and Davenant, see Wittreich, "Perplexing the Explanation," 288–90. On *The State of Innocence*, see Dryden, *Critical Essays*, I, 195.

20 Sir Roger L'Estrange, *No Blinde Guides* (London, 1660), 8. On the politics of Milton's blindness, see Wilding, *Dragons Teeth*, 237–44.

21 On Jonson's historicism and its political risks, see Worden, "Ben Jonson among the Historians."

22 Ahl, *Lucan*, 34. This paragraph is indebted to Ahl, 17–61.

23 An extreme example is the "Brave Infant of *Saguntum*" from Jonson's Cary-Morison ode, who, born during Hannibal's sack of the town, "didst hastily returne" to its "Mothers wombe" (*BJ* VIII, 242).

24 Thomas May, *A Continuation of Lucan's Historicall Poem till the Death of Julius Caesar*, 4th edn. (London, 1650), A4; italics reversed.

25 Davenant, *Works*, 2, following a tradition that extends back at least as far as Servius's commentary on the *Aeneid*. See E. M. Sanford, "Lucan and His Roman Critics," *Classical Philology* 26 (1931): 233–57.

26 See Blair Worden, "Classical Republicanism and the Puritan Revolution," in *History and Imagination: Essays in Honour of Hugh Trevor-Roper*, ed. Hugh Lloyd-Jones, Valerie Pearl, and Blair Worden (New York: Holmes & Meier, 1981), 190–91.

27 See Smith, *Literature and Revolution*, 342–44. On Milton's debt to May, see George Wesley Whiting, *Milton's Literary Milieu* (Chapel Hill: University of North Carolina Press, 1939), 324–53.

28 Marchamont Nedham, *Mercurius Politicus* (London, 1650–60), 1205–06.

29 Ibid., 1335–36.

30 On the sublime in republican literary culture, see Kahn, *Machiavellian Rhetoric*, 220–24; David Norbrook, "Marvell's 'Horatian Ode' and the Politics of Genre," in *Literature and the English Civil War*, ed. Thomas Healy and Jonathan Sawday (Cambridge: Cambridge University Press, 1990), 154–56; Annabel Patterson, *Reading between the Lines* (Madison: University of Wisconsin Press, 1993), 256–72; and Smith, *Literature and Revolution*, 214–15.

31 Norbrook, "Lucan, Thomas May," 45.

32 Sir George Mackenzie, *A Moral Essay, Preferring Solitude to Publick Employment* (Edinburgh, 1665), 58–59.

33 John Evelyn, *Publick Employment and an Active Life Prefer'd to Solitude* (London, 1667), 115, 117.

34 Brian Vickers, ed., *Public and Private Life in the Seventeenth Century: The Mackenzie–Evelyn Debate* (Delmar, NY: Scholar's Facsimiles, 1986), xxiii.

35 Thomas Hobbes, *The Iliads and Odysses of Homer*, 2nd edn. (London, 1677), B3.
36 On these debates, see Gerald M. MacLean, *Time's Witness: Historical Representation in English Poetry, 1603–1660* (Madison: University of Wisconsin Press, 1994), 26–44, who notes that Jonson "celebrates the Roman's text precisely because of its likely effect upon readers" (32).
37 Edelstein, *Meaning of Stoicism*, 31.
38 Christopher Hill, "Milton and Marvell," in *Approaches to Marvell: The York Tercentenary Lectures*, ed. C. A. Patrides (London: Routledge, 1978), 24.
39 Milton, *Complete Poems and Major Prose*, 210. See Patterson, *Reading*, 257–58.
40 Quint, *Epic and Empire*, 307.
41 Charles Martindale, *John Milton and the Transformation of Ancient Epic* (Totowa, NJ: Barnes and Noble, 1986), 210.
42 See Patterson, *Reading*, 210–25.
43 See Legouis's headnote in *Poems and Letters*, I, 303–04.
44 Wiltenburg, "Translating," 117, 124.
45 Norbrook, "Lucan, Thomas May," 45–46.

5 JOHN MILTON: THE STOICISM OF HISTORY AND PROVIDENCE

1 Francis Bacon, *The Essays or Counsels, Civil and Moral*, ed. Samuel Harvey Reynolds (Oxford: Oxford University Press, 1890), 378.
2 Christopher Hill, *Milton and the English Revolution* (New York: Viking Press, 1978), 414.
3 It is unfortunate that Stoicism is so often overlooked in Milton's texts. For instance, an otherwise helpful article on "Milton's Philosophy" states that although "Milton's references to Stoicism and Stoics are relatively numerous" and "Stoicism – usually combined with Christianity – was a real option in Milton's day," his "judgment of Stoicism . . . was preponderantly negative." Examples of this preponderance are taken from the Son's reference in *Paradise Regain'd* 4. 300 to "The Stoic last in Philosophic pride" (perhaps we are supposed to think that the Stoic is "last" on the philosophical honor role), from the ludic sixth *Prolusion* on "Sportive Exercises," and even from *Comus*: "Miltonists will recall the mention . . . of 'those budge doctors of the Stoick Furr' to whom it is 'foolishness' to lend one's ear" (*A Milton Encyclopedia*, gen. ed. William B. Hunter, Jr., 9 vols. [Lewisburg, Penn.: Bucknell University Press, 1978–83], VI, 146). But should we credit the vicious Comus as Milton's spokesman when he attacks the virtuous Lady? Frozen, motionless, bound by Comus's spell – a spell that Comus thought would be intolerable punishment – the Lady lives out the Stoic paradox of freedom in constraint, makes immobility a matter of stability, and expresses a rhetorical constancy that her body figures as emblem.
4 For a much different view of this issue see Martz, *Poet of Exile*, 247–71.
5 Malcolm Kelsall, "The Historicity of *Paradise Regained*," *Milton Studies* 12 (1978): 241. See also Stella P. Revard, "Milton and Classical Rome: The Political Context of *Paradise Regained*," in *Rome in the Renaissance: The City and the Myth*, ed. P. A. Ramsey (Binghamton, NY: MRTS, 1982), 409–19.

6 Kelsall, "Historicity," 249.

7 Ibid., 245.

8 Laura Lunger Knoppers, *Historicizing Milton: Spectacle, Power, and Poetry in Restoration England* (Athens: University of Georgia Press, 1994), 132.

9 See Kelsall, "Historicity," 242–45.

10 Bernard le Bovier de Fontenelle, *The History of Oracles and the Cheats of the Pagan Priests*, trans. Aphra Behn (London, 1688), 54, who says also that "The *Stoicks* in particular (as proud and supercilious a Sect as they were) held some opinions which deserv'd pity. How cou'd they chuse but believe *Oracles*, who believ'd *Dreams*? The great *Chrysippus* himself adopted some points for articles of his faith, which had been more suitable for the belief of some silly Old Woman" (77).

11 Edelstein, *Meaning of Stoicism*, 81–82.

12 Knoppers, *Historicizing Milton*, 133.

13 Martindale, *Milton and the Transformation of Ancient Epic*, 222–23. See also Quint, *Epic and Empire*, 140–47; and Johnson, *Momentary Monsters*, 35–66, for an engaging interpretation of Cato as caricature.

14 For a detailed account of this oracle's history, see Auguste Bouché-Leclercq, *Histoire de la Divination dans l'Antiquité*, 4 vols. (1879–82; New York: Arno Press, 1975), II, 338–60.

15 Edelstein, *Meaning of Stoicism*, 89–90.

16 *The Life, and Philosophy, of Epictetus*, trans. John Davies (London, 1670), 93–95.

17 Claudius is said to be *demens* for doing so (5. 228) and, as Bernard F. Dick observes, Lucan insists that his inaction follows, not from reason, but from "irrational impulse" and "the dictates of emotion" ("The Role of the Oracle in Lucan's *De Bello Civili*," *Hermes* 93 [1965]: 465).

18 Barbara K. Lewalski, *Milton's Brief Epic: The Genre, Meaning, and Art of "Paradise Regained"* (Providence: Brown University Press, 1966), 192.

19 Dick Taylor, Jr., "The Storm Scene in *Paradise Regained*: A Reinterpretation," *University of Toronto Quarterly* 24 (1954–55): 364.

20 Ibid., 364–65.

21 See Walter MacKellar's commentary on *Paradise Regain'd* 1. 430, in *A Variorum Commentary on the Poems of John Milton*, gen. ed. Merritt Y. Hughes, 6 vols. (New York: Columbia University Press, 1975), IV, 96–97.

22 See Earl Miner, "Milton and the Histories," in *Politics of Discourse: The Literature and History of Seventeenth-Century England*, ed. Kevin Sharpe and Steven N. Zwicker (Berkeley: University of California Press, 1987), 181–203.

23 Taylor, "Storm Scene," 363. Edward N. Hooker summarizes the political situation: "As early as 1661 a group of sober citizens, clearly opposed to the Church, some of them anti-monarchical, thinking wistfully of the good old days and the good old cause, some of them restive and sullen under the oppressions of government and magistrates, some of them pious souls genuinely horrified at the wanton conduct of King and clergy and the effect of this upon the common people, published a series of anonymous pamphlets, issued without imprint, describing many 'signal' prodigies that warned of approaching judgments or heralded 'some signal Changes and Rev-

olutions.' They were understood by the court party to be seditious, and their effect upon the people was feared. One effect which they had was to lead the English people to expect some sort of national calamity, which would appear as heaven's condemnation of the government and Church; and with such divine encouragement a rebellious people might rise again, as they had twenty-five years previously. The pamphlets were loaded with dynamite, because they strongly recalled and reinforced old prophecies, superstitions, and astrological predictions" ("The Purpose of Dryden's *Annus Mirabilis*," *Huntington Library Quarterly* 10 [1946–47]: 61–62).

24 T[homas] B[romhall], *An History of Apparitions, Oracles, Prophecies, and Predictions, with Dreams, Visions, and Revelations* (London, 1658), 343.

25 Ibid., 349–50.

26 *Mirabilis Annus, Or the Year of Prodigies and Wonders* (London, 1661), A2–A4.

27 See Michael Fixler, *Milton and the Kingdoms of God* (London: Faber and Faber, 1964), 221–71.

28 Stanley Fish, "The Temptation to Action in Milton's Poetry," *English Literary History* 48 (1981): 529.

29 Stanley, *History of Philosophy*, VIII, 94, paraphrasing Diogenes Laertius, *Lives* 7.122.

30 G[ilbert] S[heldon], *Monarchy Triumphing over Traiterous Republicans* (London, 1661), 95–96.

31 See Quint, *Epic and Empire*, 325–26.

32 See Edwin B. Benjamin, "Milton and Tacitus," *Milton Studies* 4 (1972): 129–30.

33 Stanley Fish, "Things and Actions Indifferent: The Temptation to Plot in *Paradise Regained*," *Milton Studies* 17 (1983): 175.

34 Sir George Mackenzie, *Religio Stoici* (Edinburgh, 1665), 12–13.

35 Ibid., A5v, A8v.

36 Northrop Frye, "The Typology of *Paradise Regained*," *Modern Philology* 53 (1956): 232.

37 William Kerrigan, *The Prophetic Milton* (Charlottesville: University Press of Virginia, 1974), 273–74.

38 Epictetus, *Life, and Philosophy*, 96–97.

39 Knoppers, *Historicizing Milton*, 140.

40 Ibid., 141.

41 George Plekhanov, *The Role of the Individual in History* (New York: International Publishers, 1940), 11–12.

42 The Latin text is from *The Works of John Milton*, gen. ed. Frank Allen Patterson, 18 vols. (New York: Columbia University Press, 1931–38), XII, 114.

43 John Milton, *Private Correspondence and Academic Exercises*, trans. Phyllis B. Tillyard, intro. and comm. by E. M. W. Tillyard (Cambridge: Cambridge University Press, 1932), xv.

44 "Quam si jure amari a civibus vis: fatebor, defendi, agnoscam; mortem pro ea suscipi, permittam; non illud, ut etiam doleat quis, jaceat, lamentetur" (Lipsius, *De Constantia Libri Duo*, 18).

Index

DATE DUE

OCT 1 1999	

UPI 261-2505 G   PRINTED IN U.S.A.